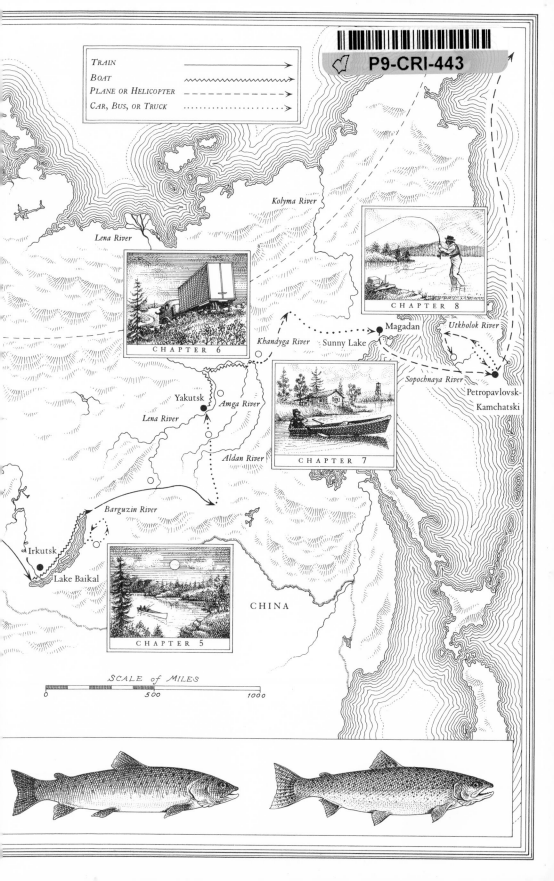

TRAIN

BOAT

PLANE OR HELICOPTER

CAR, BUS, OR TRUCK

Kolyma River

Lena River

CHAPTER 6

Khandyga River Sunny Lake

Magadan *Utkholok River*

CHAPTER 8

Yakutsk *Amga River*

Lena River

Aldan River

CHAPTER 7

Sopochnaya River

Petropavlovsk-
Kamchatski

Barguzin River

Irkutsk

Lake Baikal

CHAPTER 5

CHINA

SCALE of MILES

0   500   1000

REELING

in

RUSSIA

REELING

in

RUSSIA

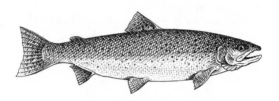

FEN MONTAIGNE

ST. MARTIN'S PRESS
New York

A THOMAS DUNNE BOOK.
An imprint of St. Martin's Press.

Design by Leah S. Carlson

Endpaper map and interior art by Laszlo Kubinyi

Library of Congress Cataloging-in-Publication Data

Montaigne, Fen.
    Reeling in Russia / by Fen Montaigne. 1st
ed.
        p. cm.
    "Thomas Dunne books."
    ISBN 0-312-18595-2
    1. Fly fishing—Russia (Federation) 2. Montaigne, Fen—Journeys—
Russia (Federation) 3. Russia (Federation)—Description and
travel. I. Title.
SH633.M66 1998
799.1'24'0947—dc21   98-10241
                                                            CIP

First Edition: June 1998

10 9 8 7 6 5 4 3 2 1

To
LAURIE

CONTENTS

ACKNOWLEDGMENTS

Dozens of people in Russia and America helped bring this book to life, and at the outset I would like to thank the Russians who inhabit these pages. Without their openness, warmth, and hospitality I would never have been able to complete the journey or the book.

In many ways, this work began with one man, Robert J. Rosenthal, editor of the *Philadelphia Inquirer*. As foreign editor, he was instrumental in naming me as that paper's Moscow correspondent at a historic time. I am deeply indebted to Rosey, a friend and mentor, for giving me the chance to work in a country I have come to love.

My longtime friend, Buzz Bissinger, played an important role in shaping the proposal for this book, and has been a constant source of support and good advice. My Moscow colleagues, David Remnick and Esther Fein, have helped me navigate the rough passage from daily newspaper writing to the world of books and magazines. I thank them all.

I would also like to thank Michael Blakely, a friend, neighbor, and ardent angler, who was indispensable in putting me in touch with Russia's small brotherhood of fly fishermen. Thanks, too, to Pete Soverel, for including me in his Kamchatka expedition. And I am indebted to Rich Turner, whose musings led to the title of this work. Many thanks, as well, to my close friends and longtime fishing and hunting partners, Grant McClintock and John Craddock, who encouraged me to write about the outdoors.

I will always be grateful to my friend Yuri Brodsky, who inspired me to take this journey. Viktor Chumak, another friend, instilled in me a love of the Russian countryside. Misha Skopets gave generously of his time to help plot the route of my journey.

I also am indebted to Leonid Bershidsky, my former translator and office assistant who has become a good friend. His continued translation help and close reading of the manuscript saved me from embarrassing mistakes. Alla Burokovskaya and Valery Kruglov, who worked for the *Inquirer* in Moscow, have been of great assistance over the past eight years. My close friends Constantin and Helen Remchukov not only opened their home to me, but also made several suggestions that strengthened the book. And many thanks to my expatriate friends in Moscow—Betsy McKay, Niel Bainton, Inga Saffron, and Ken Kalfus—for their hospitality.

My editors at St. Martin's Press, Pete Wolverton and Neal Bascomb, have been supportive, enthusiastic, and extremely patient. Pete has guided this work into print with great care. I would especially like to thank my publisher at St. Martin's, Thomas Dunne, who believed in this project from the beginning. Thanks, too, to copy editor Steve Boldt for his superb work.

My agent, Michael Carlisle, was there every step of the way as this book was conceived and written. His humor, friendship, skill, and energy have kept me going.

Finally, I would like to thank my family. My father and late mother, Gerald and Anne Montaigne, have given me a lifetime of love and understanding. My in-laws, Richard and Susan Hays, have been great fans and editors, and have cared lovingly for my daughters during my long absences. My young daughters, Claire and Nuni, have been remarkable, accepting my travels with scant complaint and greeting me with unquestioned love every time I walked back into their lives. I hope one day they will understand their father's wanderlust.

Above all, I want to thank my wife, Laurie Hays. A journalist, she has been this book's toughest editor and biggest champion. But most of all she has been a wonderful mother, wife, and companion. Her love has held us together.

REELING

in

RUSSIA

Prologue

If it had been up to me, I would never have headed into the White Sea in that little wooden boat. But I had long ago lost control of the situation. Stepan Dashkevich—a fearless, fatalistic Belorussian with a pronounced fondness for grain spirits—was at the helm. And as a storm bore down on us from the Karelian coast, thirty miles distant, Dashkevich shot a glance westward—where bolts of lightning arced down to the water out of a purple-black sky—and gave the slightest shrug of his shoulders. Then he throttled up his sputtering diesel engine and plowed into the whitecaps. As the sandy shore of the remote island of Anzer receded, I knew there would be no getting off this ride.

As a captain, Dashkevich did not inspire confidence. I had first met him several days earlier when he showed up at my friend Yuri Brodsky's apartment to take me fishing. Dashkevich was so drunk he could scarcely walk. He was not, however, too drunk to drive. I hopped into the cab of his blue Zil dump truck with my fly rod and noticed an empty bottle of Russkaya vodka rattling around on the floor. Dashkevich—an enormous man with a bovine face and beady eyes—looked faintly embarrassed, muttering something about its being Sunday, and Sunday was a day to relax. My first thought was that it was unwise to ride in a three-ton truck with a driver who had lost control of his fine motor skills. But I settled down after a few minutes, concluding the dirt roads were so potholed, and his truck so slow, that even were Dashkevich to lose consciousness, the worst outcome would be a slow slide into a ditch and a bloody nose.

Dashkevich and I bounced along in silence through a landscape of alien northern beauty. The Solovetsky archipelago, situated in Russia's White Sea, one hundred miles south of the Arctic Circle, is a windswept, heavily forested outpost dominated by a rock-walled, sixteenth-century monastery on the main island. We rumbled past the wood-domed monastery and surrounding fortress, orange lichen coating its enormous boulders. My traveling companion—*sputnik*, in Russian—was verging on a vegetative state, yet he was treating me to a view of one of the wonders of Russian architecture. In Russia, you get used to this sort of dissonance, being in a lovely spot where things are not quite right.

As we neared Dashkevich's apartment, his wife spotted us and flagged us down.

"You're already stewed, aren't you," said his wife, a lively woman with short, red hair. She looked as if she deserved a kinder fate than caring for this hulking inebriate.

"Get me some cigarettes," commanded Dashkevich.

She obliged, heading toward the brown, two-story, wooden building that housed their apartment. Nearby was a gutted brick edifice, once the headquarters of the secret police who tormented thousands of prisoners here. The Solovetsky archipelago—known by Russians simply as Solovki—was the birthplace of the Soviet gulag. In 1923, as Lenin lay near death from a stroke, Stalin and his Bolshevik cronies began shipping enemies of the people to this remote island chain. The main Solovetsky monastery, as well as numerous other monastery buildings scattered around the islands, made splendid prisons. In the late 1920s, as Stalin's terror gathered steam, the word *Solovki* became synonymous throughout the USSR with the totalitarian nightmare that had engulfed the country. Alexander Solzhenitsyn's masterpiece on Stalin's terror, *The Gulag Archipelago*, takes its name from the Solovetsky island chain.

So, as Dashkevich and I hopped out of his truck, we were landing on bones. Not far away was the site where, in 1929, guards executed czarist officers, aristocrats, scientists, merchants, and other unfortunate souls who had run afoul of the Bolshevik regime. But this little concerned Dashkevich, who was grabbing fishing nets and tossing them into the bed of his truck.

Soon, we were out of the main Solovetsky hamlet, population one

thousand, and heading toward Dashkevich's boat on Long Bay. On the half-sand, half-dirt road, we slipped in and out of craters like a rowboat riding the waves. At the edge of town, we passed two stout women in flowered housecoats weeding a large potato patch, their substantial, rounded derrieres pointing heavenward as they bent to their work. I looked over at Stepan, who was eyeing the potato weeders. I wouldn't say he had a leer on his face. Perhaps if he had been sober, his expression might have ripened into a leer. In his condition, he merely stared dumbly at the women.

We rode at a snail's pace for ten minutes through birch forests and bogs. Stepan posed rambling questions about life in America, asking about my salary, my home, and my cars, culminating in an inquiry as to whether I owned my own airplane. I asked if he wasn't worried about being thrown in jail for driving deeply under the influence. He replied that, as chief game warden on the Solovetsky archipelago, he feared nothing and no one.

"I am the main protector of the environment here," he slurred. "I am the most important person on the island. No one interferes with me, no one slows me down. I work for the Arkhangelsk regional government, and they are far away."

Then, quoting a Stalin-era saying that highlighted the independence of the gulag bosses on the archipelago, Stepan said, "Soviet land. Solovetsky power."

We arrived at the water, easing down a slippery, grassy incline to the head of Long Bay. In front of us was a coastline reminiscent of Maine or Sweden, with birch and fir trees lining a rocky shore. The water was crystal clear and inviting. We jumped out of the truck, and the wind—howling on other parts of the island on a blustery, overcast Sunday evening—was barely blowing on Long Bay, surrounded as it was by thick forest. Mosquitoes started to swarm, but that scarcely dampened my enthusiasm. I was about to fly-fish for herring on this tranquil body of water, dotted with small, picturesque islands. It would be the first time I had unsheathed my fly rod in Russia.

"The boat's not here," mumbled Dashkevich.

"What do you mean it's not here?"

"It's not here."

Stepan was swaying to and fro, staring hard at the rocky shore, where two battered wooden skiffs were tethered. I could see him struggling to figure out what had happened to his boat, his memory slogging through the vodka-sodden realms of his brain in search of an answer. Suddenly it hit him.

"My son-in-law has the boat," said Dashkevich. He wasn't at all apologetic, as if this were a fine way to end our fishing trip.

We piled back into his dump truck. Dashkevich ground the gears into reverse and floored it. We were on a steep slope, and the grass was slick from a recent rain. The wheels spun, digging deeper into the grass and mud. I hopped out to help, but Dashkevich just kept gunning the motor, turning the bank into a wallow. The tires were smoking. The engine was smoking. Dashkevich was silent as he continued revving the truck's motor. We were stuck.

Five days later, this was the man at the tiller as the storm rushed toward us off the neighboring island of Anzer. This time he was sober, but you had to wonder: How many functioning brain cells did this comrade have left?

Save for a monk or two who live there in summer, Anzer is an uninhabited island. Only ten miles long, it possesses an otherworldly loveliness. On its rocky, windswept capes, several spiral-shaped, stone labyrinths—now covered with lichen and scrub—are still visible. Russian archaeologists say they are at least four thousand years old and may have been sites where Saami or other arctic peoples communed with cosmic deities and buried their leaders. Anzer's capes are strewn with thousands of sun-bleached drift logs, piled helter-skelter along the shoreline; they are testament to the prodigality of Soviet managers, who floated the timber down northern rivers, then lost track of it when it hit the sea. On the wildest of the capes, Kolguyev, fifteen-foot, wooden Russian Orthodox crosses, some standing since before the Revolution, have been jammed into the barren ground by sailors thankful to have survived storms off Anzer's shores. The day we were there, a herd of one hundred caribou browsed lichen and tundra grasses on the cape. I am not inclined to give credence to New Age mumbo jumbo about cosmic energy. But Cape Kolguyev had an unmistakable end-of-the-earth feel to it, and if I were looking for a direct uplink to the Almighty, I think I'd start there.

After wandering around the cape, Brodsky and I walked a mile to a quiet, sandy bay, where Dashkevich lay at anchor. We were about to jump into his boat when we heard the distant thunder and first noticed the angry-looking sky. To get back to our camp, we had to navigate the turbulent waters off Kolguyev, then travel five miles west, hugging Anzer's coastline. At first, what worried me most was the lightning. You could see it from miles away, set against the dark gray thunderclouds, as it flashed over the White Sea. The storm was racing toward us, and there was no way we would outrun it. Over the clatter of the engine, I suggested to Brodsky and Dashkevich that we return to the sheltered bay, several hundred yards back, and wait out the tempest in the half-ruined boat shed of an abandoned lighthouse.

"The lightning's not a problem," hollered Dashkevich.

I wondered what water-safety manual he'd been reading.

As we rounded Cape Kolguyev, high winds and waves from the east buffeted our fifteen-foot boat. We turned nearly 180 degrees and headed directly into the storm, which was less than a mile away. Thunder boomed and the sky crackled with lightning. The White Sea turned black as I made one last attempt to persuade Brodsky and Dashkevich to head to shore. "It's too late," Brodsky yelled over the approaching gale. "It's too rough now."

Then, staring down the storm from his position at the front of the pitching boat, Brodsky—a professional photographer—snapped a picture, smiled, and said, "It's beautiful."

At the time, preoccupied as I was with the coming cataclysm, I didn't fully appreciate that Brodsky was giving me a lesson in the Russian attitude toward death. Three months later, after I had crossed all of Russia, a friend from Magadan, Misha Skopets, summed things up this way: "On the whole, Russians don't value life that much—certainly not as much as Westerners. Life is not so great for Russians that they want to hold on to it with all their might. If an American has to ride in a small boat, he'll check out its condition and see if it has life preservers. Russians are more fatalistic. They know they can expect anything from their government, or from nature."

Though they certainly valued their lives, Brodsky and Dashkevich didn't seem to view a potentially fatal dip in the White Sea with the same hysterical alarm I did. I am an upper-middle-class American, born in 1952, a product of the most pampered generation the planet has ever seen. I have a lovely wife, two beautiful young daughters, interesting work. My life is sweet, and I hold on to it with a certain maniacal zeal that I did not detect in Brodsky or Dashkevich.

The storm hit with surreal intensity. First, a white bank of clouds—more like fog—sailed just over our heads. Then a blast of hot air struck us, as if from an oven. Immediately, the wind began howling at sixty miles per hour and the sky went black. The gusts from the storm collided with the prevailing wind and waves from the opposite direction, whipping the sea into a froth. Rain, then hail, pelted the steel gray waters, turning them a sparkling silver. Water began shipping over the sides and bow of the skiff, drenching us. The gale-force winds were hitting us head-on, and I began to worry that the gusts would flip the bow and dump us into the White Sea. I scarcely took note of the lightning that sizzled around us, for at that moment lightning seemed like the least of our worries. Drowning had become my chief preoccupation. We were only about two hundred yards from Anzer's shoreline, but I quickly concluded that swimming that distance in forty-five-degree water in frenzied seas was an unlikely feat. What a stupid way to go, I thought, and so early in my trip.

Dashkevich, dressed in a heavy, camouflage coat, was standing in the stern, wiping sheets of water from his face as he tried to steer around rocks. He was quiet and steady, which gave me some hope we might get out of this mess. Then the bilge pump broke. With water rising steadily in the bottom of the boat, Dashkevich grabbed a dented tin can and started bailing. Brodsky took over, though it seemed to me that more of the White Sea was coming into our boat than going out.

Then, abruptly, the squall stopped. The rain ceased, and the storm clouds flew past with astonishing speed. Soaked, I watched in awe as the bolts of lightning continued to shoot down out of the eastern sky. The squall had lasted no more than ten minutes, and now the remnant clouds were breaking up, revealing patches of blue sky. The sea grew calm. The temperature had risen twenty-five degrees and the air felt more tropical than arctic. Brodsky was smiling, and Dash-kevich was feeling cocksure enough to say, "Really, you call that a storm? That wasn't a storm."

We chugged back to our beachfront camp, bailing as we went. I felt euphoric. It was seven-thirty in the evening, and the northern sun shone brightly. Soon, I caught sight of the forty-foot, conical, earthen mound that lay in the tidal zone in front of our hut, yet another of the little geological mysteries that graced the island. We cruised slowly over the limpid waters of the small bay, long, wide strands of brown seaweed swaying in the current. I smiled at Brod-sky. We both understood: in Russia, just when you're sure you're about to sink, things have a way of quieting down.

1.

SOLOVKI

A name can exert a strange pull. Such was the case for me with Anzer.

Four years earlier, while working as a Moscow correspondent, I had visited the Solovetsky Islands in late September with Brodsky, who had devoted his life to studying the archipelago and its role as progenitor of the gulag. Like Brodsky, I instantly fell for the place, drawn to its wild, unsullied coastline, its architecture, its crystalline northern light, its hundreds of lakes and ponds, its tragic past. Brodsky and I spent several days poking around the main island. On the day before we were to leave, we rode in a boat down the coast to a spit of land just a half dozen miles from Anzer. A nature preserve, Anzer had been uninhabited for half a century. In summer, Brodsky would live there for weeks in a nineteenth-century cabin, photographing the vestiges of monastery buildings and the gulag. He was anxious to show me the island, and we were both disappointed when the wind kicked up, whitecaps appeared on the sea, and it became impossible to motor to Anzer—plainly visible a few miles away—in a small skiff. Flying to Moscow the next day, Brodsky said to me, "Well, you'll just have to come back, and we'll make it to Anzer."

In mid-1993, after completing my three-year tour as Moscow correspondent for the *Philadelphia Inquirer*, I came home to America with my family. I did not communicate with Brodsky for nearly two years. He refused, however, to lose contact with me. Two or three times a year, I would receive a small, brown envelope in the mail. Inside would be several photographs of Solovetsky Island scenes. Scrawled on the back were short notes, ending with these words: "Anzer awaits!"

Ever since my homecoming, I had been pestered by a desire to return to Russia, and Anzer became a symbol of that longing. To some foreigners, Russia was anathema, a place grim beyond description. But to others, such as myself, Russia was an affliction, an incurable habit. From the very beginning, I was drawn to her dilapidated landscape, inhabited by people who knew hardship as intimately as we might a member of the family.

I first set foot in the former Soviet Union in November 1989, just as the Berlin Wall was crumbling and Communism was vanishing across Eastern Europe. Driving from Sheremetyevo Airport to downtown Moscow, I felt I had landed in another dimension. It was 5 P.M. and pitch-dark. Bundled-up figures with shopping bags shuffled down ill-lit, impossibly wide avenues. There was no color, few cars, oppressive Stalinist architecture. The capital reminded me of a city at war, under blackout. I loved it.

The next morning, emerging from a shoddy concrete high-rise onto October Square, I was confronted by an enormous statue of Lenin, his overcoat billowing out in a flourish of socialist realism. There were few stores, no advertisements, neat little kiosks selling *Pravda*, theater tickets, and ice cream. Black Volga sedans shot down sparsely trafficked streets, emitting a distinctive guttural, coughing sound every time their drivers shifted gears.

I walked into the metro station and was pushed toward a steep escalator, seventy-five yards long. Riding down the creaking, vertiginous contraption, I watched the parade of people coming up the opposite escalator, their worn, gray faces reflecting the toll that life in the Soviet Union had taken on its citizens. The subway station was handsome and clean. I will never forget the smell of the car as I crammed into it with dozens of Russians. It was a pungent, sour mélange of garlic, unwashed bodies, vodka, musty woolen overcoats, and Bulgarian tobacco. For me, that fragrance would forever be linked with Russia.

I spent the next several years covering the reign and fall of Mikhail Gorbachev, the collapse of the Soviet Union, and the rebirth of a capitalist Russia. Witnessing these events and writing about them made a deep impression. Once back in America, where I was edging toward leaving the newspaper business, my desire to revisit Russia grew. I missed the people, missed speaking the language. I wanted to travel through the vast swaths of territory I had not seen as a correspondent, spending time not in cities, but in the Russian countryside, a haunted, lovely place of timeworn villages, sprawling garden plots, and ruined brick Orthodox churches. It had always been my favorite part of Russia, far from the legions of mobsters and nouveau riche businessmen who had popped up all across the country. Visiting rural Russia was like time travel; much of it—especially Siberia—was reminiscent of the American West in the late nineteenth century, a boundless expanse of forests and plains where many people still lived close to the land in log cabins, growing and catching much of their food.

Unconstrained by pressures of time and work, and driven by an ill-starred desire to plumb the depths of the Russian psyche, I wanted to lose myself in the Russian countryside.

The idea for the trip came to me on a winter afternoon. Since returning from Moscow, I had combined my passion for fishing and hunting with work and had taken to writing about the outdoors. I was contemplating the fly-fishing opportunities in Russia—Atlantic salmon on the Kola Peninsula; taimen, a legendary, salmonlike fish found in Siberia; grayling on Lake Baikal; steelhead trout on the wild, tundra rivers of the Kamchatka Peninsula in the Russian Far East. I realized what I had to do. Beginning on Anzer, I would fly-fish from one end of Russia to the other. Few countries offered the angling opportunities that existed there, and with the right documents I could do what was once unthinkable—traverse all ten time zones of this enormous land, wandering where I pleased. Vast regions, as huge and wild as Alaska, were now open to anyone foolhardy enough to ramble into them.

From the start, I knew I wasn't so much after fish as I was after a glimpse of Russia from the bottom up. My fly rod would be my divining stick, defining my route and taking me places few other

Westerners had trod. Almost no one fly-fished in Russia—the practitioners of the sport numbered only in the hundreds—and I imagined that brandishing a fly rod would ease my way into village life. For Russians loved to fish, many using long poles called *udochki*. No matter how befouled a river or lake, there usually was a Russian standing on its banks, dipping his worm into a rainbow sheen of pollution in the hopes of catching some stunted perch or pike. And though fishermen are legendary prevaricators, I figured there was no finer group to guide me through this vast "wonderland," as Russians sardonically referred to their cursed, puzzling country.

As it turned out, the fly rod opened more doors than I could have imagined.

The fishing was not at all what I had expected.

And the Russian countryside? It was a world turned on its head, inhabited by people abandoned by their government and fending for themselves.

"God is a long way up," goes the old Russian proverb, "and the czar a long way off."

A dusty, golden three-quarter moon hovered over Moscow as I rode at midnight to the Leningrad Station. The Garden Ring Road encircling the city center was nearly deserted, in merciful contrast to the eye-stinging traffic jams that paralyzed the ten-lane asphalt band during the daytime. I had flown into Moscow the day before—election day—and Boris Yeltsin had just won a second term as president, soundly beating his cretinous Communist opponent. With that vote, the country may have turned its back once and for all on its Bolshevik past. But the occasion felt less than historic. Many people had cast their ballots, then headed on a sunny, breezy day to their dachas. Muscovites were weary of making history.

Leningrad Station, encased in scaffolding, was the scene of chaotic bustle generally associated with the movement of wartime refugees. Travelers staggered under the weight of massive sacks. People elbowed one another aside at ticket windows amid grunts and recriminations. Squadrons of unkempt, weary-looking Russians stood near rows of the ubiquitous kiosks, drinking beer and shots of vodka. Men hacked out wads of tubercular phlegm on the sidewalk. Gazing at these lost souls, I was amazed that the abysmally low life expectancy of Russian men—fifty-eight—wasn't even lower.

I stood by the green and red cars of Train Number 20, the overnight express to St. Petersburg. The conductors were firing up the little boilers that heated their cars' tea water, and the smell of coal smoke wafted over the platform. The scent set off a chain reaction of memories, and I recalled countless Russian train rides, nights when I stood on platforms slick with black ice, ready to board an express to some disintegrating quadrant of the Soviet empire.

This time, I was waiting for Yuri Brodsky. We were going, at last, to Anzer.

Yuri's love of the Solovetsky Islands had fascinated me ever since I had first met him five years before. In twenty-five years, he had taken thousands of photographs, spent countless hours in archives, interviewed scores of survivors of the Solovki camps, and whiled away months on the islands wandering through the ruins of Stalin's prisons. He resembled an obsessed archaeologist, slowly piecing together disparate shards of history—scrawled messages on walls, graves in dense forest, early newspapers from the camps—into a devastating picture of the genesis of Stalin's terror.

Now, his labor of love had been reposited in a dense, riveting book of more than six hundred pages, a tome crammed with photographs, archival documents, and reminiscences. It was probably the single most exhaustive volume ever produced on one of Stalin's camps, and Brodsky had absolutely no guarantee it would ever see the light of day. He had been searching for a publisher for several years, but in the jaded era that followed glasnost and the implosion of the USSR, Russian publishers were hardly scrambling to bring such material to light.

From the beginning, I liked Yuri Brodsky because he was such a gentle soul. Although I never heard him speak of God or his native Judaism, he had the tranquil air of a religious seeker. He was short and slight, with a full head of hair and neatly trimmed beard. In the time I had known him, both hair and beard had gone from salt-and-pepper to silver. Brodsky smiled often, and when he did, his head tilted slightly and his eyes nearly narrowed shut. In conversation, Brodsky, who was fifty-one, often emitted an endearing noise, a kind of throat-clearing, affirmative "Hmmmmm." He was well loved, in part because of his habit of constantly dispensing little presents to friends and strangers. His pockets were crammed with candy that he bestowed upon children, shopkeepers, and bureaucrats, friendly and unfriendly alike. Yuri's quiet charm could win over even the hardest Russian heart. Women were strongly drawn to him, and I think it was because he was simply a kindhearted man in a land where many men, often under the influence of alcohol, treated their women so shabbily.

Fifteen minutes before the train's 1 A.M. departure, Brodsky came strolling down the platform, a knapsack on his back. Piling into our two-person compartment, we talked nonstop; there was a lot of catching up to do. Yuri's life was insane in a peculiarly Russian way. He had been estranged from his wife for twenty years, yet because of the dire shortage of housing in Russia, had continued to live with her in the same small apartment in the town of Electrostal, about thirty-five miles from Moscow. Their twenty-year-old daughter was crammed into the apartment as well. Yuri had a girlfriend in Moscow, who surprised him the previous year with the news she was pregnant with his child. He was supporting his girlfriend, his baby, and his grown daughter on the 1.3 million rubles—about $260—he received each month from his job as photographer at a plant that made components for nuclear reactors. He also earned extra money from his freelance photography. This unorthodox and tenuous state of affairs seemed to trouble him only slightly. I would have come unglued years ago.

As we prepared for sleep, the conductress opened the door to our compartment. She handed us a short stick, which she told us to jam into the door to deter robbers. She said the gassings that had once plagued the Moscow–St. Petersburg trains—enterprising thieves would open the door in the middle of the night, anesthetize you, and strip you of everything but your Skivvies—had almost stopped. But common thieves, armed with master keys, were still a problem.

St. Petersburg sparkled the next morning under uncommonly blue skies and balmy temperatures. As our train moved through the suburbs, I spied fishermen with cloth caps and long wooden rods trying

13

to conjure up fish from stagnant, debris-strewn canals. Their efforts were testimony that anglers everywhere will chase fish under any conditions, no matter how dismal.

At seven that evening, Brodsky and I boarded the Polar Express, the St. Petersburg–Murmansk train that would take us up the Karelian coast toward Solovki. We headed north through a landscape of swamps and birch forests, passing villages where wooden houses and log cabins, faded to a drab gray and listing slightly, lined dirt streets. At seven-thirty, Yuri and I went to the dining car, where the service and the food reeked of the USSR.

In one booth, with red seats and a red tablecloth, a pair of policemen sat and perused the newspaper. Nearby, several young men slouched in their seats, drinking beer and soda. One of the them— a slender, dark-haired, effeminate man with a blue sport coat—was our waiter. He waltzed up and, with a frown, asked us if we wanted to eat, as if we had come to the dining car for some other purpose. He tossed two menus on the table and hovered. About twenty items were on the bill of fare, including beef Stroganoff and grilled Georgian chicken.

"Do you have all of these items?" I inquired, knowing the answer.

"All we have is chicken legs or fried eggs," he sniffed. Then he tapped his watch and said, "The time."

"But the sign says you don't close until eleven-thirty," said Brodsky.

"We're closing early tonight," the waiter shot back.

"I'd like four fried eggs, well done, not runny," I said. Brodsky ordered the same. We munched on stale bread infused with a powerful chemical taste. Even though we were the only people eating in the dining car, it took the waiter fifteen minutes to sashay back to our table with the eggs. They were nearly raw.

"I wanted these well done," I said.

He looked at me with revulsion. Then, with an impatient wave of his hand, he replied, "All you had to tell me, then, was to cook them on both sides."

We got our eggs finally, well done and foul, cooked in rancid sunflower oil with bits of tomato. I ate half the plate, then lost my appetite.

The night was restless, the train lurching, cars clanging. At 10 A.M.

on a Saturday morning, we pulled into Kem, the port on the Karelian coast that was the major transshipment point to the Solovetsky gulag. Under warm, sunny skies, we rode five miles in a taxi to the docks, where the weekly rust bucket departed for Solovki. Inhaling the salt air, gazing at the hilly islands that lay between us and the open sea, Brodsky and I began decompressing from the bustle of the mainland.

We had six hours before our departure. Brodsky had heard of a St. Petersburg man who had come to Kem, started a lumber mill, and opened a little museum about the Solovetsky gulag. We decided to find him.

The Kem port area was an odd spot, chiefly because it was built on water. Soviet engineers had dumped logs in the harbor, covered them with wood chips, then sprinkled a layer of soil on top. The entire area looked as if it were perched on a thatched roof. Near the docks, a lumber mill, built with Italian and Canadian technology, sat idle, rusting equipment littering the grounds. Farther on, weather-worn wooden cottages sprouted from the landscape. In front of them, on raised platforms, sat wooden and metal barrels, which the local government filled regularly with water, since wells were an impossibility. This section of Kem, like most Russian villages, had no running water or sewage system.

On this glorious Saturday morning, women in flowered housedresses and kerchiefs were out in force, hoes in hand, working in their potato gardens. All summer and fall, from the White Sea to the Pacific Ocean, I was confronted again and again with one enduring image: Russians tending their potato patches. At times, the country seemed like a vast potato field. People toiled for good reason: in rural Russia, a large garden meant the difference between a full stomach and a growling one.

Four young men weaved down the dirt main street, their faces assuming the crimson, contorted aspect of the hard-core alcoholic. At last we found the museum and home of Yevgeny Nikonov and rapped on the door. Nikonov answered. He was a well-built man of fifty-five with curly brown hair and mustache, blue eyes, and the de rigueur duds of Russian men that summer—a cheap, Chinese-made jogging suit. For a few seconds, Nikonov eyed us skeptically, incredulous that the Solovki expert, Yuri Brodsky, and an American journalist had actually landed on his doorstep. He quickly recovered, however, and enthusiastically ushered us into a sunny office.

Nikonov began dealing out different business cards, identifying him variously as a mining engineer, a member of an international charitable group, and—most recently—as head of something called the Karelian Fund of Humanitarian Initiatives. I began to fear we had stumbled upon a flake, but it soon became evident he was merely an affable man living a timeless Russian tale—that of a cultured, middle-class intellectual cohabitating with considerable unease among the great vodka-swilling unwashed of provincial Russia.

Nikonov had spent much of his career at a metallurgical plant in Leningrad. Five years ago, he had moved to Kem and the Karelian coast, where he received his initiation into the ways of post-Communist country living. At first, the sizable contingent of local alcoholics rapped ceaselessly on his door, seeking vodka handouts. When he opened a small lumber mill, he was plagued by drunken workers.

"The average worker typically wants to earn only enough for one bottle of vodka a day, two packs of cigarettes, and a little food," said Nikonov, as his tall, comely wife served us sausage, cheese, and bread. "If you pay him more, he'll drink a second bottle and not come to work the next day. Very few people want to work and save like in your country."

Firing dipsomaniacs and refusing them vodka had had its repercussions for Nikonov. The local ne'er-do-wells had robbed the store attached to his house—an establishment run by his sister—several times. His house and small, weather-beaten sailboat had been vandalized. Yet Nikonov claimed to be happy in this backwater on the White Sea and, like many Russians, had reconciled himself to the reality that world-class boozing and ingrained, Communist work habits had doomed the countryside to backwardness for years to come.

We toured his little museum, a modest, one-room exhibit that must have, I feared, received precious few visitors. Then it was time to go. He shook our hands passionately and left me with these words from turn-of-the-century poet Aleksei K. Tolstoi: "The country is big and rich, and there's no order in sight."

· · ·

The weekly boat to Solovki, an eighty-foot former navy vessel, shoved off at four-fifteen, stirring up a muddy backwash as the captain played Ravel's *Bolero* from a boom box. We cruised at fifteen miles an hour over the dark water, threaded our way through small, rocky islands, then emerged into the open White Sea. Arctic terns hovered frantically over the water, then plunged in, emerging with small, silver fish in their beaks. The sun went in and out behind thick, white clouds, and the air temperature fell to that of the sea—about forty-five degrees.

The trip to Solovki took two and a half hours. Ten miles from shore the monastery and surrounding walls came into view, looming larger as we approached. I had never arrived on the islands from the sea, and as we chugged toward the main harbor—the Bay of Prosperity—I understood better why this place had come to occupy the central place in Yuri's soul. All around were the frigid and vaguely menacing waters of the White Sea. And at the center of it all was a great Russian monument—the monastery—that had been the seed from which Stalin's terror sprouted. Several hundred thousand prisoners passed through the camps in and around Solovki from 1923 to 1939, when the islands' gulag was shut down. As many as forty thousand people perished. By the time the gulag had metastasized eastward, all the way to the Bering Sea, an estimated 10 million to 20 million people are believed to have died at the hands of Stalin's secret police and in forced famines.

We cruised past the ruined, whitewashed brick shell of the former gulag administration building and docked a stone's throw from the tin-roofed buildings of the monastery.

The Solovetsky Islands possess an air of splendid detachment, and life there moves at a glacial pace. There are few cars. Motorcycles with sidecars are more common, but for long stretches of time you don't hear an internal combustion engine, save for the diesel-fired generator that supplies electricity to the town. The main hamlet is a ragtag collection of old barracks, faded log cottages, tilting picket fences, peeling, whitewashed wooden barns, and here and there, long root cellars on top of which sprout yellow wildflowers. Cattle graze the hillsides. In the center of the village, by the roadside, sit long, hollowed-out cypress logs from the sixteenth century, part of the original water system designed by the island's monks. The population of the island is dwindling gradually as the Solovetsky Museum loses funding and lays off workers, the seaweed processing plant works fitfully, and the island fishing fleet, like many industries in Russia, stands idle.

We dropped our luggage at Brodsky's small apartment in a two-story, wood-frame building and headed for the weekly communal bath, a ritual in the Russian countryside. On the Solovetsky Islands, the men scrub up on Saturdays, the women on Sundays. Like nearly everything else on the islands, the Beletskaya bath is old, dating to 1717. We entered through a one-story, ash-colored, wooden building that was showing its age. A woman with gold teeth greeted Yuri with a smile and asked how he'd been; nearly everyone on the island knew Brodsky, and as we walked the dirt streets, we rarely went one hundred yards without someone stopping to say hello. The woman collected five thousand rubles, about $1, from each of us, and we entered a commodious drying room, where naked men with bright pink skin cooled off on green wooden benches. Brodsky and I stripped and walked through a door into the main washing room, a dank, steamy, cacophonous chamber with vaulted ceilings. Kids whirred around on floors slick with slime, soap foam, and bits of birch leaves.

In this outer sanctum, men grabbed metal basins and filled them with water from hot and cold spigots covered in peeling tape. They sloshed the water over their bodies, lathered extravagantly with soap, then rinsed off by overturning the basins on their heads. Some shaved, others soaped up their squirming sons. Most of the men had the wiry physiques common to members of a society where manual labor is still the norm and McDonald's and Dunkin' Donuts are not. The bathers bantered loudly; this was the communal ritual of the week, and a great leveler.

Brodsky and I entered the steam room, an inferno about the size of a two-car garage. Men sat on several tiers of benches, flaying one another with bunches of birch leaves. Occasionally someone would toss a ladleful of water on a mountain of hot stones in the corner. A long, locomotive hiss would ensue, and a cloud of hot steam would refract off the concrete ceiling and scald your shoulders. The scorching fog was so thick you couldn't make out the features of a fellow sitting five feet away. As the bathers lashed themselves with the birch twigs, bits of the vegetation and droplets of sweat were sprayed around the room. After two minutes in the steam chamber, sweat began to flow in rivulets from every pore in my body, dripping steadily from my fingertips. I endured it until I felt I was on the verge of blacking out, then exited the chamber, soaped up, and poured tubs of cold water over my burning hide. We toweled off in the drying room. Sweat continued to seep out of me long after leaving the steam chamber.

As I walked out of the drying room, the gold-toothed attendant pronounced the traditional postbath greeting—"With light steam!"—and I gulped down a glass of pineapple juice for a dime.

I had heard intriguing tales about angling on the islands, particularly that the canals of Solovki, built over the past five hundred years by monks, still held a small number of Solovetsky trout. Stocked a century or two ago, the small trout—the size of eastern-American brook trout—reportedly could still be caught on a dry fly in the narrow canals. There had been regular sightings of these creatures, but in recent years few had been caught. Some locals said the fish were long gone.

Later that night, I decided to scout one of the waterways in which the elusive Solovki canal trout allegedly dwelled. Around eleven, I walked through the quiet town. A slanting, gold and silver sunset appeared from under the patchy clouds, suffusing the landscape of gentle hills and gardens with a translucent light. A boy tended three goats near one of the small, white, stucco chapels that lay outside the Kremlin walls. Not far away, on the shores of Holy Lake, a couple did their laundry in the icy water. At the harbor, where several rusting metal boats sat at anchor, a half dozen people ringed an old, stone canal lock and jigged for herring. Little in this scene suggested the twentieth century, and this very quality drew me to rural Russia. This was the selfish conceit of the traveler. What to me was a charming lack of modernity was, to the Russians who inhabited this landscape, a world of outhouses, of water hauled from wells, of endless chopping of firewood, of constant digging in gardens so there would be enough potatoes and pickled cabbage to last the winter.

I found one of the Solovki canals around midnight and was simultaneously disappointed and intrigued. No more than five feet wide, the canal meandered through meadows, cut behind several homes, and flowed into one end of Holy Lake, in the shadow of the monastery. A rickety wooden footbridge crossed the canal, reminiscent of a stream in the English countryside. I saw no fish, but resolved to return the next day with my fly rod.

Around noon, under clear, warm skies, I stood near Holy Lake and suited up. I put on my new $365 Simms Gore-Tex breathable Guide waders and my new $90 L. L. Bean Aqua Sole wading boots. I slipped my $60 fly-fishing vest over my $85 Patagonia fleece shirt. I assembled my new $465, three-piece, Sage Light Line, 5-weight trout rod, attached my $175 Lamson reel to it, strung the rod with my new $50 Joan Wulff Triangle Taper floating fly line, and attached one of the three hundred flies I had purchased—at about $2 a pop—for the trip. I stood there in the latest, highest-tech, most expensive fly-fishing gear our great country had to offer at the end of the twentieth century and felt like a fool. Several Russians wandered by and looked at me with a mix of curiosity and alarm. The sport was so rarely practiced in Russia that it still went by the charming, archaic name of fishing "with a buggy whip."

Standing on the shore, I enjoyed the feel of the fly line unfurling on the calm surface of the small lake. I had been fly-fishing for only a few years, but one of the great pleasures—and tortures—of the sport was trying to master the art of casting. The fundamental principle of fly-fishing is that the angler uses a thick line and a long, springy rod to propel a nearly weightless fly to a waiting fish, preferably a trout. This is easier said than done, and I had spent many frustrating hours making spastic casts—snapping off flies and fouling the line in trees—before gradually beginning to feel the right casting rhythm, which was slower than my hyperactive system was inclined to permit. Now, as I ascended from the ranks of the horrible to the merely average, I began to enjoy casting, and to understand that one of the satisfactions of fly-fishing was the process itself, the act of artfully laying the fly in front of the fish.

I had hoped for a perch or a pike, or one of the elusive Solovetsky trout. But nothing was biting, or at least nothing was biting what I had to offer. I decided to try the canals. Four hundred lakes on the main Solovetsky island were connected by seventy-eight canals dug long ago by monks. Designed to supply drinking water and provide a network of waterborne transport, the canals—often lined with stones—were still remarkably well preserved. I followed one canal into the woods, hoping to pursue my quest for trout out of sight of the locals. The canal was about two feet deep, the water gin clear, the bottom sandy. Walking along this historic, man-made stream was a pleasure in itself, but fishing these waters was difficult in the extreme. The canals were simply too narrow to offer the angler a sporting chance at tossing out a fly and fooling a fish, assuming there even were fish. Overhanging trees made casting difficult in many spots. And whenever I stopped in the woods, swarms of mosquitoes emerged to harry me. I did find several clearings where I could stand in the open and cast thirty feet upstream, letting my mayfly imitation drift back over the phantom fish. For half an hour, I saw nothing. But then, as I walked near an undercut bank, I caught a glimpse of an eight-inch, spectral shape darting upstream. It looked like a trout.

Spurred by the vainglory of being the first person in recent memory to catch a Solovki canal trout on a fly, I fished with newfound intensity. I switched flies, cast dozens of times, yet nothing rose to devour my insect imitations. Farther on, another small, troutlike form shot upstream as I approached. That was as close as I ever came to this phantasmal creature.

On the ninth of July—my forty-fourth birthday—Yuri Brodsky and I set out at last for Anzer with Stepan Dashkevich. The night before, one of Yuri's friends warned him that Dashkevich was frequently hanging around Brodsky because he was a stooge for the FSB, the successor to the KGB. Brodsky seemed unconcerned.

For two decades, as he compiled material on the Solovetsky gulag, Brodsky had been a thorn in the KGB's side. In the summer of 1973, the fiftieth anniversary of the founding of the gulag, Brodsky was on the islands. It was not a jubilee that Soviet authorities were celebrating, since the history of Stalin's terror was still largely taboo. Brodsky thought the date needed to be marked, that "someone should speak up about the camps." One night, he clambered atop the monastery's belfry and painted the following words: "50th Anniversary of the Soviet Special Purpose Camp." The KGB swung into action. One of the few outsiders living on the islands that summer,

Brodsky was a prime suspect. The secret police were never able to prove he had scrawled the heretical words, but they began watching him closely.

In the beginning, he had no intention of writing a book about the gulag. He merely wanted to document what remained of the camps. But soon he found himself in a race with the local Communist Party and the KGB: as he stole around the island, photographing prisoners' inscriptions on monastery walls or iron bars on cell doors, local officials were busy rubbing out the inscriptions and removing the bars. When he returned home to Electrostal, the KGB repeatedly interrogated him about his growing work on the Solovetsky gulag. He had taken to interviewing former prisoners and witnesses and was beginning to collect documents. The KGB threatened to have him sacked from his job, even hinted he might be jailed. He avoided these dire consequences by being unfailingly polite and always playing the fool.

"In the entire country, memories of the camps were stacked into a kind of brick wall," Brodsky told me. "If one brick was allowed to be pulled out, the other bricks would have come tumbling out much easier. So they hid that wall behind an iron curtain so as not to allow anyone to pull out a single brick."

Now Brodsky was a local hero for his work, and his photographs and archival materials formed the backbone of the moving gulag exhibit in the island's museum of history. The new secret police agency, the FSB, had better things to do with its time, Brodsky reckoned. What interested me more than the possibility that Dashkevich might be spying on us was the lingering paranoia and suspicion that permeated Russian society.

Brodsky, dressed in jeans and a soiled, tan windbreaker, was smiling broadly as we shoved off from Long Bay on a luminous, seventy-degree day. Motoring along, we chased flocks of sea ducks off the water. A seal surfaced occasionally and watched us pass. Long Bay—a picturesque body of water whose shores were thick with fir, pine, birch, and quaking aspen—gave way to an inlet between the main Solovetsky island and the neighboring island of Bolshaya Muksalma. In the distance, I caught a glimpse of the brick monastery buildings that once housed women gulag prisoners. Among the inmates were about three hundred Ukrainian women who had eaten their children when Stalin starved millions in Ukraine who had resisted the collectivization of agriculture. Most of the women had lost their minds. As far as Brodsky could determine, they all perished on Solovki.

We sputtered through the inlet known as Iron Gate, where ripping currents between the islands slowed our boat to a crawl. Water boiled up from the clear, black depths of the inlet as we turned northwest and motored toward Anzer. An eagle sat on a boulder on Bolshaya Muksalma's rocky shore, guarding its nest nearby. Anzer was now in plain view, about eight miles away. Dominating the island—only ten miles long and often less than two miles wide—was the stucco and brick church on the hill called Golgotha.

We headed for a little cove called Gorodok, Brodsky's residence during his annual summer visits to Anzer. Just off the beach was an old *izbushka*, or cottage, built last century by monks for shelter during the haying season. Though no one could lay claim to the log cabin, it had, over the years, de facto become Brodsky's. As we hove to within a mile of the shoreline, dominated by rocky points of land covered in green and rust-colored scrub, Yuri confessed that he was anxious about where we would sleep. He knew that a Moscow archaeologist and a group of students were on the island restoring a monastery building. Dashkevich had also received reports that unauthorized visitors and fish poachers had been on Anzer in recent weeks.

Yuri's fears that his deserted island paradise would be crawling with people intensified when we spotted an eighty-foot vessel, a Russian-navy supply ship, anchored in the bay next to his cottage. As we rounded the next cape, we saw a sailboat at anchor in the cove at Gorodok. On the beach in front of his cabin were two long, wooden skiffs. Smoke was rising from the chimney of his shack. Suddenly, fifteen people scurried antlike out of the underbrush and lined up on the shore. Brodsky looked chagrined. His Shangri-la was as crowded as Red Square.

"Grab the rifle," Dashkevich instructed Brodsky. "They might be poachers."

We chugged into shore, where a motley-looking assortment of unshaven men, some wearing the blue-and-white-striped jersey of the Russian sailor, waited for us. Brodsky held the carbine in plain sight, and Dashkevich fingered the pistol in his holster. I feared we were about to get into a firefight with a band of White Sea poachers and braced myself.

But all I had to fear was a hangover. This was Russia, after all. Within an hour, our group would be throwing back vodka and grain alcohol with the very men we, just minutes before, had been contemplating shooting.

The desperadoes on the beach turned out to be a mixed crew of Russian-navy men and workers from the top-secret nuclear submarine factory at Severodvinsk. They had hit a squall, busted a mast on one of their dinghies, and decided to dry out—and booze it up—on Anzer. At first, Brodsky was plainly annoyed, although he managed to hold his tongue. His cabin, which appeared to be sinking into the grassy earth just behind the beach, had been turned into Animal House. The sailors had tossed their clothes on the plank roof to dry, had piled sleeping bags inside, and had spread food, luggage, and firewood all around the hut. The knee-high grass was trampled down, and some of the men had chosen to defecate a little too close to the shack.

"How's it look?" asked Dashkevich, who was on the beach radioing Arkhangelsk to determine if the sailors had permission to visit Anzer.

"How do you think it looks?" Brodsky replied calmly. "There's eighteen guys living up there. It looks like a pigsty."

The boys were on a two-week White Sea cruise, an annual ritual that enabled them to hone their sailing skills and drink oceans of vodka in as fine a maritime setting as existed in all of northern Russia. It turned out they didn't have authorization to visit Anzer, but Dashkevich quickly realized these were men with whom he could reason. First, they were hardy, happy-go-lucky Russky *muzhiks*—peasants—just like himself. Second, they were carting around a twenty-two-liter stainless steel jerry can of pure grain-alcohol spirits. Third, they had just caught a dozen palm-sized perch, which they were preparing to turn into a Russian delicacy— *ukha*, or fish soup.

"Well, we've just settled this problem with a little Asian diplomacy," Brodsky told me as we stood on the sands of Gorodok, figuring out how to reclaim his cabin. The sailors would stay with us until evening, at which point they would shove off for a neighboring bay. There, they would spend the night and the following day set sail into the White Sea.

That settled, the group got down to business. The cook—a stout, good-natured, forty-seven-year-old navy man—began peeling potatoes, singing Russian seamen's songs, and dispensing nuggets of Russian folk wisdom. Such verities as "fall in love with a beautiful woman, marry a hardworking one" tumbled out of his mouth, the more so as he drank.

The *ukha*—with perch, potatoes, bay leaf, and raw onions thrown in at the end—was sublime. First we drank the fish broth out of dirty metal bowls, then the cook ladled in fish carcasses and we ate the flesh. The sailors filled empty vodka bottles with one-third spirits and two-thirds water, shook them vigorously, then waited a few minutes until the bubbles subsided. They drank, toasted peace and friendship, and stuck a commemorative pin from their sub factory on my shirt. Soon, Dashkevich was sprawled on the ground with their leader, enjoying his buzz as he pored over nautical charts.

It was low tide. Taking leave of the sailors, Brodsky and I walked over the sand and boulders to Cape Labyrinth, a half mile away. The cape was a two-hundred-yard spit of land covered in berry bushes, white lichen, and wildflowers of violet, purple, and yellow hues. In the center of the cape sat a labyrinth estimated to be four thousand years old, one of several on Anzer. About forty feet in diameter, the labyrinth was a stone spiral, now coated with lichen and moss, its outline still plainly visible. Two boulders stood at the center. Elsewhere on the cape were a dozen piles of stones, splashed with green- and mustard-colored lichen. The cape commanded a panoramic view of the White Sea, the wooded shoreline of Bolshaya Muksalma, and the Arkhangelsk coast.

There wasn't a boat or a human being in sight. The only sound was that of the wind, the lapping of the sea on the shore, the occasional splash of a seal diving off a rock. Once, Brodsky had been on the cape in the perpetual twilight of a Solovetsky summer night when, suddenly, a Soviet submarine surfaced in the midst of this end-of-the-earth tableau. He watched in awe as the dark, evil-looking vessel steamed away.

Colossal perch were rumored to dwell in a nearby lake, nestled in a valley below the monastery on Golgotha. We hiked there through a forest of gnarled, stunted birches, mucking our way through glades aswarm with mosquitoes. The mile-wide lake was glassy, and I could see mayflies touching down on the water to lay eggs. Fish were eating the spent flies, making concentric rings on the surface, a sight that arouses the predatory instinct in any fly fisherman. It was 11 P.M., and a soft, golden light filled the surrounding woods. The mosquitoes were unbearable. Scores of them buzzed around my head and hands, and only by slathering on poisonous repellent could I keep them from driving me wild. As Brodsky walked the shoreline, waving and smiling as he tried to evade the insects, I spent an hour fly-fishing for perch.

In short order, I caught and released several small perch, pretty green fish with vivid orange fins. I deceived them with a cream-colored, half-inch imitation of the mayflies that were alighting on the surface of the lake.

The essence of freshwater fly-fishing is to mimic the various stages of aquatic insects found in streams or lakes, either the nymph—or underwater—phase, or the later stage when the nymphs pop to the surface, sprout wings, fly, then return to the water to lay eggs and die. For me and many fly anglers, catching the fish on the surface is by far the greater thrill. From the moment I first picked up a fly rod, I was mesmerized by the ritual of casting out a fly and waiting for a trout to rise and devour the deception. To witness a hatch of mayflies or caddis flies—trout dimpling the surface in a feeding frenzy—and then to cast your own fly and watch it disappear into the mouth of the trout provides a kick unlike few others in sport. It has everything—the preparation, the anticipation, the strike, and the actual fighting of the fish. Like all good sport, fly-fishing provided the ultimate in pleasure, which for me meant totally losing myself in the activity. When I was on a stream and the fish were biting, I was able—as a writer once observed—to quit dragging around the clanking chains of my mind. All thought ceased. I was utterly absorbed by the water, the fly, and the fish.

Such was the case on the lake that evening. After catching four or five small perch on the surface, I switched to an imitation of a baitfish, known as a streamer. This form of fly-angling has its own charms, the main one being the attention-grabbing "thunk" of a fish stopping your fly as you strip it in underwater. I caught several perch with a green streamer, but they, too, were small, and I let them go.

Returning to the cabin after midnight, we heard the voices of the sailors as they rowed away. In the lingering light of a white Solovetsky night, Brodsky dug up a cache of food and fuel he had stashed near his cabin the summer before. Then he went about putting his homestead back in order. He picked up scraps of litter, then dismantled and burned the makeshift tables and benches the sailors had erected. With the weary expression of a man who has just evicted a houseful of squatters, Brodsky eyed the large square of trampled grass around the cabin.

"The island is small and can't stand all this," he said. He smiled as their driftwood furniture went up in smoke. Around 2 A.M., I crawled onto one of the wooden planks in the cozy, low-ceilinged hut and fell hard asleep.

Stepan's brown, wooden craft was broad abeam and sat low in the water. It took the waves well, as I learned when we bobbed over three-foot seas on the way to Cape Kolguyev. As we headed east, the island came to a narrow point. One gulag prisoner, a musician, wrote how he enjoyed standing on Anzer's skinny eastern neck, listening to the rhythmic pounding of the surf hitting two shorelines. But such memories were scarce. Some prisoners likened being sent to the Solovetsky Islands and Anzer to crossing the river Styx. Riding a prison ship from the Karelian coast to the main Solovetsky island was like entering the outer circle of hell. Going from the main island to Anzer, you entered the inner circle, a place of isolation and torment. Cruising along the Anzer shoreline, Brodsky recalled the words of professor Ivan Ozerev, shipped to Solovki in 1930.

"They put me in a funeral ship," Ozerev wrote, "and sent me to Anzer."

At Cape Kolguyev, strolling across the boulder-strewn heath, Brodsky said, "You can see why people once built labyrinths and stone burial mounds here. It feels like the intersection of two worlds." We approached an arctic-tern colony, and more than one thousand birds took to the air. The shores of the White Sea provide one of the largest nesting areas in Russia for these birds, which circumscribe an extraordinary migration route that takes them from breeding grounds in the Arctic to wintering territory near Antarctica. Gingerly we picked our way through the colony, careful not to crush the brown-spotted eggs and furry, recently hatched chicks hunkering down in the heath. We walked through a spongy bog, past scrub grass decorated with vivid pink wildflowers. Huge, dun-colored hares bounded from cover.

That evening, Dashkevich and I motored over to neighboring Kapersky Bay, where he set out nets and I fly-fished for cod and herring. It was 9 P.M. and sunny. The bay was about a mile wide, the shoreline rocky, the wind calm. Casting into these unpolluted waters, following the progress of my brightly colored flies through the emerald sea, was soothing and pleasurable. Saltwater fly-fishing, which had become popular in America, was akin to using streamers to catch trout, only in the ocean you fished with flies that imitated baitfish, eels, and shrimp. I had no idea if cod could even be caught on a fly, or how to go about doing it. Predictably, I landed nothing. Dashkevich was beginning to take delight in watching this well-outfitted foreigner get nowhere with his pricey equipment.

"God, who dreamed up this way of fishing?" said Dashkevich. Sport fishing was not his métier. He preferred the surer results that came from using a net. "You'll never catch a damned thing with that outfit."

I was beginning to like this man. That night, dining on fat-studded morsels of canned Great Wall–brand Chinese pork and hurling back shots of vodka, I told Dashkevich that my compatriots had become a health-obsessed lot, fretting about what they ate and drank.

Flushed from the alcohol, his belly stuffed with camp chow, Dashkevich—a forty-seven-year-old who stood five feet ten inches tall, weighed 220 pounds, and was going bald fast—said, "Why would I want to live to some old age? I prefer to live a good, full life and not grow real old. Shit, another ten years is plenty for me. That's all I need. Why do Americans want to live forever?"

He slept with us that night in the cabin, deafening snores escaping from his hulking form. A violent storm roared over Anzer, and at 3 A.M. the dusky sky was riven by lightning.

• • •

Drenched in sunlight, the waters of the White Sea lapping on its stony shores, Kenga was a benign, bucolic spot. Located on the southwestern tip of Anzer, Kenga was a long, sloping heath, with a twenty-foot bluff on its south side and a pebbly beach on the west. Daisies and purple wildflowers trembled in a soft ocean breeze. Plainly visible across the Anzer Straits, five miles away, was the village of Rebalda on the main Solovetsky island.

Sixty years before, this was the debarkation point for inmates who came to Anzer. At first, the Communist commissars who established the prison camps on Solovki and Anzer didn't realize they were laying the cornerstone for what would eventually become a network of hundreds of camps spread across the Soviet Union. In 1923, when the first prisoners began trickling in, the Soviet regime was six years old. It had survived a bloody civil war, and with Lenin incapacitated by a stroke, Stalin was consolidating his power. He and his fellow Bolsheviks began rounding up their foes: the former nobility, czarist officers, Russian Orthodox priests, members of vanquished political parties. Already, the guiding principle that would give birth to Stalin's totalitarianism—anything goes in furtherance of the Revolution—was operational. An early Soviet banner summed things up: "With an iron hand, we will drive humanity to happiness!"

For the first few years, conditions on Solovki and Anzer were relatively benign. Inmates had their own newspapers, magazines, scientific societies, theater troupes, and libraries. Gradually, however, as Stalin assumed absolute power and more prisoners were sent to Solovki, the camps began to take on the brutal character of the later gulag. "The Solovki camp was like a tree growing," said Brodsky. "Nobody knew where its branches would go, but it was all worked out in the tree's genes. The entire system was like that. Nobody knew what it would do next, but it was genetically programmed to make its every move."

By trial and error, the masters at Solovki laid the foundation for what would become the largest system of labor camps and prisons the world had ever seen.

In 1929, one incident highlighted the difference between the old

Solovki and what was to come. Camp bosses wanted to rid themselves of some of the islands' most respected prisoners, including
czarist officers. The commissars trumped up charges against the inmates, accusing them of plotting to kill camp guards, commandeer
a steamer, and flee overseas. The prisoners were sentenced to death.
Among them was Georgi Osorgin, an officer who had been awarded
a gold sword by Czar Nicholas II for his heroism during World
War I.

Several days after Osorgin was sentenced, his wife, Princess Lina
Golitsyna, visited him on the main Solovetsky island. After promising to tell his wife nothing of the death sentence, Osorgin persuaded
camp authorities to let him see her. The couple spent three days
together—probably in a room rented from a guard—and Osorgin
kept silent about his fate. On the third day, he waved farewell as
her steamer sailed out of the Bay of Prosperity. That night, October
29, 1929, Osorgin and thirty-five other prisoners were led to a pit
and shot by torchlight.

Alexander Solzhenitsyn wrote about the incident in *The Gulag Archipelago:*

"Those three Osorgin days show how far the Solovetsky regime
was from having donned the armor of a *system.* The impression is left
that the air of Solovki strangely mingled extreme cruelty with an
almost benign incomprehension of where this was leading."

As Brodsky and I stood on the shores of Kenga, he recounted an
event that occurred there in 1938. One of the witnesses was Olga
Manet, at the time a young Polish Jew who had been arrested in
Minsk on her way to visit her sister in Moscow. Her crime? Suspected
espionage, based on the fact she was a Pole and a student of Espe-
ranto, an international language in vogue at the time.

Manet arrived on the main Solovetsky island in 1935 and was
transferred to Anzer in the summer of 1937. In a conversation in
1992, Manet—then eighty-seven—described to me the surreal mix
of beauty and cruelty she encountered on Anzer. She and a group of
women prisoners had been sent to the island to gather seaweed used
in the production of iodine. Decades later, she still remembered what
a natural paradise Anzer was, its waters teeming with herring, its
forests filled with berries, mushrooms, and wildflowers. The women
had been hungry when they arrived on Anzer. But one of them was

adept at catching and killing baby seals, and the inmates feasted on seal flesh cooked with berries. "We stuffed ourselves until we could eat no more," Manet recalled.

In the early spring of 1938, Manet and her group were brought to the dock at Kenga—where Brodsky and I were standing—for the return trip to the main island. The ice pack in the Anzer straits was breaking up, and blocks of ice were piling atop one another, grinding and crashing against the shoreline. Placing a narrow plank between the rickety wooden dock and the boat, the guards then forced the women to crawl along the board, which was being buffeted by ice floes. One of the women in Manet's group was Olga Rimsky-Korsakov, niece of the famed Russian composer. She began inching over the icy plank, but soon slipped into the water and drowned. The guards roared with laughter. A second woman tried. She, too, drowned. Finally, Manet and the remaining women managed to safely negotiate the plank and were transferred back to the main island.

The wooden pier had long since crumbled into the White Sea, replaced by a stone jetty. On the day we visited Kenga, two terns sat on the jetty, facing seaward. I walked along the heath, and a large brown bird with webbed feet, a parasitic jaeger, did a broken-wing display to draw me away from her nest.

That evening, on the north side of the island, Dashkevich and I competed to see who could catch the first cod. He steered the wooden boat close to a rocky ledge on the shoreline, cut the engine, and we drifted and fished. After fifteen minutes, no one had caught a thing. Then I heard Dashkevich cursing mightily and figured he had snagged his big, shiny lure on the bottom. I looked over and watched as he hauled a two-foot, green, bug-eyed cod out of the bay and flung it on the floor of the boat.

"Hey, American," said Dashkevich, "how do you like that?"

Over dinner, Dashkevich told me he had wound up on Solovki fourteen years ago after leaving his job as a factory worker in Belorus. Like many who had come to the islands, he was drawn to their faraway feel, and the sense that a man was his own master. There was some poaching on the archipelago, he said, more since the Russian economy had gone to hell. Only recently, Dashkevich had apprehended two people as they plundered eggs from a seabird colony. They were planning to eat them.

. . .

The church atop Golgotha—named for the hill where Christ was cru-
cified—was in ruins, its floor littered with bricks, wood, and other
debris. Pastel frescoes of saints were reemerging on the walls as the
Stalin-era whitewash faded. Everywhere were the vestiges of the gulag—isolation cells, bars on windows, holes in doors through which
prisoners were fed. Three mass graves were located near the monastery, one believed to hold eight hundred prisoners. Standing in the
cool, damp church, Yuri looked out through a smashed window frame
and surveyed the sweeping panorama—the indigo sky, the dazzling
sea, the forests of Anzer. He recounted the words of Pavel A. Flo-
rensky, a renowned inventor and theologian who was imprisoned on
Solovki and shot in 1937:

"This is a beautiful place. But only my eyes can see it. Not me."

Walking through high grass to an adjacent building, we shimmied through a hole in the debris and scrambled over dirt floors to
a wooden door barely hanging on its hinges. Brodsky pulled back
the door, revealing a note hastily scribbled by a prisoner sixty
years ago:

"12th November 1936. A group of 205 counterrevolutionaries and
counterrevolutionary terrorists arrived. On May 17, 1937, removed
to an unknown location."

Brodsky had discovered the note a few years earlier after pulling
off an old bulletin board. As far as he could determine, the entire
group was executed.

"Every person was a world, a cosmos, with children and families,"
said Brodsky as we returned to his cabin. "It's difficult to compre-
hend. The very best people were destroyed. They were the conscience of the country, and the conscience had to be destroyed first
of all."

He talked, also, of how many of the guards, secret-police officers,
and all but one of the camp commandants were eventually executed,
devoured by the very system they had served. "All who came in
contact with this system turned out unhappy," he said. "Everyone
was eventually vanquished. Literally everyone."

Around 1 A.M., taking advantage of the round-the-clock sunlight,
I walked alone to neighboring Kapersky Bay with my fly rod, deter-

mined to prove to Dashkevich that I could catch a cod with my silly rig. But the tide was too low, and fishing was impossible. I sat instead in the center of an ancient labyrinth. The sea and the sky were a uniform shade of gray, and a few faint beams of sunlight protruded through the overcast sky. I watched seals sitting on rocks, their blunt, glistening heads slowly rotating like gun turrets. Far off, I heard the hum of a boat engine. I wished that a black Russian nuclear submarine would surface just offshore, rising out of the water like a whale. I could wave to the crew. But it never came to pass.

The following afternoon, in a thick fog, we boarded Dashkevich's boat and crept back to the main island.

Galya Kozmin was an uncommonly attractive woman. About thirty, with pale, translucent skin, gray-blue eyes, dark blond hair, high cheekbones, and a delicate nose of perfect proportions, she was a classic northern-Slavic beauty. She would have turned your head in Moscow or St. Petersburg. On the Solovetsky Islands, she was a vision.

Galya lived one floor below Brodsky and worked in the local telephone station. Her husband was in Arkhangelsk, recovering from an operation, and she lived with her son, a towheaded toddler whose nose ran prodigiously and who played outside the apartment as mosquitoes feasted on his chubby, pink face. Her yearning to flee Solovki was palpable.

One night, she invited Yuri and me to dinner. Her willowy sister, Lena, was there with her boyfriend. Galya's apartment was typically Russian, a small, two-bedroom affair with cheap, factory-made oriental carpets on the walls and a large, glass-front cupboard filled with wedding crystal and china. Her balcony betrayed her peasant roots. It was a riot of cucumber and tomato plants, the fruits of which we enjoyed for dinner. A table placed in the center of the small living room was covered with dishes—fried pork, potatoes, salads, sardines, cheese, and sausage. We toasted with beer and vodka, and I marveled at Galya, who exhibited that pouty, feline, hyperfeminine flirtatiousness common to many young Russian women.

After dinner, we repaired to the island's only nightclub, a place called Max. Located in a neglected wooden building, across the street from a Stalin-era barracks, Max was a study in boredom and bad taste. A handful of inebriated young men hovered sullenly outside the front door. Entering the bar, I was struck by a blast of heat and smoke as I paid the five-thousand-ruble cover charge for each person in our group. Flashing lights ricocheted around the dark interior, and deafening Russian pop music—there is none worse in the world—blasted out of fuzzy speakers. About forty people were in the club, most of them women. They danced together on a wooden floor ringed by tables where men sat slumped over tumblers of vodka. Galya said the place was so crowded the previous New Year's Eve that people had had to bring their own chairs.

I bought our drinks from a barmaid proffering Baltika beer, counterfeit vodka, and a sickly German port wine that was destined to make Galya's sister ill by the end of the night. The barmaid was a squat woman who wore a miniskirt, brilliant gold panty hose, and several pounds of makeup. Her long hair was died a gaudy henna color, and it framed a puffy face grotesquely painted with crimson lipstick and dismal eye shadow. She had a personality to match.

As I jitterbugged with Galya and Lena, the locals eyed us with curiosity. Lena, a slender woman of five feet nine, was getting drunk from the German port and was sticking quite close to me as we danced. "The women here are very loose," lovely Lena warned me. "You've got to be careful." Indeed, the Solovki maidens were casting come-hither glances at both Yuri and me, a testimony not to our good looks, but to the dismal state of manhood on the island. Yuri and I had talked about sex earlier in the day, and he was surprised to learn that I had been faithful to my wife of fifteen years. He said that nearly everyone he knew had cheated on his or her spouse. We agreed that Soviet power had not had a salutary effect on the morals of its citizens.

By 1 A.M., inebriation had reached critical mass in Max's. Several young men pulled up chairs to our table and began shouting rambling, unintelligible questions into my ear. Belligerence was rising with the overall blood-alcohol level. Lena could barely walk. It was time to go.

The next morning, a Monday, Stepan Dashkevich showed up to collect the money I owed him from our excursion to Anzer. He and a friend sat down at Yuri's kitchen table and drank grain spirits mixed with cold tea. It was 10 A.M. After only a week in rural Russia, it was beginning to dawn on me why the country functioned so poorly. At any given time, half the male population was either drunk or hungover. So widespread was the practice of curing a hangover by boozing it up again in the morning that the Russians had a special verb for it: *pokhmelitsa*. It was a word, and a ritual, I would encounter repeatedly in the next three months.

Since its founding in 1425, the Solovetsky monastery had been one of the northernmost outposts of the Russian Orthodox Church and had played a leading role in the country's spiritual life. It was virtually a state unto itself, complete with its own army of monks. In 1854, during the Crimean War, the English fleet blockaded the strategically located archipelago. A British armada sailed into the Bay of Prosperity and, in eight hours, lobbed eighteen hundred shells at the monastery and surrounding village. But the archimandrite, Father Alexander, a former army priest, mounted a spirited defense and returned fire. The English fleet withdrew without landing a party of marines.

In the 1920s, the Bolsheviks crushed the five-hundred-year-old religious institution as they closed the monastery and ushered in the gulag. The Solovki prison was closed in 1939, and monastery buildings across the archipelago fell into disrepair. In 1991, the monastery reopened. The giant bronze bells—which mariners could reportedly hear twenty-five miles out to sea—rang again for the first time in seventy-one years. Every evening when I was there, a monk would climb to the top of the decaying bell tower, which was encased in scaffolding, and play a rapid-fire, melodious serenade. The sound washed over the Bay of Prosperity, fading into silence somewhere over the White Sea.

Father Archimandrite Iosif took over the monastery in 1992 with the charge of revitalizing an institution that was physically and spiritually in decay. Yuri and I sought him out, walking through a gate in the massive kremlin walls and into the crumbling inner compound, which occupied an area the size of two city blocks. At the entrance to the three-story building that housed the monks' cells, a brother stood in front of an icon and sang out prayers in the sonorous,

35

haunting tone of the Orthodox Church. A young apprentice monk, with an unruly black beard and grim expression, sat in a guard booth silently mouthing a prayer. He let us pass with a sullen nod. Later, Brodsky informed me that this young seeker was known for skulking around the monastery, hounding women visitors in miniskirts and shouting, "Get off of these grounds!" Brodsky had nicknamed the kid the Ayatollah.

Walking up two flights of wide, stone steps, we opened a heavy wooden door and were greeted by the smell of incense. Along an empty corridor hung portraits and photographs of well-known monks who had died on the island. Brodsky, who knew Father Iosif, called out his name. Soon, a stout young man in a floor-length black robe appeared. He had a round, full face, a reddish brown beard, and light brown hair pulled back in a ponytail. Smiling, he ushered us into his office and sat down in a thronelike chair ornately carved with the double-headed Russian eagle. His face was gentle and alert. Folding his hands on his belly, he leaned back, propped one leg on the bottom of a table, and announced he was ready for questions.

"The history of the monastery was unfortunately abruptly ended in the 1920s, and we must now rebuild the traditions here all over again," Father Iosif said as a cold rain drummed on the monastery's tin roofs. "I myself am doing my best to learn the old monastic ways. The main thing has been to restore the daily schedule of prayers and religious devotions. Any private company could oversee the physical restoration of the monastery, but the most important thing, the foundation of the monastery, is to restore the daily religious rituals and prayers. I am trying to tie all these things together—the prayers, the physical restoration—to point the life of the monastery toward its main goal, the worship of God."

He would need the Almighty's help. The monastery, on the United Nations' list of worldwide architectural monuments, was in appalling condition. Windows were smashed, roofs leaked, beams sagged. A huge mound of trash sat in one corner of the grounds. Neither the Moscow Patriarchy nor the Ministry of Culture was sending Father Iosif the money he needed to keep the monastery from falling down around him.

Still, Father Iosif, who was thirty-nine, said that something about the remote splendor of Solovki continued to attract the faithful. Fifteen monks and fifteen apprentice monks were serving at the monastery. "Well, if you compare us with Danilov monastery in Moscow, for example, then the Solovetsky monastery is heaven. There are tourists everywhere at the Danilov monastery, moving around the place like ants. You can't go out by yourself and be left alone. Here, of course—especially in winter—there is solitude."

Unprompted, Father Iosif volunteered what was widely known about the old Orthodox Church but little discussed: that it was controlled, top to bottom, by the KGB.

"When I graduated from the Moscow Spiritual Academy, I came into contact with the three initials that all priests and students of the academy come in contact with: K-G-B," said Father Iosif. He said KGB officers approached him and asked him to inform on fellow students and priests at the academy. He refused.

The friendly visage sitting across from me was the new face of the Russian Orthodox Church, and it was a welcome change from the corrupt, sinister stool pigeons who passed for holy men in the Soviet Union. Brodsky said Father Iosif was often mentioned as someone destined to move up in the Church ranks. Some even thought he might one day become patriarch.

Before leaving, I asked him about the quality of young men who came to Solovki to enter the monastery. Many, he acknowledged, had come for the wrong reasons. Some, fleeing the disorder that prevailed across Russia, were seeking three square meals a day and easy work. "They thought they would be free of the responsibility of caring for a family or of having a wife who was always sawing on their neck," said Father Iosif. "They thought they could turn life here, as one father superior put it, into a society of bachelors. That's not the way it is."

Chuckling, the archimandrite said, "As they say in the New Testament, 'Many are called. Few are chosen.' "

Getting off the Solovetsky Islands is not a simple matter. A boat customarily runs weekly to the Karelian coast, but there are no guarantees. Yuri had a friend with a vessel and suggested I ask him for a ride. But Yuri alerted me: this man had been flattened by his foray into Russia's topsy-turvy market system, and I could expect to hear about it.

Igor Kurochkin's ship, a former navy tender, was docked at the main harbor. A chilly rain fell as I stepped aboard. Entering the mess cabin, located above deck, I ran into a stocky man with brown, curly hair and green eyes. It was Kurochkin. He had an intense, harried look, not unlike that of an American small businessman struggling to survive in the entrepreneurial jungle. He couldn't give me a ride. But over plates of goulash, he gave me a full accounting of his life.

For twenty-five years, Kurochkin had toiled in the one realm of the Soviet state that had functioned relatively well—the military. He was assigned to the Northern Fleet, based near Murmansk, and worked on a variety of warships as a surgeon. He rose to be a second-rank captain and served on the front line of the Cold War.

Although he served with distinction, he realized for years that he was trapped in an inane, doomed system. "The potential that was in me was not used before I retired in 1990," said Kurochkin. "I used a certain tiny fraction of that potential in the navy. The rest was wasted on idiocy."

Shortly before retiring, Kurochkin bought a mothballed tender. In his spare time, he renovated it himself, and in 1990, at the age of forty-five, he began to navigate the harrowing course his country was taking from Communism to capitalism. His plan was simple: working with foreign partners, he would develop tourism and light industry along the scenic White Sea coast.

"Then, as now, I saw unlimited possibilities here," said Kurochkin. "I saw that five or six bold and energetic people could conquer this whole stretch of coastline. I saw a beautiful sea, untouched nature. But there was a conflict between the unlimited potential I saw in Russia and my complete ignorance of my own people. I suffered from naïveté. I didn't know my own people. They didn't want to work honestly."

Kurochkin found a Norwegian partner, and together they built a small prefabricated-housing factory. They produced and exported eighteen prefab homes to Norway before the venture began to come apart under the pressures of the chaotic Russian market. Employees stole and drank. His on-site manager slacked off.

Kurochkin, several days' stubble on his face, popped open a bottle of beer with his fork. The cap ricocheted off the cabin's wooden walls.

"The country's best people, its potential, have been lopped off. Look at history. Who died? The very best people. Who remained? The biggest problem today is post-Communism. What the Bolsheviks did was take away all the initiative from people, leaving a nation of parasites. To find energetic, innovative people is very difficult. People have forgotten how to work. They only pretend to work. They take no pride in doing a job well. People have become deformed. Under the Communists, things worked because of fear. Now there is no fear and no discipline."

He sighed and seemed near tears. The sphere of his business activities had contracted to his boat, which he used for carrying passengers and cargo.

"This will go on for another thirty or forty years until we replace a couple of generations. I'm tired of fighting with people. From the dirt that was Communism, you can't do anything. The alcoholics will die out and gradually a generation will rise up that will be able to do something. I consider myself fertilizer for those who will come after me."

The conversation returned again to the country's monumental vodka problem. Kurochkin let fly with a line that rang in my ears for the rest of my trip:

"The country is under narcosis."

That evening, my last on Solovki, Brodsky and I set out at midnight for the monastery. We walked along the stone-floored ramparts, passing moldering brick walls and rooms littered with debris. Stooping, we entered the barnlike chamber that once housed the gulag theater, a fixture of the camp in its early days in the 1920s. The room, its walls covered with graffiti, was cool and gloomy. Once, it held up to six hundred inmates, many of them intellectuals who came to the theater to forget that they had been wrenched from their old lives and were now prisoners in Comrade Stalin's brave new world. Standing in a rectangle of dusky light near a smashed window, Brodsky recalled the visit to Solovki of writer Maxim Gorky, who had become an unabashed propagandist for the Bolshevik regime. Visiting Solovki, he extolled the virtues of reeducation camps. One night, he came to the theater and sat in the front row as prisoners recited verse that demonstrated how loose things were in the early gulag.

We're prisoners of the country of Soviets,
Where there are no prisons and no torture.
They don't punish us, they correct us,
And therein lies the truth, and the whole secret.

Brodsky recounted what happened after the performance:

"Gorky went out to the smoking area, and prisoners, not realizing at that point what he truly was, came up to him and began slipping notes into his pocket. These notes described the real conditions in the camp. Gorky smiled, as if to tell the prisoners that he would read the notes later and look into their problems. In fact, he gave all the notes to the Chekists [secret police].

"All this happened right here, just that way."

We walked past the building housing the monks' cells. Out of a third-floor window drifted the dark, otherworldly, basso profundo voice of one of the brothers singing evening prayers. An old woman, dressed in a long black skirt and kerchief, plucked green onions and lettuce from the ample monastery garden.

In front of an adjacent whitewashed, brick building, a black-robed monk stood before a wooden door, waiting to enter. He raised his head heavenward. For the first time that day, the heavy, gray overcast was breaking up. Low, leaden clouds were scattering swiftly to the east. In their wake the sky opened up dramatically, and an ethereal, rose-colored light spread across the heavens. The retreating clouds caught fire. Soon the entire sky was lit with shades of orange, pink, gold, and silver-blue, the memorable hues of a Solovetsky sunset in July.

2.

WAITING FOR MIKHAIL'ICH

 In the angling world, there's no snob like an Atlantic-salmon snob. And while being mindful not to tar all Atlantic-salmon fishermen with the same brush, the truth is this: many devotees of the "sport of kings" are insufferable, tweedy, elitist, name-dropping bores.

For years, the American sports who pursued *Salmo salar*, arguably the finest northern game fish, did so primarily on pricey, private rivers on Canada's Atlantic seaboard, waterways with lyrical names such as the Grand Cascapedia, Restigouche, and Miramichi. They inherited spots in turn-of-the-century camps by a sort of droit du seigneur. Or, if rich enough, they simply bought their way onto a stream. But in the 1990s, the Atlantic-salmon brotherhood discovered a new playground. It was Russia's Kola Peninsula, and wealthy Western anglers flocked there for one reason: the place was teeming with fish.

As I left the Solovetsky Islands and journeyed north by train on the Arctic express, I was determined to give my moneyed compatriots a wide berth. I wanted to fish for Kola salmon on the cheap, and among the Russians. It was for that reason I found Uncle Vasya so appealing. Clearly, here was a man at the nadir of the Kola Peninsula food chain.

Uncle Vasya caught my eye the moment I stepped off the train at Kandalaksha, a port city on the northwestern edge of the White Sea, about seventy-five miles from the Finnish border. He and a female companion were standing on the platform, looking as if they had stepped out of a sepia-tinted photograph from St. Petersburg, 1918. Uncle Vasya was a gnomelike creature of about seventy—short, skinny, and tightly wired. He was dressed in a beat-up, gray cotton jacket, thick layers of wool sweaters, brown canvas pants, and black rubber boots. On his back was a large aluminum pack, the shape of a half-cylinder; I learned later it was full of fish. He was trying to talk his way onto my train, bound for Murmansk, and was jabbering intently to the conductor, who was playing hard to get. Both men knew Uncle Vasya—who didn't have a kopek—would eventually get on the Arctic. It was only a question of what he would have to barter in exchange for a seat, and how long the conductor would toy with him before relenting.

His sidekick—who turned out to be his daughter—was a tall, handsome woman of about forty, dressed from head to toe in rough, olive green pants and jacket. She wore knee-length, black leather boots and a green cap like those popular with the early Bolshevik commissars. On her back was a hefty army-issue, cotton knapsack that sagged to her waist. She had a smooth, tanned complexion, blue eyes, light brown hair pulled back in a ponytail, and high cheekbones.

Uncle Vasya temporarily gave up on the conductor. Wheeling around to see what other opportunities might present themselves on the platform, he spied me and made a beeline in my direction.

It was nearly 5 P.M., the weather was brisk and clear, and I was in high spirits. My train had crossed the Arctic Circle about fifty miles back, and I was heading at last to Kola to fish its renowned salmon rivers. I had left Solovki early in the morning and was trying to make it to Murmansk—350 miles to the north—by midnight. We had stopped for thirty minutes in Kandalaksha, the gateway to the Kola Peninsula.

"Hey, son, would you have any matches?" the old man asked.

I handed him a glossy white box of matches from the Ebbett Grill in Cape May, New Jersey. He slowly turned over the box in his gnarled hands, admiring the raised lettering.

"Hey, my friend, I haven't seen anything like this in sixty years. No, sir, not in the Soviet Union."

"They're from America," I said.

"America?" he inquired, arching his bushy eyebrows. "You're

from America? Hey, maybe you have another present, just a little one for grandfather? I've been a woodsman for more than fifty years, most of it here on the Kola Peninsula. I'm a fisherman, too."

"It's beautiful country."

"Yeah, but it's all gone to hell now. The water? The rivers? They're crap. Look at the shit the Communists pulled. And now the 'democrats' are doing the same thing."

I returned to my compartment and grabbed two packs of fishhooks for the old man. He looked slightly disappointed when I placed them in his hand, expecting, perhaps, something grander from an American. "Okay, thanks," he said, marching back to the conductor. Just as the train was about to pull out of the station, he talked his way onto the car ahead of mine.

Back in my compartment—which I was sharing with a well-fed Armenian textile merchant from St. Petersburg—I continued thinking about the old man and decided to pay him a visit.

Kola's undammed rivers harbor the largest concentration of Atlantic salmon in the world. This, in turn, has attracted a host of well-heeled anglers, men and women willing to pay dearly to catch—and release—Atlantic salmon. This gold-plated passion is understandable. Hatched in undefiled rivers and streams in Canada and northern Europe, the salmon spend a few years in freshwater before migrating to the open Atlantic, where they fatten up for a few more years before returning again to spawn in their natal streams. On their spawning runs, the salmon—which often weigh twenty pounds—do not feed. Yet, out of a primal feeding instinct or territorial aggression, these powerful fish attack beautiful, man-made flies with names like the General Practitioner and Jock Scott, giving the angler one of the great thrills in sport as the fish hurls itself out of the water and makes dramatic dashes up and down some of the prettiest rivers on the planet.

There's a catch. In today's world, this thrill is hard to come by. Of the hundreds of thousands of Atlantic salmon that once migrated in and out of the rivers of the northeastern United States, only a few hundred wild fish remain. The rest were wiped out by dams, pollution, and commercial overfishing. Canada still has a run of several hundred thousand wild salmon, but their numbers are steadily dwindling and most of the prime water is private.

Every schoolchild knows Mikhail Gorbachev changed the world. Few realize he also made it a better place for salmon fishing. Once, the Kola Peninsula had been an armed, arctic camp closed to the prying eyes of foreigners. The Northern Fleet was based near Murmansk, and the rest of the peninsula was lousy with Red soldiers, rocket forces, and air defense squadrons. But in 1989, sensing they'd lost the Cold War anyway, the Soviets opened up Kola to foreign fishermen, and a few intrepid Westerners armed with fifteen-foot Spey rods hit the beaches. They discovered an angling paradise, a place where a good fly fisherman could catch and release a half dozen Atlantic salmon a day, about five more than on most other salmon rivers in the world.

Beginning in 1992, a volatile combination of elements converged on Kola's scenic, arctic rivers. Russia's wide-open, bribe-ridden market economy began to take wing at the same time as more than a thousand American and European fly fishermen flocked to Kola each year, eager to shell out $4,000 to $8,000 a week to dupe a fish into devouring a gaudy wad of fur and feathers. As Samuel Johnson once wrote, "Angling or float fishing I can only compare to a stick and a string, with a worm at one end and a fool at the other."

Such a collection of fish nuts from the West inevitably attracted a cast of Russian and Western characters, some of them unsavory, eager to cash in on this magnificent obsession. There ensued a series of unseemly financial and territorial squabbles that came to be known as the Kola Wars, during which massive bribes allegedly changed hands, leases were signed and abrogated with alacrity, and shell-shocked groups of naive, moneyed, indignant American anglers were kicked out of their cushy camps because their Russian sponsors had wound up playing for the losing team. Still, the fishing was spectacular, particularly on rivers like the Ponoi, which were little touched by scandal.

All of this was of marginal interest to me. It boiled down to one thing—greed—and I was far more intrigued by the rivers, the fishing, and the ordinary Russians who lived amid this commercial comic opera. I set two goals for myself: not to ride helicopters into swanky camps on far-flung rivers, and to fish only with the natives. Landing a salmon under these circumstances would prove trickier than I had imagined.

I found Uncle Vasya and his daughter in the last compartment of the adjoining car. Sliding open the door, I inhaled the sour smell of clothes that had gone unwashed for weeks. The pair waved me in and announced they were hungry. I returned with apples, cheese, and bread, and they ate with appreciation.

Uncle Vasya's full name was Vasily Volkov, and he was born in Kirovsk on the Kola Peninsula. In 1937, when he was a boy, Stalin's secret police sent his family into exile in Siberia for fifteen years. In the 1950s, he made his way back home, where he worked for decades as a lumberman. Now, Uncle Vasya received a pension of about $60 a month. His daughter, Yelena, was unemployed. So they did what an increasing number of rural Russians were doing as they wandered around in the rubble of the Soviet economy: they turned to nature.

"Only the woods feed us," said Yelena. "We live thanks to fish, mushrooms, and berries."

Uncle Vasya and Yelena were returning home to the Kola Peninsula following a month of camping and fishing in the forests of Karelia, near Finland. They caught hundreds of perch and traded them for bread and cured pork. Uncle Vasya had charmed his way onto the train by giving the conductor a sack of fish. Now they were returning to Kola to cash in on the berry season, picking raspberries and whortleberries and selling them for seventy thousand rubles— $14—a bucket. "In a week, the money will be pouring in," said Uncle Vasya.

I asked Uncle Vasya if he had heard of the Americans and Europeans who were paying $1,000 a day to fish for salmon in his backyard. He mulled over this astronomical sum for a moment. "Are they really so rich that they can afford that?" he asked. He said he didn't begrudge the foreigners their passion, but resented that many of the best salmon rivers were closed to Russians. Even those that remained open required that anglers fish with a license, a concept that was alien to Uncle Vasya, a natural-born poacher. "Oh, if they nab you catching those salmon, you'll get it," said Uncle Vasya. "They'll cut your boots off, confiscate your nets, and make you walk home bare-foot. No, Uncle Vasya has to catch these little perch. The salmon are for the czars."

He harbored no great love for the old system, but thought even less of the new one. "At least under the Communists I had sausage—two to three sticks, always," he said. "Now, with the democrats, I have nothing. Absolutely nothing. We've hit a dead end."

For people like Vasya, life had been crummy under the czars, it had been crummy under the Bolsheviks, it had been crummy under the princes of perestroika, and it was crummy under Mr. Yeltsin. "No one," said Yelena, "believes in anything anymore."

As the train traveled north, the landscape grew hillier, and three-thousand-foot mountains—their summits treeless and still partially covered in snow—rolled by our window. At 6:30 P.M., the train lurched to a stop at Uncle Vasya's station. I gave him a dollar bill as a souvenir and thirty thousand rubles—about $6—for the road. Standing on the platform, Uncle Vasya invited me to come visit. "I'll show you around, and I'll tell you the truth," said the old man. "No one likes to hear the truth. But when Uncle Vasya tells you something, it's true."

He shook my hand and adjusted the straps on his aluminum back-pack.

"Go with God," he said, and was gone.

Around 10 P.M., I caught my first glimpse of the Kola River. Steady summer rains had sent a surge of water into the stream, and it roared through a rugged landscape of gorges and high valleys. We passed several villages, the brightly colored wooden houses built with steeply pitched roofs to shuck off heavy winter snows. Where the river widened and settled down, scattered fishermen prospected for Atlantic salmon. The Kola River ran from the Barents Sea, past Murmansk and a handful of other towns. It was the most industrialized and heavily poached salmon river on the peninsula, but it still had a sizable run of fish and—unlike the remote, high-priced rivers—was open to anyone who bought a license.

A look at the port city of Kola left me astonished that salmon still migrated up the river. A twenty-mile industrial zone began there, running all the way to the Barents Sea, and the waterway's banks were lined with towering cranes, docks, and factories. We headed toward neighboring Murmansk, through a striking natural landscape that had been blighted by Soviet-era sprawl and neglect—decaying concrete factories and fish-processing plants, lots littered with scrap metal and lumber, rusting tugs and trawlers. Murmansk, a town of about five hundred thousand, was located in a splendid setting on hills overlooking the Kola River and Bay. But Soviet concrete towers had been deposited on the slopes like piles of guano. Communist architects and planners had displayed a remarkable ability to transform the most awe-inspiring landscape into a bleak tableau guaranteed to weigh heavy on the soul.

The Communists did not view fly-fishing as a particularly worthy pursuit. Indeed, to them it reeked of the ruling class. There weren't many fly fishermen in Russia before the Bolshevik Revolution. Afterward, there were almost none. It was the kind of hobby that could get you shot.

In 1929, an American journalist and angler, Negley Farson, discovered that the Reds considered the sport highly suspect. He was fly-fishing in the Kuban region of southern Russia, in the shadow of the Caucasus Mountains. One evening, he caught seven trout and fried them up for the local comrades.

"That night a Cossack, who informed me that his official status was Instructor in Communism, ate one of these, pronounced it marvellous; but said that I was a Capitalist because I used the fly," Farson recounted in his book, *Going Fishing*.

If you were second secretary of the regional Communist Party Executive Committee, and you were gunning for that top spot, you didn't exactly want to be seen streamside tying on a Royal Coachman to outwit a trout. Besides, in the Soviet Union, there weren't many trout left anyway.

Russia's fly-fishing fraternity was so small I had little trouble locating Alexander Starikov, a man variously described as the best—or the only—Russian fly fisherman in Murmansk. He was a tall, lanky, easygoing man of forty-two with thinning, dark blond hair. He could loosely be placed in that class known throughout the land as New Russians, a hodgepodge designating anyone flourishing under the new capitalist order. Its members included mobsters, government officials living off graft, and honest businessmen who had found a niche in the emerging chaos of the reborn Russian market. Starikov was in the latter category, a representative of a middle class that had begun to appear in cities across Russia. He and his partners made their fortune in an odd way: they imported huge quantities of Norwegian ice cream to a peninsula that was frozen nine months a year, as well as importing farmed Norwegian salmon to the wild-salmon capital of the planet. Things were going well for Alexander, who, when I showed up, was about to take his wife and two children on a three-week vacation to America.

The Cold War was over, but I soon discovered that vestiges of it would hinder my pursuit of salmon near Murmansk. Two good salmon rivers were not far from the city, the Titovka and Western Litsa. But to reach them you had to travel on the highly restricted road that ran west out of Murmansk to the Norwegian border. The region still bristled with military installations, and foreigners needed permission from Russian border troops to set foot there.

Starikov suggested we pay a visit to the FSB, the federal security service, seeking authority for me to travel the highway and fish the two rivers. Holding a meeting with the FSB ran counter to all my better instincts. Although I was legally in Murmansk, I thought it highly unwise to march into the FSB offices, announce my presence, and say I wanted to go fishing along one of the most tightly controlled highways in all of Russia. Fishing? Somehow, I doubted the boys at the FSB would have believed me, considering they were firmly convinced that representatives of Western "special services" cruised the road whenever possible, eavesdropping on Russian military communications. I still had all of Russia to cross—about three months and six thousand miles of travel—and my inclination was to slip under the FSB's radar screen.

But the desire to catch Atlantic salmon can cloud a man's judgment. The next thing I knew, Starikov and I were walking into the imposing stone building that housed the FSB. Starikov asked the soldier on duty to summon one of the officers dealing with border issues. In a few minutes, a short, stocky man appeared in the waiting area. He was scowling. Starikov explained our predicament. I caught snatches of the conversation: "American journalist . . . salmon fishing . . . Titovka . . . restricted highway." The FSB officer was

scowling fiercely now. Any second, I expected him to lead me upstairs, where I would be interrogated for days. I couldn't believe my
stupidity. Smiling at the officer, I tried to maintain an expression of
eager politeness, while silently cursing myself and Starikov. But it
turned out the Cold War really was kaput. The officer didn't even
ask for my name or my documents. He was merely annoyed and sent
us on our way, saying the only way to get to the rivers would be
to apply, in writing, for permission. A response would take a minimum of two weeks. I could not have cared less. I was elated not to
be in FSB custody and would fish the Titovka and Western Litsa in
another lifetime.

Starikov and I were not yet finished with the bureaucracy. We
had to procure licenses at the state fish inspectorate, and there I first
heard of an intriguing character on the peninsula. His name was
Svyatoslav Mikhailovich Kaluzhin, known to locals by his abbreviated patronymic, Mikhail'ich. Kaluzhin was chairman of the Shoots
of Communism collective farm, a wildly anachronistic misnomer. For
Kaluzhin was lord and master of a small, capitalist empire that included the farm, a handful of high-seas fishing trawlers, a salmon-
processing plant, and several salmon camps for foreign fishermen.
When people spoke of Kaluzhin, they tended to use words like
"prince" and "fiefdom." His domain was the Varzuga River on
southern Kola, accessible by a bad road. I decided that, after Murmansk, I would go there.

On a clear, cool evening, Starikov and I drove south out of town,
along the way stopping at his modern, warehouse-sized freezer. One
of his partners had spent the day selling ice cream and fish to local
retailers, and he was carting around a bulging sack of one-hundred-
thousand-ruble notes. "Cash and carry," remarked Starikov, who had
a fine command of the English language.

We passed the billboard-sized "Order of Lenin" medals and "Hero
City" signs paying tribute to Murmansk's role in World War II as
the Soviet Union's vital northern port. The city had been bombed
by the Germans at the start of the war in 1941 and was nearly burned
to the ground. Turning off the main road to our fishing hole, we
followed a dirt track and soon found ourselves in a garbage dump.

There were mounds of trash, scrap metal, construction debris, fifty-gallon drums oozing unknown substances. A shabbily dressed couple sifted through the refuse, looking for bottles, aluminum, anything that might fetch a few rubles. Continuing on, we bounced over washed-out portions of the road before arriving, finally, at the river.

We walked to the riverbank, which was littered with vodka bottles, cans, and paper. The river fell steeply out of the surrounding hills and surged past us, the water a tea brown color. The Kola was about one hundred yards wide, the middle churning wildly and the edges a succession of boulder-strewn eddies and pools, where we would be fishing. This was pure urban angling. Across from us was a large quarry and what looked like a gravel-processing plant. The main Kola Peninsula railroad tracks ran down the opposite bank. Above them lay a succession of industrial buildings and, higher up, apartment blocks. A sprawling pig factory sat on a nearby hill, about a mile away. The air was redolent with the sickly smell of swine dung.

I strung up my fly rod, tied on a dark fly, and waded into a backwater. Starikov, employing an odd rig in which he used a spinning rod to toss out a salmon fly, was standing on a rock, forty yards downstream.

Fly-fishing for Atlantic salmon is a ritualized, time-tested affair. The angler searches for sections of the river where salmon are likely to be resting on their upstream migration—in pools, behind rocks, at the seams where fast water meets slow. He then casts his fly downstream at a forty-five-degree angle, lets the current swing the fly until it is parallel with the shore, strips in the fly a few yards, pulls in much of his line, takes a step or two downstream, and begins the entire process over again. This is known as covering water. To many fishermen, covering water is hell, boring beyond description, a colossal waste of time. To the avid salmon angler, covering water is heaven itself, a repetitive, peaceful ceremony that allows a person to admire the unfolding of his line, the movement of the water, the subtleties of the surrounding landscape, the antics of osprey and waterfowl. A salmon angler can cover water for days without a bite. And then, just as his casting arm is aching, his palm blistering, his mind drifting back to the umpteenth insignificant episode in his life, his line will abruptly stop. A weighty tug is felt. There is no more daydreaming. Reality has arrived. The rod bends sharply, a silver fish boils at the surface, and the angler has got a wild salmon on the line. The fish streaks up and down the river, shearing line off the reel. He might lose this fish, but ultimately he reels one in, lets it rest in shallow water on the gravel, removes the hook, and looks into that wild eye staring up at him. Once this happens, the angler is hooked. Ever after, he knows that on the 277th cast of the day, his line might stop, signaling that another wild creature has come in from the ocean and, quite inexplicably, attached itself to his resplendent fly.

I cast for fifteen minutes, but failed to find a rhythm. The water toward the center of the current was too swift, the water on the edges too slow. I snagged my fly twice in the willows at my back. Then I heard an exclamation. "Fen!" hollered Alexander. His spinning rod was bent sharply. "Five kilos!" he yelled. The fish propelled itself out of the river and splashed down again. It looked far larger than five kilograms (eleven pounds).

Starikov fought the fish for an hour, an excessively long time, but his line was light and he was fearful of breaking off the salmon. Finally, he dragged the exhausted fish onto the bank, where it flopped a few times, then lay still. The salmon was nearly forty inches long and weighted twenty-two pounds. It was a gleaming silver color, fresh from the sea, with a faint pink cast to its flanks. The salmon's sides and dorsal fin bore fresh net scars from poachers who had tried to snare it on its upstream migration. Unfortunately, this fish would not be the beneficiary of catch-and-release angling. Starikov put his left hand around its thick body and, with his right, jabbed a knife into its brain, sending a series of spasms down the glistening length of the salmon. Grabbing the fish by the tail, he turned it upside down and slit its gills. As blood trickled onto the sand, I felt a pang of sadness over the death of this magnificent creature, which had migrated thousands of miles—probably to the Faeroe Islands, in the vicinity of Iceland—had avoided the nets of trawlers in the North Atlantic, had narrowly escaped the nets of the poachers on the Kola Peninsula, had swum through a wall of pollution in Kola Bay, had leapt through rapids—only to be hooked by a sport. I wished Starikov had let this one go, for Atlantic salmon, unlike Pacific salmon, often survive the spawning run and return to the ocean.

Then Starikov split open the fish, revealing thousands of orange-red, pea-sized eggs within. Heaven knows how many new salmon fry she would have produced had she lived to spawn. The sight of the eviscerated fish, the color already draining out of its chrome flanks, depressed me. I was a hunter, I killed fish and game, but wild salmon somehow belonged in a different category. Their numbers were dwindling, done in by all the scourges of the modern world—overcrowding, overfishing, pollution, the genetic engineering of their fish-farmed cousins, which was watering down wild stocks. But it was more than that. Anything that completed a journey that heroic deserved, in my opinion, to live.

A half dozen fishermen had arrived as Starikov fought his salmon, and no sooner had he gutted his fish than they displayed the curious mob psychology of the angling brotherhood. Four men stood shoulder to shoulder in the exact spot where Starikov had stood, believing, somehow, that all the salmon in the river had congregated in the same location. I moved upstream and saw, thirty-five yards out—beyond my casting range—a salmon jump. For an hour I tried in vain to catch the fish.

Shortly after midnight, we stopped fishing. Driving back to Murmansk, on a road high above the river, I watched as a prolonged arctic sunset painted the drab, industrial waters of Kola Bay a brilliant gold. Even the concrete monotony of Murmansk looked lovely, bathed in the pastel colors of a sunset that, over two hours, imperceptibly turned into a sunrise.

The following night, Starikov and I headed again to the Kola River. We ate first at Starikov's, consuming, among other things, the caviar of the salmon from the previous night. We talked briefly of the catch-and-release fishing ethic that had become so prevalent in America, yet which most Russians viewed as bizarre. Volodya Goncharov, a seventy-year-old angler who had accompanied us the night before, thought it enlightened. "You know what it's all connected with?" said Goncharov. "The fact that in your society you have full stomachs, and that here we don't. You're forty to fifty years ahead of us."

Returning to the same spot, we fished for two hours without success. Behind me, a couple cooked chicken over a fire. At first, I suspected they were using plastic bottles as fuel, but soon came to understand that the acrid odor filling the air was courtesy of the pig farm. Downstream, a group of men caroused, lobbing vodka and beer bottles into the river.

Around 11 P.M., three fish inspectors roared up in a small, green van to check our licenses. The head man said theirs was a Sisyphean task, for the Kola River was packed with poachers.

"All along the river, the poachers know where we are and where we just left," said the inspector. "We leave, and then they set out their nets. We need to be a lot tougher than we are. In the old days, they'd give a repeat poacher a couple of years in jail and that would be the last time he'd do it. Now, they just give them a little fine and let them go. So of course they do it all over again."

I would soon discover that poaching was rampant on much of the Kola Peninsula. Some poachers were netting salmon to feed their families. Some were small-time businessmen making a quick profit on the salmon, which they could sell for up to $5 a pound. And some were members of large rings that strung nets across the mouths of rivers and made hundreds of thousands of dollars a season. All of them operated because many Russians believed that laws were obeyed only by fools, and that nature's bounty was inexhaustible. They flourished, also, because a sizable number of the state's fish inspectors could be bribed to turn a blind eye. Biologists estimated that poachers killed up to 50 percent of the salmon run on the Kola River, and as much as one-third of the run on rivers such as the Umba, Kharlovka, and Rynda.

A half dozen men stood beside me along a short stretch of riverbank, bombing the water with lead-weighted gadgets. Although the weather was sublime—clear and sixty degrees—fishing this stretch of the Kola was rapidly becoming unpleasant. Of course, had the salmon been biting, I would have thought everything was swell.

I pulled out of Murmansk early the next morning, on a southbound train. My destination was the southern coast of the peninsula, where I could legally fish for salmon on two major rivers, the Umba and the Varzuga. Near an old dam on the Kandalaksha River, several men fished in the warm sun on a quiet Sunday morning. Four boys stood next to the tracks and gave our passing train the finger—another import from the West.

I had one remaining fly-fishing contact on the peninsula, and he lived in the village of Umba, where I was heading. His name was Artur Turkin, and an acquaintance in Moscow had described him as a fisherman who could help me find salmon. Little did I suspect that Turkin was an operator with the scruples of a used-car salesman and a desperate need for cash. Nor did I suspect that my acquaintance in Moscow, one of Russia's best fly fishermen, was in business with Turkin and would be getting a cut of whatever could be extracted from me. A flicker of doubt arose when I called Turkin from Murmansk and he said he'd pick me up in Kandalaksha, a two-hour drive from Umba. But I figured he was just a friendly, unemployed fellow curious to meet an American.

Sometimes, first impressions are infallible. Such was the case with Artur. I saw him as I was shuffling across the parking area in front of the Kandalaksha station, a fifty-pound pack on my back, a fifteen-pound gear bag in my left hand, and a featherweight fly-rod case dangling from my right. Artur hopped out of an olive green van and rumbled my way. He was as round as he was tall—about five feet seven, easily 220 pounds—with curly, greasy, gray hair, a jowly face, and shifty eyes hidden behind thick, plastic-rimmed glasses. Greeting me perfunctorily, he grabbed the lightest thing he could, which was the rod case. Then he was off at a near run. I marveled at how quickly a fat man could move. Simultaneously, I was overcome by a feeling that I was sliding into an extremely disagreeable situation. But I tried to exhibit Yuri Brodsky's peculiar Russian-Jewish brand of Zen Buddhism. Go with the flow, I told myself as I trudged after Artur.

Sitting behind the wheel of the van was a thin, laconic, worn-looking man. His name was Viktor Shmelyov, and at first I mistook his weary silence as hostility toward foreigners, or toward me personally. Later, I learned his taciturnity on our ride to Umba was attributable to his intense dislike of Artur. Fate had thrown this odd couple together. Both were unemployed, Viktor had a van, and Artur occasionally had clients and schemes that required wheels. But Viktor later confided that Artur had stiffed him before, and that only a grave shortage of money had persuaded him to work for Artur once again. Later, Viktor would be instrumental in delivering me from Artur.

We drove along the southern shore of the Kola Peninsula, a place known as the Tersky coast. As we rode up and down hills covered in pine and fir, we caught dramatic glimpses of the White Sea coast-line, dotted with rocky islands. The Solovetsky Islands lay far to the southeast. The warm, sunny weather continued, and I longed to be outside, away from Artur, as he leaned into the front seat and re-counted his life history. Nearly everything he had touched seemed to have turned to dust, most recently a quarry project and a salmon-fishing venture for foreigners. Then again, as he rambled on, it be-came clear that the economy of virtually the entire Tersky coast was in ruins. In Umba—the main town, with a population of 8,500—the fish collective farm was near bankruptcy, the lumber mill worked with a skeleton crew, and the quarry was out of business.

Artur held my attention only once, when he mentioned the name I had first heard in Murmansk: Svyatoslav Mikhailovich Kaluzhin, the overlord of the Varzuga River. He ruled with absolute authority, said Artur. All Kaluzhin touched turned to gold.

At midafternoon, we pulled into Umba, a collection of weathered wooden homes and concrete apartment blocks strung around a small bay that flowed into the White Sea. Viktor turned the van into the yard of a cozy, blue cottage on the water's edge. Walking in, I was warmly greeted by a bedraggled woman with an appalling mane of bleached-blond hair. She was fixing soup, sausage, and fried eggs. The table in a small dining room was set with juices, salads, and vodka. Artur informed me that the cottage used to belong to a now-defunct state construction organization. Suddenly, it dawned on me. I would be paying for all this—the driver, the van, the cottage, the cook, the food, the sleazy services of Artur. I had expected a few days of peaceful fishing with a simple Umba angler. Instead, I found myself in the clutches of a small-town loser who evidently thought that an infusion of capital from my pockets might tide him over for the summer. He was putting on the dog, Umba style, and I was footing the bill. I was seized by a desire to grab my gear and bolt.

"Artur," I said as we waited for lunch, "we've got to talk."

"After lunch," he said. "Let's let you relax a little before we talk money."

The food was awash in grease. And even by the low standards of table manners common to men in the Russian heartland—deafening slurping and bone sucking are evidently signs that one is simply wild about the fare—Artur was a pig. Inhaling the soup off his spoon, he created a whooshing gurgle like that of a bathtub being drained. He smacked emphatically and declined to wipe the layers of grease off his fat lips. We drank one desultory toast, but mainly I sulked and waited for a chance to sever ties with Artur.

After lunch, we repaired to the living room, where Artur got things off to a good start by asking me for $70 for food. He eagerly explained that he had worked out a terrific five-day program of fishing and sight-seeing. He informed me that he would accompany me everywhere, keeping me out of trouble. He had contacts along the entire southern coast. And the bill for this unforgettable excursion—now he whipped out a handwritten, itemized list of his eminently reasonable charges—was only $950. I blanched. *Nine hundred fifty dollars!* This was my budget for a month! This was a Russian pensioner's income for an entire year!

"But you see," he began, as he sensed my rising consternation, "I have a lot of expenses: amortization of Viktor's van, fuel charges, the cost of—"

"Artur," I interrupted. "Is this some sort of a joke? I told you on the phone I wanted to fish the Umba on the cheap."

"Why, is something wrong?"

"Artur, you're asking me to spend in five days what I had planned to spend in Russia for a month. I don't have this kind of money. Plus, I don't want this kind of program. I don't need you with me, especially if I go to see Kaluzhin on the Varzuga."

"But I thought you wanted—"

"Artur, forget it. I can't afford this. I just wanted someone to fish with on the Umba for a couple of days."

"All right, all right. I'll work up a revised bill for a scaled-down trip."

Crestfallen, Artur rose and left the room. His cash cow was slipping from his grasp. I walked to the kitchen, where Viktor the driver and Nina the cook were eating. They gave me a look that said, "So, you've just figured out whom you're dealing with. Good luck."

The door opened and through it walked a tall, well-built, young man with blue eyes and light brown hair. He was Andrei Yeshenko, my fishing guide. At last, I thought, something good might come of this day.

Around 6 P.M., Viktor deposited Andrei and me at a bridge north of town. The plan was to walk along the river and fish our way to the settlement of Old Umba, about six kilometers downstream. Two things soon became evident. The first was that it was not the peak of the salmon run. The second was that it *was* the peak of the mosquito season.

We scrambled down a bank and plunged into a thick, boggy wood that ran along the river. The mosquitoes were so numerous they emitted a chain-saw-like whine as they thronged around us. Moving briskly helped, so Andrei and I fought our way through creeks and thickets and swamps at a rapid pace. Clothed in chest-high waders, I was soon soaked with sweat. The walk was so uncomfortable that I scarcely noticed we weren't doing any fishing. As we plunged through the bush, Andrei pointed out numerous places where poachers had earlier placed nets in the river or built campfires to dry nets at the conclusion of their business day.

Andrei, who was thirty-two, had lost his job at a quarry in 1990. Since then, he had fielded odd jobs as an electrician, construction worker, and occasional fishing guide. His wife worked as a hairdresser, and together they made enough to support their nine-year-old son. One of Kola's fishing camps for Westerners was just a few miles upstream, but Andrei said that—other than for the creation of about fifteen jobs at the nearest camp—the locals benefited little from the presence of the wealthy foreign anglers. "It's a drop in the ocean," he said. "It just doesn't get to us."

As we moved downstream, the Umba became narrower, the scenery more dramatic. The river was high, and after two hours we came to a cascade, where a torrent of brown water tumbled over enormous boulders. This section of the Umba looked nothing like classic salmon water, which customarily has deep pools and long riffles. Just above the cascade, Andrei—leading me by the hand through deep, fast water—dragged me ten yards from the bank to some downed trees, from which I was able to cast to the edge of a surging current. I caught nothing, but the exercise focused my attention, which had been flagging due to the heat and mosquitoes: had Andrei let go of me, I would have been sucked like a leaf into the short, explosive falls.

We walked on a path through the woods, emerging fifty yards below the cascade. The river opened up, offering a sublime view of steep, wooded slopes tumbling down to the dark, clear water. Across the Umba, about one hundred yards away, was a government salmon hatchery. Just in front of it, we saw two poachers at work, apparently unconcerned that they were breaking the law within sight of the hatchery. They rowed a small boat as they checked their nets.

"The fish inspectors give them the okay," said Andrei. "The police are corrupt. The hatchery has been bought off. The whole place is corrupt. It's big money. In a season, a good poacher can catch two tons of salmon with a retail value of ten dollars a kilo. Part of this money goes to the police, the fish inspectors, regional officials in Murmansk. It's all corrupt and it's all tied together. If they catch a corrupt official, they just move him to another town. This is all done right before our eyes."

Official corruption had become particularly brazen since the collapse of Communism, but then again it had always been as much a part of Russia as long winters and cheap vodka. As one nineteenth-century foreign traveler remarked, "Russia? They steal, and the roads are bad." An adviser to Peter the Great once said, "We all steal. The only difference is that some of us steal larger amounts and more openly than others."

Our excursion had come to more closely resemble a forced march than a fishing trip. But four hours into the evening, we finally came to a lovely stretch of water that held salmon and offered an opportunity to cast without snagging my fly in a tree. The spot was a granite shelf that jutted into a long, deep pool. Just upstream were high, rocky cliffs that towered over a crescent-shaped, pebbly beach. The river narrowed to about fifty yards at the ledge, and opposite was a precipitous incline. Below the shelf were a series of riffles and pools, followed by another cascade, which rumbled soothingly in the distance. "There are usually salmon here," said Andrei.

I cast for an hour, slowly working my way down the granite outcropping, changing my fly several times. It was nearing midnight, and the sun threw a warm, orange light on the opposite cliff. A salmon showed itself closer to the far bank, out of my casting range. A mink skittered onto the ledge, circling in an effort to drive me out of its territory. I never had a bite, but the place was so peaceful, the water so fishy looking, that I almost didn't mind. After midnight, we walked the remaining two kilometers to Old Umba, a White Sea village of listing, wooden houses. We crossed a decrepit, wooden bridge with gaping holes that provided a fine view of the river smashing through the rapids below. Less than a kilometer away, the Umba flowed into the White Sea.

Back at the cottage, Nina served an early-morning meal that was even less palatable than the afternoon one—fish sticks fried in sunflower oil, accompanied by sausage that was more fat than meat. After a few shots of vodka, Artur presented his revised bill. Instead of charging me $950 for five days, he proposed $700 for two and a half days. I was flabbergasted. But you had to give him credit. He was a tenacious bastard.

"Artur, I told you I don't have this kind of money. I'm staying one more day, and after that I'm going to Varzuga by myself. Give me a realistic bill for two days and I'll pay it."

Holding up his hands, Artur said, "Oh, I didn't understand before. Now I see."

Nina reached new lows with breakfast the following morning. The first course was macaroni in boiled, sweetened milk. The second was eggs and sausage in grease. But she was a hard worker, caring for her two grandsons when she wasn't cooking for me. She also couldn't abide Artur, which gave us something in common. Artur showed up and slurped down his breakfast. Afterward, he presented his last, best offer—$400 for two days of fishing, sight-seeing, and transportation. I extracted a promise that Viktor, whom I had come to like, would drive me first to Varzuga and then back to Kandalaksha at the end of the week. Then I relented. Losing Artur had become a priority.

I paid a visit to the head of the Umba regional government, hoping to get a sense of just how bad things were along the Tersky coast. On the town's dusty main street, I walked along a raised boardwalk built for the springtime, when the mud was ankle deep. The local boss's office was located in a two-story, brown, wooden building. Inside, the nerve center of the regional government was as dark and quiet as a crypt. I saw no one, heard nothing, as I shuffled down a wood-floored hallway and up the steps to the second story. This scene greeted me whenever I walked into a rural government office that summer, and there was a reason for it. In the old days, the local Communist government could actually do something for its constituency. Now, the folks in rural Russia were on their own.

Rumors of corruption and bribe-taking swirled around the person of Viktor Vladimirovich Didenko, the local head of administration. But such gossip was repeated about nearly every elected official in Russia. Greeting me in a spacious office, Didenko turned out to be a slender, pleasant-looking figure of fifty-two, with graying hair and mustache. Like many rural officials, he was the former chairman of the local Communist Party. He struck me as articulate, personable, and overwhelmed by the staggering problems that had steadily multiplied in his region since the bloom had gone off the Gorbachev rose in about 1990.

The Communist economic structure that had supported the Tersky coast for decades had collapsed. The largest employer, the local lumber mill, had laid off hundreds of workers and hadn't paid its skeleton crew a full salary in eighteen months. The largest collective farm, which used to have 300 workers and 210 cows, now had 36 workers and 25 head of cattle. Officially, 1,200 people were unemployed—more than 20 percent of the workforce—but actual unemployment was higher, Didenko said. About a third of the region's population lived at or below the poverty level, defined as a per capita income of about $50 a month. The scattered villages along the remote Tersky coastline were slowly being abandoned. Nearly 90 percent of the region's budget was now made up of subsidies from Moscow and Murmansk. Some pensioners were subsisting mainly on bread. Alcoholism and child abuse were increasing.

More people were turning to fishing to survive. Some had obtained licenses to harvest cod and other fish in the White Sea. Others had taken to poaching salmon, and Didenko worried that stocks on the Umba would plummet if the illegal netting continued. That could drive away the roughly three hundred foreign anglers who came annually to the Umba to fish in seven different camps. Their arrival had helped the region, Didenko said, creating more than one hundred seasonal jobs, a handful of year-round ones, and generating about $50,000 in lease revenues.

"We have so many riches in this area—fish, timber, minerals—and yet we live in poverty," he said. "When it will all stabilize here, I don't know."

I wandered over to the territory of the old timber mill, a patch of blight in the center of town. Once, Soviet lumberjacks had clear-cut forests throughout the Tersky region and brought trees to the mill to be turned into boards and telephone poles. Several years ago, however, some of the mill's buildings had burned down. The rest had been left to rot. The grounds were strewn with rusting bulldozers and the wood-frame skeletons of old assembly lines. The guardhouse had been stripped of every valuable morsel of metal and wood. Two boys were at the entrance to the mill, ripping a wooden gatepost out of the ground. Near them stood an eight-foot concrete monument, on which was painted a red hand holding a red torch. There was no inscription; it was merely a woeful example of socialist art, a nonsensical signal from a lost world.

In the middle of the grounds sat the long, low-slung remains of a building. Only the wooden frame—chunks of the roof dangling from it—was still standing. Nailed to the top of this carcass was an old, red sign, its lettering nearly indecipherable:

"Work and fight according to Lenin, live according to Communism."

Later that day, I came across two babushkas standing in the sun amid the shin-high plants of their potato patch. I commented on their fine garden. One of them, Lydia Shevelyova, responded that she and other Russian peasants were living thanks only to their gardens, chickens, cows, pigs, and goats.

"In the countryside, we still live by the old ways, relying only on ourselves," said the seventy-one-year-old babushka, her hair covered with a white kerchief, her eyes a brilliant blue set against her tanned face. "Let them keep carrying out perestroika all they want in Moscow. We will live our own way here."

. . .

Andrei the fishing guide was back that night at 5 P.M., this time with vodka on his breath. I was disappointed when I got a whiff of him. This was, after all, his work. I liked him and worried that perhaps he, too, was just another village sot. Then again, the alcohol on his breath and the unopened bottle in his bag may merely have signified that he felt comfortable enough with me to fish Russian style, which meant doing more drinking than fishing. "Fishing is drinking with hip boots on," Russian anglers were fond of saying.

Walking from the Old Umba village to the ledge where we had been the night before, we spotted a poacher's net stretching a third of the way across the river. On the granite bench, I fished for forty-five minutes, casting my fly halfway across the Umba and watching as my line swung back toward shore. At the lower end of the shelf, a salmon grabbed my fly. The next few seconds were a blur. The line went ripping off my reel. The reel handle spun wildly, smashing my knuckles. The salmon ran a few yards toward the center of the river, then jumped. I was struggling to get hold of the handle and haul in the fish when the line went slack. The salmon was gone. I had been connected to it for no more than five seconds. Two evenings of fishing had, in an instant, gone up in smoke. "You should have given the fish some slack when it jumped," said Andrei, who had been sitting on the ledge, watching the show. "It threw the hook right out of its mouth."

We stayed at the ledge until midnight. I caught a fat trout and took pleasure in watching Andrei surmount the little obstacles that presented themselves in an evening of fishing. When I snagged a fly on an underwater obstruction, Andrei fashioned a crown of twigs, slipped it over my line, let it float in the direction of the hook, and, somehow, freed it. Later, when I entangled one of my flies twenty-five feet up in a fir tree, Andrei scrambled through the thick branches and retrieved the fly. After I lost the salmon, we drank a few swigs of vodka. Russian vodka bottles often lack screw caps and are equipped only with a piece of tin that is yanked off and can't be used again. (Once opened, a bottle is supposed to be drained.) Andrei sat for ten minutes and whittled a four-inch cork out of a birch branch. The wooden stopper fit hermetically; even when I turned the bottle upside down and shook it, not a drop sprinkled on the granite ledge. The stopper sits now on my bookshelf, a reminder of my two nights on the Umba and of this young man, who could take apart a car engine, build a house, or seal a vodka bottle with equal alacrity.

Most Russian men are similarly handy; life forces them to be. Even the Marquis de Custine, a French dandy who traveled through Russia in 1839 and found much to dislike, had to tip his hat to this national trait.

"With a Russian by your side, were you to lose yourself in a forest, you would in a very few hours have a house to pass the night in," the marquis wrote in *Empire of the Czar*.

The poachers were out in force as we walked back to Old Umba. In one section of the river, where high granite cliffs flanked the far side of the mist-covered water, two teenaged boys stood by a camp-fire on the bank. They looked at us nervously as we approached, but upon learning I was an American and hearing my accented Russian, they relaxed. One of them pointed out their net. The other, a slender boy of about seventeen with an acne-scarred face, said they would sell the salmon to buyers who came to Umba from Kandalaksha. "We're not greedy," he said. "We only want a few."

As we crossed the decayed wooden bridge over the Umba, two men in a small boat rowed out to check nets heavy with a few, fat salmon. They were in plain view of the village and the bridge, yet seemed unconcerned, and with good reason. Some fish inspectors on the Kola Peninsula had been attacked by poachers. Afterward, the inspectors had been ordered not to work late at night.

The contrast between the scene at the Umba bridge and the com-fortable "Flyfishing in Kola" camp, a dozen miles upstream, was extreme. As the Western anglers caught and released Atlantic salmon, they handled the fish with a care bordering on reverence. Down-stream, where the Russians ruled the river, the salmon were little more than slabs of meat to be sold, fried, or salted.

Back at the cottage, I drank vodka and ate sausage and bread with Andrei, Nina, and Viktor, the driver. Viktor was a scrawny man of forty-three, with blue eyes, greasy brown hair, and a pale, lined face. He cut a somewhat pathetic figure in his soiled blue jeans, scuffed brown shoes, and old, brown suit coat. But he was a likable man whose fall from grace had been steep. For years he had labored as a truck driver, hauling logs from clear-cut sites to lumber mills on the

Kola Peninsula. He spoke with pride about the long hours he had worked and the princely salary he had earned before the collapse of Communism—eight hundred rubles a month, about four times the national average. He had had everything he needed—food, a car, furniture—until a few years ago, when he lost his job.

"Now," he said, talking freely after a few shots of vodka, "I'm scratching for kopeks. I have a twenty-two-year-old son and a fifteen-year-old son. I have to feed them and dress them. My wife is the yard woman at an apartment block and hasn't been paid in four months. I've got to get by somehow."

The conversation returned inevitably to Artur Fokich Turkin, who had gone home. Nina interjected, "He's a tricky Jew." With that remark, I began to feel guilty about slandering Artur. My comments that he was a leech had probably fanned the already substantial anti-Semitic flames burning in Nina and others in Umba. Viktor refrained from ethnic slurs, satisfied to label Artur a delusional dreamer, a "teller of fairy tales."

"You know what kind of guy he is?" said Viktor, pulling on cigarette after cigarette as we sat in a smoky, enclosed porch. "Artur is the kind of guy who would crawl up your ass without using soap."

The road to Mikhail'ich's domain was paved with the leavings of Communism. Gutted wooden cowsheds, wrecked barns, broken-down tractors and trucks, fields gone to seed—clusters of this flotsam greeted us as we rolled down the hundred-mile dirt road to the Shoots of Communism collective, run by Svyatoslav Mikhail'ich Kaluzhin. We left at noon in Viktor's 1983 Uaz van, a relic that by some miracle had survived nearly two hundred thousand miles on Russian roads. The windows were wired shut, the shock absorbers had long ago expired, and dust seeped into the rattling hulk from a multitude of holes and crevices. Every twenty minutes or so, the van would sputter to a stop. Viktor would flip open the engine cover between the front bucket seats and squeeze his broken fuel pump twenty times to enable us to go another ten miles. The metal dashboard was plastered with stickers of naked women, their enormous bosoms and curvaceous derrieres beckoning.

Artur was not yet out of my life. We had to drop him off at his dacha, and he rode with us for the first twenty miles. On the way, he showed me his dream project, the Kuzver quarry, proof that sometimes even staggering natural wealth was no match for the Communist economy or the corruption and anarchy that had followed in its wake.

The Kuzver quarry, with more than 2 million cubic meters of high-quality pink granite, was Artur Turkin's shot at the title. In the Communist era, Turkin had worked there as an engineer. With the collapse of Communism, he helped create a Russian-Italian joint venture to exploit the deposit. Turkin became general director of the new company, traveling to Italy and employing thirty people at the quarry. Soon, however, things went sour. As Turkin tells it, he was pushed out by a scheming Russian partner. As Viktor tells it, the Italians eased out Artur, convinced he was a slippery, incompetent manager. The joint venture hit the skids, the quarry closed, and Artur was out of a job.

Viktor parked the van at the gate, next to an old, metal trailer where the quarry's one remaining employee—a guard—lived with his family. Artur shot out of the van and barreled into the quarry. He was dressed in a camouflage jacket, brown plaid shirt, white suspenders over baggy brown trousers, and tennis shoes. As I struggled to keep up with him, Artur came to a stop in front of a pit the size of a football field. The walls had been neatly sheared off by explosions and excavating machinery. In and around the crater were scores of massive granite blocks, about ten feet high and five feet wide. They were the color of a deer's flanks, streaked with rose hues. Scattered among the granite cubes were rusting orange bulldozers and tan dump trucks.

"Why isn't this quarry working?" sputtered Artur. "Russian idiots!"

He ricocheted closer to the excavation site, scanning the remains of his dead enterprise.

"Can you imagine what a huge quarry site this would be if I were still here! My heart aches. My dream was to create this quarry! From studying the geology to excavating the stone, I did it with my own hands."

Turkin pivoted and headed for a cluster of granite blocks. He patted a big slab of stone, worth about $30,000. "More than one million dollars in granite is lying around here, already cut. Look how beautiful this granite is. It meets world standards. Our economy in the region is falling apart and here sits beautiful, world-class granite that we could sell on the world market for a nice profit. Sell it! Ship it!"

He was yelling and spitting now in a paroxysm of frustration.

"This is real production! Sell it! Sell it below world prices if you have to! Sell it! It's all falling apart from wind, rain, and freezing temperatures. . . . I could do this! Excuse me if I am being emotional, but this is my life. I opened a world-class quarry and now it is closed. In the whole world, there are practically no unprofitable quarries!"

We continued eastward along the coast to the settlement of Kuzreka, where Artur had built a spacious log dacha a few yards from the White Sea. The sun was shining and the temperature in the seventies as I gladly bade him farewell. This was one of the joys of travel—jettisoning, for all time, the likes of Artur, and then moving on.

Viktor had his own beachfront dacha not far away—a one-room shack the size of a walk-in closet, plopped down on the pebbles and rough sand. The White Sea glistened just a few yards from his hut. Inside, there were two single beds, on which we sat and ate the pink-fleshed trout I had caught the night before.

"People don't live now," said Viktor. "They just exist. They survive. I am barely scraping by. It is a hopeless situation. I now keep a cow and goats. Actually, the animals are good for my soul. The cow has horns, but sometimes she is better to talk with than people."

The Varzuga road led us through pine groves carpeted with green and white lichen. A caribou bolted across the road and disappeared into the woods. From time to time we caught a glimpse of the White Sea. Mainly we bounced along, breathing clouds of dust, occasionally passing another truck or car. As we cruised by the wreckage of a dismantled fishing collective, the White Sea Fisherman, Viktor said, "Now everyone lives by his own wits, and with his own hands."

At five-thirty that evening, we arrived at last in Varzuga. Ascending the top of a muddy rise, I saw a village of faded wood and log homes strung out along a bluff over the Varzuga River. The cabins were surrounded by picket fences and ringed by conical haystacks and long rows of firewood stacked neatly for the winter. Dominating the scene was the hundred-foot, wooden Uspensky Cathedral, built in 1674 without nails and topped by a shingled cupola. The settlement, spread out under a vast, low, azure sky, looked similar to others we had passed, with one notable exception: there was life. Workers were building several large structures for the collective farm, as well as a half dozen two-story, wooden houses. Hammer blows resounded throughout the village.

To get to Kaluzhin, I had to go through Gennady Popov, a fish inspector who officially worked for the state, but who was de facto in the employ of Mikhail'ich. He was, in effect, Kaluzhin's river keeper. And the river was indisputably Kaluzhin's: the governor of the Kola region had leased the Varzuga—a public river—to Kaluzhin for ten years.

It turned out that Kaluzhin was in Murmansk, buying another trawler for his North Atlantic fleet. He might be back the following night, perhaps the day after. As for fishing, the state inspector would not let me on the river without Mikhail'ich's permission. If I wanted to fish the Varzuga, I'd have to wait.

Later that night, we followed Popov's brother to a two-story, wooden building perched on a hill overlooking the hamlet. Occasionally used by biologists from Murmansk, the dwelling was empty. A four-foot heap of bottles, cans, and trash sat just outside the front door. Viktor and our host pried plywood boards from the windows to provide light for the house, which had no electricity. Inside were piles of debris and scientific equipment. Bread crusts, cigarette butts, unwashed dishes, and other detritus were scattered around the kitchen. There were two dirty rooms upstairs with foldout couches and soiled sheets; I began to suspect that this scientific station doubled as a bordello. The inspector's brother informed us that the toilet was the woods, the well was one hundred yards downhill, and the price was $10 a night.

Before turning in, I remarked to Viktor that Mikhail'ich did seem to wield absolute authority in Varzuga. He laughed and said, "Not only in Varzuga. He goes to the offices of the big shots in Murmansk, kicks open their office doors, and yells, "Hey, you goats! What's up?"

Shortly after 2 A.M., I sat at a table in front of the window and gazed at the Varzuga River, three hundred yards away. As the sun skirted the horizon, the sky above the river turned vivid shades of pink and gold. The village was just a few miles south of the Arctic Circle, and in mid-July the sun scarcely set. I had never spent a prolonged period in the far north and was discovering the pleasures of the white nights. With so much light, time seemed to expand, and the pace of life to slow. You didn't have to rush, for without the prospect of darkness curtailing the day's activities, there was time for everything. Sleep became less important, and four hours a day was ample.

Surveying the quiet village and the bluffs on the far side of the Varzuga, I heard a distant splash. Scanning the river, I saw in midstream the spreading, concentric circles created by a salmon that had leapt out of the water on this still, summer morning.

That night, I found Viktor at a cottage in the center of the village, drinking vodka with five of his friends from Umba. Walking down a darkened hallway, I entered a hot, dusky kitchen with green walls, a filthy linoleum floor, a scarred wooden table, and a stucco fireplace. The men were all in their late forties and had worked with Viktor in the Soviet timber industry, felling trees and driving lumber trucks. They, too, had lost their jobs, but for the last six months had found temporary employment hacking a right-of-way for a power line to Varzuga. They had labored in forty-below-zero weather in winter and in mosquito-infested swamps that spring and summer. But the work paid 2 million rubles a month—$400—and they were glad to have it. "Being healthy is the key," said one logger, a blue-eyed forty-eight-year-old with three grandchildren. "If you get sick now, forget it. It's over."

Unshaven, their hair uncombed, their clothes soiled, their hands cut and dirty, their mouths glistening with gold and silver teeth, these were working stiffs sharing their first drink with an American. They welcomed me exuberantly, pushing piles of canned beef, raw onion, and bread my way, and pouring vodka into thick, grease-smudged shot glasses.

I had long ago learned not to try to match men like this drink for drink. There is no way to keep pace. A normal shot for a sturdy Russian *muzhik* is about four ounces. He can drink, with little difficulty, a half a fifth of vodka in one night. A fifth—about two Russian bottles—is not out of the question. Through bitter experience, I knew the best course was to throw down the first few toasts *do dno*— to the bottom—and then sip at my own speed. (In 1990, in Kazakhstan, I ran headfirst into a deadly combination of Russian drinking, Communist protocol, and Central Asian hospitality. The first American ever to visit a remote, agricultural region, I was feted grandly and told that if I didn't drink each toast to the bottom, I would be insulting all at the table, and their ancestors, as well. There were about twenty toasts. At one point, I remember eating—whole— a sheep's eyeball, tendrils and all. I ate sheep's ear and brain and drank some more. I threw up violently and awoke with the most brutal hangover of my life.)

Satisfied I had properly demolished the first few shots of their harsh vodka, the lumbermen let me drink according to my abilities. The group of six quickly emptied two bottles. Someone went out, and soon two more bottles were on the table. There was a good chance that what we were drinking wasn't really vodka at all, but a mixture of grain spirits and water, produced by an underground factory. The country was flooded with fake vodka, manufactured and distributed by organized-crime groups. Their enterprise wreaked havoc on the national treasury, depriving Moscow of desperately needed revenues from vodka taxes. At the turn of the century, vodka sales made up half the state's revenue. By 1996, only about 5 percent of the Russian government's revenues came from the sale of vodka.

After two hours of boozing and eating, I suggested some fresh air. As the men puffed away on malodorous Russian cigarettes, I glanced at a green Ural truck parked nearby—a mustard-colored passenger cab affixed to its back—and remarked that it certainly was a brawny-looking vehicle.

"You ever drive one?" asked one of the boys.

"No," I replied.

"Would you like to?"

"Why not?"

"It doesn't have any brakes, but you can control the speed with the gears."

Before I knew it I was sitting high up in the seat of the Ural truck, a black steering wheel the size of a hula hoop in my hand. Three loggers joined me in the cab, babbling instructions. It was midnight and the village was asleep. There wasn't a car on the move within twenty-five miles. And Mikhail'ich, the only law in town, was in Murmansk. With enormous effort, I shoved the gears into first, and we lurched forward onto a rutted mud track.

"Second! Second!" the boys hollered as the engine whined, and I jammed the heavy stick shift into second gear. We were out of the village now, rumbling down cratered roads at about fifteen miles an hour. We hit a straightaway. I shifted into third and cranked the Ural up to about twenty-five miles an hour. Ashes from their cigarettes flitted around the cabin. I glanced over at the boys and saw that great, demented smiles had spread over their faces. I hadn't had so much fun in months. Finally, after ten minutes, we came to their work site, and I pulled into a turnoff and relinquished the wheel to Volodya, a gravel-throated man with pendulous bags under his eyes. He got us home safely.

My first spin behind the wheel of a Ural was cause for real celebration. The lumberjacks found more vodka. Soon, the singing started. The men crooned Cossack songs, their voices rich and emotional, their harmonies surprisingly good, if slightly off-key. Viktor, my driver, was a former Spetsnaz—special forces—trooper, and he began bellowing commando songs.

"The greatest pleasure of the people is drunkenness; in other words, forgetfulness," the Marquis de Custine noted a century and a half earlier. "Unfortunate beings! They must dream if they would be happy. As a proof of the good temper of the Russians, whenever the *muzhiks* get tipsy, these men, brutalized as they are, become softened, instead of infuriated. Unlike the drunkards of our country, who quarrel and fight, they embrace each other."

By 2 A.M. I'd had enough and suggested to Viktor it was time to go. He was very drunk, and we crept home in his van to our shack. "You'll forgive me if I'm drunk," mumbled Viktor, "but sometimes you just want to sit with friends and drink a glass of vodka."

The next morning, his hangover was profound. Viktor was subdued as we dined, for the fifth time in Varzuga, on canned sardines and bread. That he hadn't brought a toothbrush, towel, or change of clothes only added to his dishevelment; how he stood the taste in his mouth I'll never know. I stripped naked in front of our cottage and washed myself with two buckets of frigid well water.

Mikhail'ich had returned, and everyone knew it. Around 3:30 P.M., with low, lead gray clouds spitting rain, I walked to the small, green, wood-frame house where Kaluzhin lived. From a distance, I saw his light blue jeep parked next to the house, which contained not only Kaluzhin's apartment but those of three other families. The door was open. I stuck my head inside and shouted hello.

"Come in," came the reply. The voice was deep, confident, and sober.

I walked into a tiny kitchen and saw no one. Hearing a man speaking on the phone in the next room, I poked my head through the door. There, sprawled sideways on a single bed, was a burly figure with curly, brown hair that fell to his collar, a ferocious-looking Fu Manchu mustache, camouflage pants, a blue jean shirt open to his navel, and suspenders. He looked my way and nodded. I retreated to the kitchen and sat down.

The man in the next room hung up. A few seconds later, Svyatoslav Mikhail'ich Kaluzhin shuffled up to me in a pair of bedroom slippers and extended his hand. He truly was a bear of a man, standing five feet ten inches tall and easily weighing 240 pounds. His gut was prodigious, but he was not flabby. His arms and hands were thick and powerful, his neck stubby, like that of a linebacker. As he led me into his kitchen, I sized up his demeanor. Friendly, but skeptical. He didn't show the least concern, but he had to be wondering why a Russian-speaking American journalist had come all the way to Varzuga to meet him. He was plainly a figure of gravitas. In the abstract, I had thought of Kaluzhin as the sachem of a small tribe. But his confident gaze and deportment intimated that this was a man whose influence and experience extended beyond the sleepy Tersky coast.

"Help yourself," said Kaluzhin, sliding a teacup and a can of instant coffee my way. He tossed a heap of black powder into his cup and filled it with steaming water. The phone rang and he shuffled off to answer it.

71

Returning, he announced his readiness to answer any questions. I paid homage to him by saying that his fame had reached to Murmansk and beyond, and that I had come to meet him in the flesh and see his business empire. Then I let slip that I might like to fish for a day on the Varzuga. Instantly, I knew this was the wrong approach. Too direct.

He furrowed his brow.

"Well, I have a little problem with that," said Kaluzhin, slurping his coffee. He extracted a lemon peel from the bottom of the cup, popped it in his mouth, chewed twice, and swallowed. "You see, I just had a few Finns come to the river by themselves, not through my camp. And they were going to go back and tell everyone that you can come fish on the Varzuga for forty dollars a day. And now you show up, wanting the same thing."

I could see my dreams of fishing the Varzuga going down in flames. Backpedaling, I told him how hard it had been to catch a salmon on my own, and how I would write that freelance angling for Kola salmon was only for the foolhardy. He shot me a disbelieving look. The phone rang once again. When he returned, I dropped the fishing request. I would bide my time.

We talked for two hours. Kaluzhin, who was forty-two, was actually from Ukraine. Born in a village not far from Odessa, he eventually went into the Soviet fishing industry, along the way earning three college degrees—one in economics, one in the maritime sciences, and one from the Communist Party's Higher Party School. In 1987, he was working as first mate on a large fishing trawler when Party bosses requested him to move to Varzuga and take over its decrepit collective farm, the Shoots of Communism. (He has steadfastly refused to change the outdated appellation. "It's part of our past. Why erase it?")

When Kaluzhin hit Varzuga—there was no road then, and he arrived by airplane—he found a collective farm with forty-four employees, a few dozen cows, a meager potato crop, a small salmon-fishing operation, and huge debts. The place was utterly cut off from the outside world. "The first thing I did was to institute some order," he said. "I had to impose some discipline upon the place."

Desperately in need of income, he bought a used trawler in 1987 and began fishing in the White Sea. In 1989 he bought a new fishing vessel, and in 1993 added two more. He sent his trawlers to the North Atlantic, and the money poured in. The day before I met him, he closed the deal on his fifth oceangoing trawler. He paid $3 million. In cash. His fishing fleet now employed 250 people.

"Soon after I took over as chairman here, I told people I had a plan of development through 2010," said Kaluzhin, warming to his Horatio Alger story. "They all laughed. They called me the Varzuga dreamer. But look. Now we—I—have created a fleet. We've built a road to Varzuga that's almost finished. We're putting in an electric power line to the village. We're building lots of new houses. We're increasing the population of the village and now have five hundred employees at the farm. The average age of collective farm members is twenty-six, and people are having two, three, and four children. I encourage large families. We've built a sausage-making plant. We're putting in a big refrigeration plant for our salmon fishery."

There was a knock at the door and a man of about forty walked in. He was the director of the state fish hatchery in Umba. Kaluzhin excused himself and repaired with the man to his bedroom. I eavesdropped.

"So what do you need?" asked Kaluzhin. "Tell me."

"Twenty lemons." A lemon is a million rubles. The man was asking for about $4,000.

"I can give you twenty lemons, but they'll only be here on Tuesday. I'll transfer it through the bank."

The phone rang. It was the director of the collective-farm store. She wanted Mikhail'ich to okay dispensing beer to a gang of construction workers. He did. A second man knocked on the door. It was a foreman, coated in mud, asking Kaluzhin to approve disbursing food to another brigade of temporary workers in the village. He gave his permission. Mikhail'ich dismissed the worker, shook hands with the head of the hatchery, and returned to the kitchen table.

His farm, which now had four hundred head of cattle, was still losing money. The commercial salmon and high-seas fishing operations were major profit centers, generating about $9 million in income a year. And the salmon-fishing camps were beginning to turn a profit, with nearly all of it being invested in developing new sites on Kola.

Back in 1989, when Atlantic salmon fishing on the Kola Peninsula was first opened to Westerners, Mikhail'ich had the foresight to go to his cronies in the Murmansk regional Communist Party and ask for control over the Varzuga and three other rivers along the Tersky coast. At that time, connections were everything, and Kaluzhin got his wish: a ten-year lease on the Varzuga and two other rivers, and 50 percent control of the Umba. In 1990, working with foreign partners, he opened the main Varzuga camp to 38 Western anglers. By 1996, with a British partner supplying clients, he was hosting 175 anglers at the main Varzuga camp, as well as scores of other fishermen at six camps on nearby rivers, including the Umba. His biggest problem was poaching, and—contrary to the word of his villagers—he said he had it under control on the Varzuga, thanks to dozens of paid wardens and police. "Poachers know that if they get caught here, I'll tear off their heads," he said.

I asked him where the bountiful profits from the Shoots of Communism conglomerate went. People whispered in Murmansk and Umba that Kaluzhin was a wealthy man with fat overseas bank accounts. He certainly wasn't spending it on himself in Russia. He lived in a minuscule apartment, dressed like a farmhand, didn't smoke or drink, drove a Russian jeep, and paid himself about $300 a month, half what his construction foreman earned. So where were all the rubles, and to whom did they belong—Kaluzhin, or the workers of the Shoots of Communism?

I didn't expect the answer to be straightforward.

"It all belongs to the collective—all the capital. We're still building up this enterprise, investing in it. We're not going to cut it into little shares. All we make we plow back into the business."

I posed the question another way, but got the same answer. Everything belonged to everybody. The collective owned the money, but a member could not cash in his share if he quit. Kaluzhin was not a rich man. He lived like the other comrades.

Inquiring as to how working today compared with toiling under the Communists, I elicited from Mikhail'ich a weary smile. "To be honest, when the Communists were in power, I worked. Now the democrats are in power, and I work. Everything depends upon how a person works. We live completely on our own means. The main thing is not to interfere with us."

Occasionally nibbling on his mustache, he continued, sounding like one of America's great apostles of the flat tax and free enterprise, Steve Forbes.

"People in government often don't understand business. The worst thing is taxation policies. They're killing us. For every ruble we produce, they take eighty-five kopeks and leave us fifteen kopeks. You have to give freedom to producers. Right now I pay thirty-two different taxes. Can you imagine? They ought to have one flat tax on income of ten to twenty percent."

Mikhail'ich acknowledged that he was thinking of expanding his empire, possibly to mine for diamonds on the Tersky coast or revive viable yet defunct enterprises, such as the pink-granite quarry. I remarked how bizarre it was that a region so rich in natural resources should be so impoverished. "It's idiocy," said Kaluzhin, raising his voice for the first time during our talk. "Everyone wants to make money quickly, not to produce things. They want to buy a car, build a fancy cottage, and earn fast money. We need good brains, good managers, people who can create, who can do things. Unfortunately, there aren't enough of them yet. People can learn to work. Unfortunately, we have people in this country who are used to walking around with an outstretched hand. That's not the way it is on our boats. Our men earn based on the quantity of fish they bring in, and they can make seven thousand dollars for a four-month trip. They all work hard and take good care of the ship. Paying them this way increases productivity. It's good for everybody."

Mikhail'ich offered to show me his village. Walking outside, we were met by a six-year-old boy in a ski cap. The waif had been waiting for the boss and thrust out a picture of a truck. "Mikhail'ich," he said. "I have a drawing for you."

"Wonderful, very nice, thank you," said Kaluzhin, patting the boy on the shoulder.

"Can I have a soda?" asked the boy.

"A little later. Come on back. I'll give you one then."

Disappointed, the boy walked away. Already, he had learned about favors, and who dispensed them along the Varzuga.

Bumping along in his jeep, gesturing left and right, Kaluzhin sketched out his dream. A factory to make bricks would go there. That white structure would soon be a 250-ton refrigerated building. Over here, the new collective-farm workshop was being built. That building would be the new diesel-fired generating plant. There would be a smokehouse, a brewery, a restaurant. The smaller church was being restored. A priest was arriving by the end of the year.

We stopped at the site where a half dozen two-story, $20,000 cottages were being built for his workers, including Popov, the fish inspector. Scrambling through the nearly completed houses, Kaluzhin was like a hot-wired American realtor, pointing out the spacious kitchens, the roomy bedrooms, the view from the second-story veranda.

"I promised when I came here that I would develop the village," said Mikhail'ich as he drove me back to my hovel. "Look, I could do a lot of things. I could go to Murmansk and become governor if I wanted. But I want to stay here, to finish what I started and fulfill my promises."

Before I realized it, we were at my cabin and he was shaking my hand and bidding me farewell. I still had not received permission to fish. Instantly, I became another supplicant, gently nudging the Prince of the Varzuga into doing me a favor.

He gave me a long look.

"All right," he said. "You can fish. I'll tell Popov about the license. But you go back and write that we will not take any more clients if they come here on their own. If they arrive on their own, they will have to live in the camp and pay two hundred and fifty dollars a day. They can do that and get all the services the regular clients get."

He did suggest that I enlist one of the lodge's guides to help me, and I agreed. I thanked him, we shook hands, and Mikhail'ich was on his way, his jeep bumping over the rutted roads of his half-finished domain.

Gathering up my gear, I raced down to Popov's and bought my license. It was the low point of the salmon run, and Mikhail'ich's lodge—about a mile from the village—was empty. I hired one of the lodge's guides, a kid fresh out of the Russian army, to accompany me.

Directly in front of the lodge were several deep, fast-moving pools, and I began casting into them. The water was whiskey colored, the wading difficult. The Varzuga was studded with boulders and rocks, their surface coated with slick algae that bloomed at the height of summer. Twice, I nearly fell into the water. My guide, Dima, was a handsome boy with fiery red hair and blue eyes. He also was sullen and ignorant and spent most of his time sitting or standing on the bank, watching me cast. He knew almost nothing about flies, little about the water and its lies, and responded to my questions with grunts or shrugs. But even Dima could not cast a pall on this evening, for after forty-eight hours of waiting for Mikhail'ich, I was fishing for salmon in the famed Varzuga.

A salmon flashed on the surface, seventy feet away. I cast my fly over it several times, to no effect. After two hours of fishing in front of the lodge, Dima and I moved upstream, where a gentle, deep current—an excellent spot for salmon to rest on their migration— lay just fifty feet from the bank. In the middle of the current was a boulder, a prime holding spot for salmon. I only had pursued salmon once before, on the Margaree River in Nova Scotia, but I knew that the downstream side of the boulder might hold fish.

Wading out, I cast several times toward the rock, letting my fly swing closer to the downstream lie where I felt sure a salmon would be. I dropped a cast upstream of the boulder and watched as my line moved briskly over the rock. Suddenly, just upcurrent of the boulder, a large, silver salmon thrashed and sped to the safety of deeper water. Searching for a fish behind the boulder, I had allowed my fly-line to touch a salmon holding in front, scaring it. I had forgotten a fundamental of salmon angling—that fish can hold above rocks as well as downstream of them—and blown yet another opportunity.

Dima and I were on the river at nine the next morning. The weather had deteriorated while I had waited for Kaluzhin, and the wind was blowing hard, making casting difficult. But several fish soon showed themselves in the pool in front of the lodge. I cast over a salmon, which swiped the fly but didn't grab it. About thirty feet upstream, a second salmon leapt and splashed down hard in the water. Wading slowly upstream, I made a decent cast over the second salmon. It grabbed the fly, leapt, and spit it out. I was not deterred, however. There were salmon everywhere, and I had attained that state to which all fishheads aspire: utter concentration on the matter at hand. No thoughts entered my brain, save those of the fish, the fly, and the water.

A salmon leapt into the air on the opposite bank, where a sandy bluff fell into the Varzuga. Dima ferried me across the river in his long, wooden skiff, and I began casting into a pool close to the bank. Ten minutes passed. I kept my casts short in the brisk wind. My fly drifted over a small boulder and I felt a gentle tug. For a split second I thought I had snagged the rock, but then the water boiled, and a salmon raced downstream, leapt once, and continued on. The reel handle scraped my knuckles. The fish took all my fly-line and had just started to unspool the backing underneath when it stopped. The salmon leapt twice more, but within five minutes Dima had it in his net. It was a female, silver with small, black spots, about two feet long, and weighing six or seven pounds. I wanted to release it, but as we retrieved the orange fly, I saw that the fish was hooked in the gills and was bleeding. There was no way she would survive.

Dropping her on the bank, Dima knocked her in the head several times with a stone. She flopped on the pebbles, quivered, and died. I felt faintly ill at having brought her epic cycle of migration and spawning to an end. I felt even worse when we returned to the lodge and the cook cut open the hen salmon. Inside, were two six-inch-long egg sacks. They represented thousands of fish, although I knew the vast majority would never reach the fry stage, let alone maturity. That night, before leaving Varzuga, Viktor and I ate the fish—her salted caviar, her baked flesh, nicely prepared by the lodge's cook.

By the time Viktor and I were ready to leave that night, word had filtered back to Kaluzhin that the American had caught a salmon. Through the fish inspector, Popov, word got back to me: Mikhail'ich was pleased.

A Moscow-bound train was leaving early the next morning from Kandalaksha. Viktor drove hard, a wall of brick-red dust forming behind us as we rumbled west toward Umba. In the back of the van was a burlap sack filled with illegally caught salmon, a gift to Viktor from a friend.

Around 10 P.M., we reached the coastal hamlet of Moiseyeva. It was Friday night, and the boys from Varzuga had come to their dachas to be with their wives. One of them ran out as we passed and invited us in for a shot of vodka and some food. Picking our way through a potato field, Viktor and I walked into a dimly lit cottage, where the lumbermen and their wives were seated around a large table. Greeting me like an old friend, they nudged me toward a seat. In the center of the table, in a massive iron skillet, were small chunks of blackened meat. One of the men had slaughtered a pig that afternoon, and they were feasting upon a delicacy—pig heart, spleen, liver, and kidney, sautéed in blood. Men and women shouted and filled shot glasses to overflowing. One of the men pushed me into a chair and handed me a fork. We all stabbed chunks of the pig's innards and washed it down with three quick toasts. The meat was surprisingly good; within ten minutes, I was full and mildly inebriated. I had grown fond of this crew. As we stood for the last toast, one of the men's wives lifted her glass and said, "We're friendly people." Then she added, "We're still not spoiled by capitalism."

Viktor and I continued on to Umba, where he took me to his house for dinner. He lived in a log cabin at the end of a dirt road, his neighborhood a muddle of shacks, barns, haystacks, log piles, and garden plots. I met his two gangly sons, aged fifteen and twenty-two, and then I met his cow, Zorya, to whom he spoke with great tenderness. His wife was a plain-looking woman with thick glasses and light brown hair, and she seemed uncomfortable with my presence in their small, low-ceilinged dwelling. We quickly ate a plate of beef goulash. Then we were off to Kandalaksha, Viktor's two sons in the back of the van.

We cruised at 1:30 A.M. into Kandalaksha, through a sleeping city center of drab, gray, Soviet-era office buildings. A small crowd waited for the Murmansk-Moscow express, and I secured with ease a first-class ticket. I was just about out of cash and—in addition to the $200 he had received from Artur—gave Viktor nearly all I had left, about $60. I threw in a new pair of polarized sunglasses. When I asked Viktor what he was going to do next, he replied, "Whatever comes up."

Waiting on the platform, I felt the awkwardness of the traveler in a poor land. I was about to catch a train out of this beautiful, economically depressed territory, bound for more adventures and, eventually, a soft life in the United States. Viktor was staying behind, left to piece together a meager living by working with the likes of Artur Turkin. We both sensed this divide as the train rolled in. We shook hands warmly, and I boarded the express.

To my relief, I had the two-berth compartment to myself. For weeks, I had constantly been in the presence of other people, speaking Russian nonstop. I looked forward to a thirty-hour train ride, to sleeping, to not opening my mouth and reading a collection of Chekhov's stories. The first-class wagon was only half-full, and I slept soundly until eleven the following morning. Early that afternoon, a voice that would be a constant companion on the trip to Moscow came over the train intercom. The deep, soothing male voice, like that of a professional announcer, was informing the passengers that *Independence Day*—a film that had debuted in America only a few weeks before— was being shown in the "video salon." Russians excelled at selling bootlegged videos of recently released American films. These pirates could be proud of their turnaround time with *Independence Day.*

The "video salon" was several cars ahead of mine. It was a Soviet-era railway wagon reconfigured with airplane-like seats, about six abreast. The shades were drawn, and in the semidarkness twenty travelers sat in comfort, watching the flickering images of space aliens attacking Washington. The salon's manager sold beer, peanuts, soda, and candy. Most customers sipped bottles of Russian Baltika beer.

"Bootlegged film?" I asked the manager.

"Of course," he replied.

I never uttered another word the entire train ride.

Around three, the announcer got on the intercom to crow about an even greater video coup: the salon was showing the Mel Gibson thriller *Ransom*, which would not be released in America for another five months.

"This film is interesting because it has a scheduled 1997 debut in America and it's already on our screen," said the announcer. "We're the only ones who can bring it to you."

How they pirated the film and were screening it on a Murmansk-Moscow train a half year before its release, I will never know. But the announcement—brimming with pride that they had engineered such a bold rip-off of Hollywood—filled me with joy. Who dare accuse the Russians of lacking entrepreneurial spirit? They were showing a film that officially did not even exist. And on a state-run train, with great fanfare.

I slept much of the afternoon and evening. At one station, workers with long-handled hammers patrolled the platform, striking the wheels to check if they were cracked, the resonant *pock-pock* of steel mallets on steel wheels filling the air with a reassuring rhythm. Not far outside Petrozavodsk, a half dozen blond girls stood on the platform, selling basketfuls of blueberries, raspberries, and strawberries.

Around 9:15 P.M., the announcer was back, unveiling the centerpiece of the evening's viewing—an "erotic detective" film.

"Please don't bring the kids," said the voice on the intercom. "There are a lot of erotic scenes. But it's fine to watch. It's decent."

I dozed again. At twilight, we stopped at the town of Volkhovstroi, east of St. Petersburg. Soon, the voice was back. This time it had lost its honey-accented pitchman's tone. It was angry.

"Conductors of the fourteenth wagon! Why are you letting your passengers run around on the platform! It's time to depart! The green light is on! Immediately escort your passengers back onto the train!"

This was not a train boss infuriated that he was behind schedule. This was a man with a theater to fill. The train lurched and began to roll. Five minutes later, the voice returned: "We invite all lovers of erotica to the video salon for a showing of an erotic crime movie. All lovers of erotica!"

Outside, the Russian countryside rolled past, a tapestry of birch forests and cabins and potato fields. Only eight hours from Moscow, and relatively far south, I experienced darkness for the first time in a month. The sun had set, leaving a faint splash of pink on a bank of clouds. Gradually, the light drained out of the sky, and a deep, northern dusk obscured the landscape.

3.

PRINCE KURAKIN'S MADHOUSE

Southern Russia was in the throes of a heat wave. Poking my head out the window, I inhaled the parched winds as the long, green train rolled south over a flat landscape. We passed fields going a burnt gold in the August sun, rumbled over stagnant canals and rivers, their algae-choked surfaces a far cry from the crystalline streams I had just fished north of the Arctic Circle. The train, from Moscow to Almaty, the capital of Kazakhstan, was full to overflowing, and passengers stood in the corridors as a desiccated breeze riffled flimsy curtains. The toilet was a chamber of olfactory horrors where the ammoniac fetor of urine joined forces with the effluvium of uncut disinfectant to knock you to your knees. But I was not going far. At the next stop, Rtysheva, I planned to disembark. Meeting me there was Viktor Chumak, an old friend.

Viktor stood on the platform, scanning the wagons as they eased into the station. His bull-like silhouette was unmistakable, and I spied it from afar. His big belly was covered in a black T-shirt, his powerful legs in cheap, blue track pants. His arms were tanned and massive, and his granite-block face more creased and menacing-looking than ever. He still had his Fu Manchu mustache, though his hairline had retreated significantly, leaving a brown ducktail marooned on his broad, sunburned forehead.

Viktor, who was forty-five, spotted my head protruding from the window and raised his arm. I extended mine, and we high-fived as the train came to a stop.

On the platform, Chumak enveloped me in a crushing bear hug. On my way east, I had decided to check in on Viktor, and to fish the Serdoba River, which ran past his house. I had last visited him five years ago, in June 1991, two months before the botched coup that led to the collapse of the Soviet Union. At that time, he was one of the first private farmers in the USSR, a profane force majeure who had assembled an agricultural empire—sixteen hundred acres, one hundred head of cattle, twelve tractors, two harvesters, and three trucks. He labored with maniacal zeal, making more than eighty trips to Moscow to beg and badger government ministries for equipment. He had hired three coworkers and built new houses for them and his own family.

His optimism had been catching. Private farming was going to resuscitate the Russian countryside, and he would be in the vanguard. After all, before the advent of Communism, Russia had been—in the words of a Western traveler—"one vast village." At the turn of the century, 90 percent of Russia's population lived in the countryside. Many in this agrarian society led lives of squalor and ignorance, in part the result of serfdom, which ended only in 1865. But conditions began to improve early in the twentieth century as Pyotr Stolypin, Czar Nicholas II's prime minister, introduced reforms to encourage private farming.

By 1913, Russia was exporting wheat, flax, butter, and other products to Europe. Chumak believed the countryside could rise again and recapture the momentum that had existed before the Bolsheviks took power. His personal goal was to erect a $5.5-million, American-designed complex that included a dairy, meat-processing plant, and greenhouse.

"I have this dream and I want to see it come true," Chumak had told me. "And I won't give up."

Things had not worked out the way Viktor had foreseen. I knew the general story from a mutual friend in Moscow. Interest rates had hit 200 percent. Chumak couldn't make his bank payments. Much of his equipment had been confiscated. Viktor had nearly been thrown in jail, but was still hanging on to the farm. All I knew as I pulled into Rtysheva was that if Viktor Chumak was a casualty of Russia's new Mad Max market, then the situation in the countryside was grim indeed.

Disappearing for a few minutes to run some errands, Viktor left me in the company of a sidekick named Sasha, a young man who had about him the unmistakable whiff of the Russian mobster. Perhaps it was his crew cut, all the rage that summer with racketeers. Perhaps it was his formidable physique. Perhaps it was the way he responded when I asked what he did for a living.

"It's hard to explain, really," said Sasha. "Partly, I collect debts."

Later, I would learn that Viktor, like many Russians struggling to survive in the perverse, post-Communist marketplace, had turned to the likes of Sasha and his pals to grease the wheels of commerce. Chumak gave them sides of beef or construction materials. In return, they helped Viktor shake loose a debt or sell a few tons of sugar that a collective-farm director had dumped on him in lieu of cash.

Dealing with men tied to organized crime was not what Viktor had had in mind when he set out in 1989 to become a farmer. But to remain standing in the whirlwind, you needed a little support.

"We have excellent relations with the right people, here and in Moscow," he said.

Sasha was behind the wheel of a Volga sedan, and Viktor in the front seat, as we drove to Chumak's farmhouse in the hamlet of Alexandrovo Rostovka. Viktor looked tired and distracted, and though still humming with energy, it was clear that some of the air had gone out of this dynamo. As before, he cursed with relentless, poetic intensity. Passing a collective farm, its dilapidated machinery strewn around a concrete barn, I asked Viktor how this former Communist enterprise was faring.

"They're barely breathing," he replied. "They're eating the last dick without salt."

Turning off the asphalt highway, we rattled down the dirt roads that led to Chumak's house. In one village, we passed the remains of a nineteenth-century Russian Orthodox church. Splotchy with faded whitewash, the red-brick church was topped by a three-story bell tower, a chunk of which had tumbled onto the main roof. The onion domes had long since disappeared, their wooden ribs rotting in the open air. Clumps of grass sprouted from the roof of the church, used during the Communist era to store grain.

Alexandrovo Rostovka was a sleepy village strung for more than a mile along a rutted dirt track. About one hundred wooden cabins and shacks, some dating to before the Revolution and faded to an ash gray, lined the road. Listing picket fences surrounded many of the homes, nearly all of which had a large garden plot out back. Behind the plots were weather-beaten outhouses. Residents drew their water from the old, iron well pumps that dotted the roadside every hundred yards or so.

Before the fall of Communism, the residents survived thanks to the nearby Lenin Collective Farm, which paid them a meager salary every month to milk the cows and tend the fields. They collected their pay whether they worked well or poorly, whether they showed up drunk or sober or not at all. The workers—somehow the word *farmer* didn't leap to mind—received slightly more than one hundred rubles a month, but in an era of controlled prices that was enough to keep the family in sausage, bread, and vodka.

This was the way it was in 1986 when Chumak, his wife, Olga, and their two daughters showed up in Alexandrovo Rostovka to live with Olga's ailing grandmother. Everyone, Chumak most of all, knew that this state of affairs couldn't go on forever, that the old system was winding down like some Rube Goldberg contraption. In 1989, when the Soviet government passed a law legalizing private business, Chumak came home and told his wife he was starting a farm.

"From the very start I believed in this law like in God," Chumak once told me.

By the time I pulled into the village in 1996, the Lenin Farm had not officially been declared dead, but had it been hooked up to an electroencephalograph, you would have detected no signs of brain activity. The government had stopped pouring in subsidies. Workers had not received a full salary in eighteen months, surviving instead on the sugar, flour, and other goods occasionally parceled out by the director. Every so often he would toss a few hundred thousand rubles their way. Some pensioners were subsisting on two hundred thousand rubles a month, about $40. "They have just enough money for milk and bread, that's about it," said Chumak.

This disintegration was the logical end result of seven decades of Soviet agricultural policies, particularly the forced collectivization that saw millions of peasants murdered, shipped to Siberia, or wiped out in government-created famines. Stalin made sure that energetic, thriving farmers—the spiritual forebears of Chumak—were the first to be crushed.

The Chumak conglomerate occupied one end of the village, and though he had clearly run into tough times recently, Viktor's spread had grown since my last visit. His sixteen hundred acres had expanded to more than four thousand, and he had built a horse stable, a cattle shed, and a grain-storage bin. A sixty-foot tower supplied running water to his house and those of his workers, a grand convenience in a settlement where people had been hauling water from wells for centuries and had every expectation of continuing to do so for decades to come.

Under a fierce sun—the temperature had risen into the low nineties—Viktor showed me the new additions to his homestead. All that was missing were his tractors, trucks, and combines, most of which had been confiscated by the bank. He didn't seem to want to dwell on the subject, and so we went in for lunch.

Olga was as robust as Viktor. Powerfully built, with short brown hair and blue eyes, she had the mettle needed to withstand the strain of living with Viktor, whose zeal could no doubt wear thin on those closest to him. Over borscht, sausage, and salad, we talked of our children. But the unspoken subject was the near ruination of their farm, and Viktor's battle with the bank.

"These past five years," said Olga, "have flown by like one day."

It was harvest time. The bank had left Viktor two combines, and he was bringing in cash by cutting rye for one of the marginally solvent collective farms left in the region. Chumak was padding around barefoot in the dirt, searching for something as he prepared to jump into his Kamaz truck and head to the fields.

"Olga! Olga!" he bellowed, hoping his wife could find the lost object. His voice boomed through the lower end of the village, but he was not concerned about disturbing the neighbors. There never seemed to be enough room for Viktor, or for his cannonlike voice. In America, he would have come across as a man bristling with energy. In the Russian countryside, he was a force of nature. All around was a vacuum, a landscape of dazed and passive individuals groping

to come to terms with a world that had been turned upside down. Chumak barreled like a dervish through this entropic void, leaving stunned peasants in his wash.

The fields of the former Peace collective farm were twenty-five miles away. Halfway there, Viktor's flatbed truck overheated and lurched to a stop. "Motherfucker!" he muttered as he plucked a pack of Prima cigarettes from the dashboard and lit up for the tenth time that day.

Heat shimmered off the yellow fields—many of them fallow—that stretched to the horizon. A few fleecy white clouds meandered across a still, blue sky. Conical haystacks dotted a nearby meadow. Grasshoppers droned. This was classic, unbounded Russian steppe. I half-expected to see a squadron of Cossacks thundering toward us in the distance. Instead, an old man clopped past in a horse-drawn, rubber-wheeled cart.

I asked Viktor a question about the local economy, and he was off.

"You developed your capitalist markets in the West over hundreds of years, and our government wants our people to go to sleep one night in a Communist world and wake up the next morning in a capitalist one. They want to go to bed and wake up with a fucking market! We're a long way from the market. Shit, we don't even know what the word means. We don't have a market. We have a fucking bazaar. In a split second we wanted to be on the same level as Western countries, but instead of democracy we got anarchy.

"What does democracy mean to us in Russia today? It means I can call you a dickhead and there will be no consequences. To me, democracy means a person has freedom to be a farmer if he wants, and if he doesn't, he can be part of a collective farm. But being able to call the farm director a fucking goat? That's not democracy."

Chumak was knitting his formidable brow. After a brief silence, he professed admiration for Alexander Lebed, the former general who had become one of the most popular leaders in the land. Lebed, like Chumak, was a free marketeer, but one who believed Russia needed an iron hand. Recently, according to news reports, Lebed had headed off a potential coup against Yeltsin. During the 1991 coup against Gorbachev, the plotters had taken over state radio stations and begun playing *Swan Lake*.

"Lately, I like Lebed," said Viktor. "You want to pull off a coup? Fuck you! To the dick with your coup! Fuck! You want to play *Swan Lake*? Fuck your mother! Play *Swan Lake*, you fuckers, and see what happens!"

He flicked his cigarette out the window of the orange Kamaz cab and climbed down to look at the engine. A shimmering, chartreuse liquid was dripping onto the pavement.

"Oh, that cocksucking, motherfucking driver! Shit! Mother-fucker!"

We reached the rye fields an hour later. Coming over a low rise, he saw that his son-in-law, Andrei, and his sixteen-year-old daughter's boyfriend, Sergei, were mowing at a Stakhanovite pace. "Motherfuck, they've done a lot," he said.

Chumak was a believer in free enterprise. But five years before, his convictions were tinged with traditional Russian communalism. He tried to make partners of his three hired workers. It was a disaster. He said they wanted ever-larger shares of the farm while doing less and less work. Eventually, he sacked them. Now, he was the sole owner. He hired workers when he needed them. Otherwise, he counted only on his family.

Pulling into the shade of a row of trees, Viktor hauled out jugs of water and soup for the boys. They clattered over in their combines and hopped down. Drenched in sweat and dusted with rye husks, Andrei and Sergei were tanned, sinewy, blue-eyed blonds. Praising their work, Viktor seemed in a fine mood until Andrei told him the farm manager wanted them to mow another section of land.

"Cocksucker!" shouted Viktor. "Fuck him! We've got to finish this first. Son of a bitch doesn't understand . . ."

Andrei gazed at his father-in-law with equal parts respect, awe, fear, and amusement.

Grabbing a few combine parts that needed welding, Chumak rode over to the garage of the Peace farm. More than a dozen dead, dying, and cannibalized tractors lay scattered outside a cavernous concrete shed. Chumak and the gold-toothed farm foreman held a good-natured discussion of plowing schedules, during which, in the space of five minutes, they used several dozen variations of the Russian verb *yebat*, which means "to fuck." In the end, Viktor relented and agreed to move his boys to another field.

In the shed, Viktor guzzled water from a dirty black hose. Passing a grease-smudged worker, he said, "You old dog, why don't you work?"

"Look at my hands? You don't think I'm working?"

Chumak laughed. "In the old collective farm where I used to work, the guys used to show up in the morning, slather their hands and face with axle grease, then stand around and smoke all day, doing nothing."

"Fuck you!" the worker said, laughing.

After welding a broken hunk of his combine, Chumak bolted for his truck. A half dozen farm workers stared dumbly at his fast-moving, 200-pound frame. Settling into his Kamaz, he glanced at the men and said, "They're lost."

As we drove back to the rye fields, Chumak talked about the confiscation of his equipment the previous year. The very banker who had given him his start had turned on him, Chumak said. Chumak had borrowed several hundred thousand dollars, at 28 percent interest, to buy tractors, combines, and trucks. When inflation drove interest rates to 213 percent, the banker gave Chumak no reprieve on his debt. Despite a Russian law prohibiting banks from confiscating equipment of working farmers, bank officials—accompanied by about twenty security guards, police, and drivers—showed up one morning in October 1995 and drove away with Chumak's equipment. His wife wept. Chumak could only watch as his dreams went up in smoke. Later, the bank president sold much of the equipment to his brother, a farm director, for a mere $30,000, Chumak said.

But it was unwise to cross Viktor Chumak. His early farming success had left him with friends in high places in Moscow—in the parliament, government, and the press—and he was raising the alarm about the dismantling of his farm. Russia's leading agricultural expert had written a story in *Izvestia* expressing dismay over what had happened. A local government commission was investigating the case. Chumak was determined to get back his trucks and tractors. If I were the wagering kind, I would have laid odds on Viktor, not the banker.

We passed the Bolshevik, one of the more robust of the collective farms, and its fields were aswarm with combines and trucks bringing in the harvest. Back at the rye meadow, Viktor went to work on one of his broken combines. A bolt had sheared off a harvesting blade and was stuck fast. He grabbed a hammer, a steel awl, and began pounding. He whacked the bolt thirty times. The veins in his head bulging, sweat flying onto the combine, Chumak kept at it for a couple of minutes. Finally, the bolt yielded.

That evening, Chumak stopped back at the garage of the collective farm, where six workers squatted in the shade and swigged a murky, homemade brew—about 20 percent alcohol—from a battered plastic soda bottle. Viktor and I refused their moonshine, but he passed out cigarettes and bantered with the men. The chairman of the farm appeared in a green jeep, prompting one of the workers to stash the bottle behind a stack of tires.

"You don't have bosses in the U.S., do you?" asked a rheumy-eyed mechanic.

"Sure we do," I replied. "Most people work for a salary and have bosses."

"But I thought everyone worked for themselves."

I set him straight. Many Russians' views of America were as skewed now as they were under Communism. Before, they had been told we were all slaves, working for hard-hearted robber barons. Now, from sketchy TV and newspaper reports, they had gleaned an equally fallacious impression—that we were all self-starting Rockefellers, working only for ourselves, answering to no one.

Judging from the vodka fumes, the collective farm chairman—a short, trim man with dark hair and gold teeth—had raised the cocktail flag, as well. We talked as the sun set, and he told me that only about six of the region's thirty collective farms—*kolkhoz*, in Russian—were still in decent shape. The structure of the farms had remained, but the federal government had turned off the tap. Most subsidies were history. Now the Peace collective farm had officially been turned into a "limited corporation."

"It's the same old collective," interjected Viktor. "But the new name allows the government to chuck off the farms and say, 'Fuck you. You're on your own.' "

Prices for grain and sunflower oil were so low it didn't even pay to grow them, and thousands of acres lay fallow. Five or six private farmers in the area had gone under. Only Chumak remained standing.

Viktor and I rode most of the way home in silence. The sun eased below the horizon, throwing a soft golden light over the fields. Workers had set fire to hundreds of mounds of rye and wheat stalks, and as far as the eye could see, black piles of chaff smoldered, sending plumes of smoke into the still evening air.

The milk run began early. Olga applied lipstick in her darkened hallway as Viktor, who had woken up worrying at four and had not gone back to sleep, shuffled into the tiny kitchen for another cup of coffee and a cigarette. Shortly after 7 A.M., Olga, her seventeen-year-old daughter, Natasha, and Natasha's three-month-old son climbed into the cab of the family's blue Zil dump truck.

When I last saw her, Natasha wasn't even a teenager. Now, five years later, she was a mother, bouncing her infant son on her lap as we drove into the town of Serdobsk with fifty gallons of milk and a big jug of sour cream. Russians married early and reproduced early, an understandable tradition when you considered that life expectancy—fifty-eight for men, seventy-one for women—was far below that of the West. Most Russians I knew were already grandparents by their mid-forties. Marrying at eighteen had its advantages from a procreative point of view. But it made for many miserable unions and contributed to one of the highest divorce rates in the world.

As we drove along on a warm, clear morning, Olga told me that Viktor had been away almost constantly in the last year, mainly to Moscow to try to win back his farm equipment and secure loans for his $5-million, American-made agricultural "complex." She had run the farm in his absence.

"Viktor's been working on this American deal for five years," she said. "Sometimes I think it's never going to happen."

In a shady courtyard flanked by five-story brick apartment buildings, two dozen people, mainly elderly, had gathered. Some had waited since 6 A.M. to be at the head of the line for Viktor and Olga's milk, delivered fresh seven days a week. The women wore flowered housecoats, sandals, and kerchiefs over their hair. The men were outfitted in tattered suit coats and short-sleeved synthetic shirts. At four thousand rubles—about eighty cents—a gallon, the milk was a staple in the diet of retirees, whose monthly pensions rarely exceeded $100.

As babushkas fussed over Natasha and her baby, Olga stood in the bed of the Zil and accepted the empty glass jars proffered by her customers. Filling them with milk and wiping the lips dry, she handed down the vessels and took battered ruble notes in return. People talked quietly as they waited their turn, and other residents moved slowly about the courtyard on a lazy Sunday morning in August. Within an hour, the milk and sour cream were gone.

Serdobsk, a provincial center of perhaps forty thousand, was a town in deep economic trouble. The two main industries—a clock factory and a plant that made spare parts for the Zil automotive giant—worked only sporadically. Thousands were unemployed. Yet as we drove through the town to the open-air market that Sunday morning, I got no sense that this was a city in crisis. Neatly dressed families strolled the streets and filled the cupolaed, nineteenth-century brick cathedral. At the outdoor market, shoppers clogged the aisles as they sized up goods at more than one hundred stalls. The tranquil scene in Serdobsk was typical of Russia that summer. In most countries, a 20 percent unemployment rate, endless factory closings, and the near-universal practice of not paying salaries would have sent the masses into the streets. But Russians demonstrated a boundless ability to absorb shock and suffering. The collective memory had a lot to do with this. To a people who had lost 27 million citizens in World War II and as many as 20 million to Stalin's terror, a pink slip was no big deal.

The street market, located across from the church, was the domain of the ubiquitous *chelnoki*, or shuttle traders, who traveled to Korea, China, Poland, and Turkey, loaded up on piles of cheap clothes and food, and returned to peddle them to their compatriots. This had been going on for several years, and many Russians were fed up with Chinese garments that fell apart after two washings. But Russian industry had yet to fill the breach.

Two menacing-looking young men, one with the squashed nose of a boxer, made the rounds of the booths, collecting a few thousand rubles in tribute money from each of the sellers. A half dozen Vietnamese stood near the entrance to the market selling rip-off Reebok track suits and sweatshirts plastered with Sino-English gibberish like "Beer Child."

We returned around noon to the Chumak home, where I ate lunch and lay down for an hour in the living room. As I was drifting off to sleep, I caught snatches of a fierce argument between Viktor and Olga in the kitchen.

"How much have you been here in the last year!" Olga spat out. "Maybe three months? You're never around!"

"Ahhh," yelled Viktor, "what kind of woman are you anyway!"

A door slammed, and Viktor stormed out.

High on a bluff over the muddy Serdoba River sat the ruined estate of Prince Kurakin. A grandiose, gutted brick reminder of the lost world of czarist Russia, the mansion dominated the landscape near Alexandrovo Rostovka and was visible for miles around. If you stood in the field behind Viktor's house and looked at the imposing, columned edifice in the distance, it was not difficult to conjure up the scene from two centuries ago—the grand manor house, the semicircle of outbuildings, the river meandering far below, with serfs scything hay in the fields. I had briefly visited the estate five years before, and the image of this gracious wreck had been with me ever since. The interior of the mansion had been destroyed by fire after the Revolution. But the shell of the palace still stood, and the low-slung outbuildings had been turned into a mental asylum in the 1950s.

In late afternoon, Viktor's sixteen-year-old daughter, Galina, joined me on a walk to the estate. My plan was to tour the grounds, talk to the staff and villagers about the prince, then fly-fish the Serdoba River at dusk. Galina—a bright, wide-eyed girl with honey blond hair—was amused and mystified that a stranger would take such a keen interest in the sprawling remains that locals had long ago ceased to notice.

We wandered down the dusty road that ran through Alexandrovo Rostovka, past villagers tending gardens and gaggles of geese. Ahead, a fisherman returned to his wooden cabin on a bike, a pair of bamboo poles lashed to the back. I quickened my pace, eager for angling advice.

"Good day," I said to the man as he hunched over his bike, untying a sack.

He mumbled hello and didn't look up.

"I'm an American writer and fisherman, visiting Viktor Chumak. Do you have any idea where the best place to fish on the Serdoba is?"

"Fuck if I know," the bent figure replied.

He straightened up, a disheveled fellow of about fifty in a threadbare sport coat, with clumps of brown hair sticking out from under a cloth cap. A half-empty vodka bottle protruded from his left coat pocket. Looking me over, he evidently decided I was indeed a foreigner and softened slightly.

"I caught these up at the lake near Kurakino," he said, opening a satchel containing about seventy-five goldfish-sized creatures. I wondered how he was planning to prepare these pitifully small prizes. "It only took me one and a half hours."

The man began talking about his life, telling me he and his wife both worked at the Lenin Collective Farm and hadn't been paid a regular salary in three years. "From time to time the farm gives us sacks of sugar and flour, sausage, and hot dogs. If we need medicine, we go to the farm director and he gives the okay to the nurse. But that's about it."

Upon first hearing such tales, you marvel at the passivity of Russian peasants, stuck in a decaying village, waiting patiently for an authority figure to dole out scraps of food and drugs. Why don't they just pick up stakes and move to greener pastures? But then you realize he's flat broke, that the situation is bad almost everywhere, and that housing in most cities is ridiculously scarce. In light of his options, staying put and waiting for better days didn't look so moronic.

I said good-bye, and as Galina and I walked away, he let loose with the fishing advice.

"Try above the bridge on that flat near the island in the river."

I thanked him. When I turned around to wave good-bye, I saw he had extracted the half-full bottle of grain alcohol and was holding the mouth up to the pump, diluting his evening libation.

We continued on through Alexandrovo, a village reportedly named for the daughter—Alexandra—of the prince who had built the mansion on the hill two hundred years before. Although nearly 5 P.M., the temperature was still in the eighties, and the sky clear. As we walked, I was overcome by thirst, the beginnings of a fever that would hound me that night. I stopped at nearly every pump, gulping mouthfuls of water and splashing it on my face. The village's pre-Revolutionary church was a forlorn relic, rising above the flat farm-land below the palace. Alexandrovo's tiny House of Culture, the center of the hamlet's social life in the Soviet era, was shuttered, a casualty of the demise of Communist institutions and the arrival of the VCR, which had killed the House's once-popular movie night.

At the far end of the village, in full view of Prince Kurakin's palace, I spied two older women and a one-armed man sitting in the shadow of a barn. Interested in divining what myths and facts about Kurakin had filtered down to the masses during seven decades of Communist rule, I approached the trio. They were cordial.

"The prince named three villages for his daughters—Alexandra, Sofia, and Nadezhda," said one of the women, a stout soul with black hair and silver teeth. "Once, the prince traded the whole village of Nadezhda and all the people in it for a dog."

She continued, "He buried one of his lovers behind a wall in the palace. They brought in a craftsman, blindfolded him, and he covered her up behind the plaster. The prince, he was a very clever man."

The old man—a talkative fellow of about seventy with pinched, birdlike features and a week's stubble on his face—chimed in.

"The prince had eight mistresses in nearby villages and children by all of them. They say that he built a tunnel from his estate to the river, and that when people went into the passageway years later, they found all sorts of skeletons in it."

The trio paused, as if for effect. I was beginning to understand that Kurakin's reputation had suffered somewhat under the Bolshe-viks. Four small, dirt-smeared children with white-blond hair ap-peared, the youngest wearing nothing but a shirt. His tanned legs were extraordinarily bowed. Stopping in front of us, he bent his knees slightly and unleashed an impressive stream of urine that splatted into the dust.

"There used to be a lot more houses and people in the village," said the older woman, who wore a white kerchief and flowered house-coat. "People were always visiting one another as if it were their

95

own house. They were more sociable and friendly. They were kind. Now they have become a lot more closed, and ill-tempered."

We moved on, walking to the Serdoba, just below the mansion. The enormous residence was rectangular and roofless, its brick surface pocked but solid, its riverfront side decorated with a six-columned portico capped by a pediment. Sixty gaping window frames stretched across the river facade, blue sky visible behind. Gazing at this relic, Galina recounted how she had ridden on horseback through the grounds recently, spying one of the patients—dressed in a ragtag uniform and armed with a toy gun—herding fellow inmates into military formation as they walked to the dining hall.

We crossed a footbridge over the Serdoba, unidentified fish dimpling the surface of the warm, murky river. Walking up a hill to the palace, I saw a stuccoed archway in the center of the horseshoe-shaped outbuildings. Standing guard beneath the arch, surreal in the vivid evening light, was the patient Galina had seen. He stood erect, his right arm stiff to his side, a plastic shotgun—held together with tape—slung over his left shoulder. He was about twenty-five, dressed in gold, corduroy pants and an old, olive-drab Soviet-army jacket secured around the waist by a wide, brown belt and a gold buckle with a red star. His uniform was completed by a brick-red shirt, a soiled tie, felt boots, and an army forage cap with a hammer-and-sickle emblem.

His getup was sufficiently strange. But what was truly unsettling was his gaze. His brilliant blue eyes glowed with a mad, unblinking intensity. He stared at us as we strolled his way, his young face tanned and flecked with sparse whiskers. When I got close, he saluted.

"Do you live here?" I asked.

"*Da!*" he bellowed.

"May we go in?"

"*Da!*" he boomed, saluting once again.

Inside, in front of the buildings flanking the ruined palace, patients sat on benches and shuffled to and fro. They stared at me and my garish green fly-rod case with interest and incomprehension. Many of the women were dressed only in robes, their scalps shorn to prevent outbreaks of head lice. Some men smoked, some mumbled to themselves, some rocked back and forth on the benches. In the middle of the main courtyard stood an apple orchard, where a bony horse reached up and tore fruit from the trees.

Dilapidated wooden sheds had been grafted onto the exterior of the stately mansion. On the eastern side, the asylum had erected pigsties, and the stench was overwhelming. Swine squealed, and thousands of black flies hummed in rooms where the prince once entertained the Russian nobility, an ensemble of serf musicians playing on a balcony above the dining room. Now, the once ornate parlors were the domain of goats and stray dogs, which nosed around the rubble. I wondered what was attracting them, until I saw that someone was using the prince's abode as a garbage dump.

Galina and I walked to the side facing the river, and before us opened up a bucolic vista. The Serdoba meandered through a landscape of swampy meadows, patches of forest, log-cabin villages, and golden fields dotted with grazing cattle. A hawk glided overhead, and the sun perched low over the horizon.

From a safe distance, the young guard was surveilling us. Standing behind one of the auxiliary buildings that housed patients, he drew a toy pistol from his coat pocket and began silently firing into the first-floor rooms. I stepped inside the mansion, picking my way through timbers, bricks, garbage, and a dead goat. Despite its ravaged condition, you could still sense the grandeur of the place. Though no floors were left in the palace and you looked straight up into a cerulean sky, you could tell that the ceilings had once been high, maybe twenty feet, and the rooms spacious. Mostly the interior was exposed brick, but high up on some walls, far from the hands of vandals and souvenir hunters, were clues as to what had once been: a faded, eight-foot swath of a mural, a few chunks of marble moldings, faint glimpses of colors—deep reds, warm oranges—from another century. Many of the roof timbers were charred from the 1920s fire that had finished off Prince Kurakin's residence after years of neglect.

Returning to the main courtyard, we passed a man of about thirty sitting in a wheelchair in the small orchard. He reached up and shook a branch vigorously, sending a half dozen apples thumping to the ground. I walked a few yards farther and began to pick an apple for myself.

"Don't take one of those," said the man in the wheelchair, who had dark, curly hair. "Here, take one of these. They're the sweetest."

He squeezed his hand into his pocket and extracted four green apples with tinges of rose in their skin. "Just one will be fine, thanks," I said.

He smiled, shook his head, and dropped all the apples into my cupped hands. "In Russia, we don't give a guest just one."

An old woman with shorn gray hair and a green robe appeared. "The best apples are on this tree, over here," she said. "Pick one right here. These are the juiciest."

Galina plucked one for me as the woman—a half dozen of her fellow female patients looking on in dull-eyed befuddlement—told me about the asylum.

"I live in a room with two other women. They're a little retarded and they look up to me. They obey me. They say, 'Mama gave me some sugar. Mama gave me some fish.' I like it here. There are good doctors."

I smiled, and Galina and I headed for the entrance. The old woman, missing her upper teeth, followed, earnestly describing how she had been a tank driver in World War II, had served at the front for three years, and had fought in the Baltic states, finally rising to the rank of lieutenant colonel. She said she had recently received the coveted Zhukov medal in recognition of her service. "My name is Nadezhda Alekseyevna Ushakova, and this all happened the way I described."

She seemed credible, and I started to ask her a question. Just then, a white-coated woman doctor appeared and led her back to the entrance of her building. Returning, the doctor looked at me coolly and said, "Excuse me. She's schizophrenic."

Walking through the crumbling, neoclassical arches, I took a deep breath. I needed to get to the river.

The sun was setting, the evening still, the riverbank deserted. I rigged up my trout rod and tied on a grasshopper imitation. I had seen grasshoppers pinging around the fields on our walk to the Kurakin estate and was confident that one of my little deceptions would do the trick on the Serdoba.

Standing on the muddy bank, I cast a third of the way across the river, which was about sixty yards wide. The setting, just below the mansion, was splendid, and not a breath of air rose to bat down my fly. My deer-hair grasshopper floated serenely on the lazy current. Occasionally I tugged on my fly-line, conveying a twitch to the bogus insect twenty yards in front of me. I knew from Chumak that the Serdoba was home to pike, perch, and other less glamorous species that—unlike trout—can survive in warm, turbid waters. But whatever was in a Serdoba was not rising to my grasshopper. I switched to a fly known as the Stimulator, a colorful imitation of no particular insect, but one that often coaxes a strike from the most reluctant fish. No luck. As the sun went down and twilight deepened, I tied on two different minnow imitations and hauled them through the water at an alluring rate of speed. Not a bite.

The truth was, in my five weeks in Russia, I had not distinguished myself as an angler. At this point, I was uncertain where the problem lay. No doubt a large part of the blame was mine, for I was a mediocre fly fisherman. Throughout my trip, I didn't know the water and often hadn't a clue as to what flies to use. My bait-slinging Russian angling buddies told me to quit tormenting myself with the fly rod and haul in some fish with a net or a worm. But I persevered, and gradually—as the polluted waters of western Russia gave way to the more pristine waters of Siberia, as my skills and angling intuition slowly improved—I actually began to catch fish.

Usually I knew when to quit, and that evening on the Serdoba, after an hour without a bite, I broke down my fly rod. Twilight settled over the landscape, and the air was fragrant with summer grasses. The scene at the edge of the village was timeless, reminiscent of an evening described by Ivan Turgenev nearly a century and a half before.

"The immaculate dark sky rose solemnly and endlessly high above us in all its mysterious significance," Turgenev wrote in *Sketches From a Hunter's Album*, describing his native province of Oryol. "My lungs melted with the sweet pleasure of inhaling that special, languorous and fresh perfume which is the scent of a Russian summer night. Hardly a sound was audible around us. . . . Now and then a large fish would make a resounding splash in the nearby river and the reeds by the bank would faintly echo the noise as they were stirred by the outspreading waves."

Galina and I moved quickly home, and she surprised me by crit-
icizing her father, saying her mother held everything together, while
Viktor spent months on end chasing his dreams.

"And what is he doing there in Moscow?" she said. "Trying for
years to get credit from America that never comes?"

After working more than twelve hours in the fields, Chumak was
eating dinner with a couple of friends, including Anatoly Ustinov,
former chairman of the Lenin Collective Farm and currently the director of the asylum. Chumak declined a shot of vodka because his
heart had been skipping beats the last few weeks. The men wandered outside for a smoke. Lighting up a nonfilter cigarette, Chumak
said, "Maybe this will be the year I get out from under all this
crap."

"I hope so," replied Ustinov. "You deserve it, after all the heart-
ache I've seen you go through."

That night, my guts boiled and sharp pains shot through my in-
testines. Experiencing the onset of diarrhea, probably giardiasis, that
would plague me for weeks, I passed a short, feverish night of sleep.
At 5:30 A.M. I woke up wrung out and soaked with sweat. Walking
out of Chumak's small living room, where I had slept on a couch, I
found the master of the house standing bare-chested in front of a
hallway mirror, smiling and combing his wet hair.

"How'd you sleep?" I asked.

"Wonderfully," he replied. "I haven't slept so well in years. It's
odd. I have a strange sensation I slept with my wife."

"Viktor!" barked Olga, laughing and swatting him on the shoulder.

I whined a bit about my stomach, but Viktor, like many Russian
peasants, tended not to fret much about the human body unless
portions of it were missing, bleeding profusely, or had ceased functioning altogether.

"Ah, it'll be better in a little bit. Go on back to bed for a while."

The asylum director, Ustinov, had promised me some material on
the Kurakin estate and sent a jeep at eight. Wobbly with fever, I
rode in a daze over dirt paths to the asylum, where Ustinov greeted
me warmly. After tea and biscuits, he handed me a brown leather
scrapbook detailing the history of Kurakin—the "Diamond Prince"—
and his palace. Written in 1968, it was a tale seen through a Communist prism and warped accordingly. But that small book, coupled

with visits months later to the Slavic Division at the New York Public Library, enabled me to piece together a picture of the rise and ruination of the magnificent estate on the Serdoba.

The Kurakins were one of Russia's most venerable families. Perhaps the most notable of the clan was Boris Ivanovich Kurakin (1676–1727), a soldier, diplomat, and historian who was a trusted adviser to Peter the Great. Boris Kurakin's wife and Peter the Great's first wife were sisters. Among the prizes that Peter bestowed upon his friend was a sixty-thousand-acre tract of land on the Serdoba and Khopr Rivers, the same property upon which one of his descendants would eventually build a grand manor house.

The man who erected the palace on the Serdoba was Prince Alexander Borisovich Kurakin, born in Moscow in 1752. His grandfather was the tutor to Pavel Petrovich, son of Catherine the Great and heir to the Romanov throne. The young Prince Kurakin studied with Crown Prince Pavel and became his fast friend. Prince Kurakin was a fixture at the Romanov court in St. Petersburg, but being Pavel's chum was not destined to endear him to Catherine. The empress had seized power illegally—leading a coup in which her husband was killed—and Pavel came to hate his mother with increasing intensity as the years passed. Given Catherine's heroic sexual exploits, Pavel didn't even know for certain who had sired him. As the crown prince moved into his twenties, Catherine the Great became increasingly suspicious that he and his pals—Prince Kurakin included—might try to depose her.

In 1782, when Prince Kurakin was thirty, he unwisely wrote a note critical of the empress's favorite paramour, Grigory Potemkin. Catherine's loyalists intercepted it, and the handsome and vain Prince Kurakin was booted out of St. Petersburg.

Prince Kurakin traveled awhile in Europe, living at the French court and charming Louis XVI and Marie Antoinette. But eventually he returned to Russia and his ancestral lands. What a dump it must have seemed, this flat, sparsely inhabited territory on the Russian steppe. One minute he was hobnobbing with royalty, living in palaces from the Baltic to the Seine, enjoying his role as dandy and courtier. The next minute he was exiled to a remote hamlet, Borisoglebskoye, surrounded by a crude cast of Russian country bumpkins—small-time merchants, filthy, vodka-swilling serfs, provincial nobility.

But Kurakin was determined to make the best of his rustic purgatory. After living several years in a wooden house, he resolved in the late 1780s to build a grand palace in the Greek Revival style. If he couldn't go to St. Petersburg, he would bring the majesty of St. Petersburg to the Serdoba. He decided to call his new estate Nadezhdino, from the Russian word for hope, *nadezhda*. The name symbolized his longing to return to his friend, Crown Prince Pavel, and the court.

Prince Kurakin is believed to have commissioned the famed Italian architect Giacomo Quarenghi—designer of such St. Petersburg landmarks as the Smolny Institute and the Academy of Sciences—to help build Nadezhdino. The prince chose a site high on the bluffs over the Serdoba, hired craftsmen from the surrounding regions, and set to work constructing his enormous, three-story mansion. He used seven hundred thousand bricks in the main house and another seven hundred thousand for the outbuildings. The palace itself had a majestic staircase, reception rooms, a ballroom, a chapel, and—on the third floor—small rooms for servants and his harem of serf girls. (Prince Kurakin was a lifelong bachelor, so if he did, indeed, sire many children—as the locals had told me—they were born out of wedlock.) The neoclassical architecture extended to the auxiliary buildings, which featured triumphal arches, porticoes, and colonnades.

Inspired by the parks he had seen on his travels to England, Prince Kurakin created a garden, three and a half miles in circumference, that was no less impressive than his manor house. Seven alleys—with names such as Pleasant Enjoyment, Difficulties Overcome, and Memories of Past Consolations—radiated like spokes from a central point in the park. Among the oaks, lindens, and elms, he built gazebos and a summerhouse.

When all was done, Prince Kurakin had built one of the most splendid palaces in the Russian provinces. Now he set out to enjoy himself and impress fellow noblemen from near and far. That he had a whopping ego seems little in doubt. He loved nothing more than to have his picture painted, and all the leading portraitists of the day took a whack at him. One work, by the English artist Brompton, shows a handsome, slightly effeminate grandee in silk breeches and knee-length silk coat. He has a straight, finely sculpted nose, a small mouth, dark hair that falls to his collar—pulled back in a ponytail— and a warm, if slightly smug, expression. Like all his contemporaries living on country estates, he was supported by hundreds of serfs, many of whom worked at the palace as cooks, maids, valets, hairdressers, butlers, tailors, dressmakers, and musicians. Prince I. M. Dolgoruky visited Nadezhdino and reported that there was a constant round of guests at the estate, and that the prince would make ceremonial entrances and exits, ushered in by uniformed lackeys. Musicians serenaded Kurakin's company from a balcony in the dining room. A bust of Marie Antoinette stood not far from the main table; the prince liked to gaze upon her while he ate.

In 1912, a journal called *Bygone Days*—which wistfully chronicled the decline of the Russian aristocracy and its estates—ran a feature on Nadezhdino. The author had this to say about Prince Kurakin: "Generally good humored, Prince A. B. Kurakin was notable not so much for his ambition, as for his empty vanity. He loved to do things for show; as a result he did a lot of silly things and, not surprising, while some of his contemporaries called him 'marvelous,' others compared him to a peacock."

The Communist author of the brief history of Nadezhdino was even less charitable. He noted that Prince Kurakin bestowed upon himself the titles *admiral, kapellmeister,* and *stallmeister* and used to tool up and down the Serdoba in yachts, often running aground in the shallow river. He got his nickname, the Diamond Prince, because of his habit of donning a blue caftan with two rows of large diamond buttons. He was shod with slippers studded with smaller diamonds.

Prince Kurakin liked to tell his friends in St. Petersburg how delighted he was living on his estate, comparing himself to Roman senators who used to withdraw to their country villas. The truth was, however, that he pined for Pavel and life at the court. When Catherine the Great died on November 5, 1796, and Pavel ascended to the throne, Prince Kurakin wasted no time fleeing his beloved Nadezhdino, setting in motion a long, slow decline of the estate. He set himself up again at the side of Pavel—known in the West as Czar Paul I—and eventually became a diplomat under Pavel and Alexander I.

From time to time, Prince Kurakin returned to Nadezhdino, but even in his lifetime the estate began to fade. In 1816, Prince Kurakin wrote to his caretaker, upset that his park was being used as a cow pasture and its gazebos and pavilions turned into pigsties.

After Prince Kurakin's death in 1818, other members of the Kurakin family lived off and on at Nadezhdino throughout the nineteenth century. In 1848, a man named Kartashov, hunting on the Serdoba, toured the estate with the permission of the caretaker. He found it still in fine shape, the walls and floors covered in marble, the rooms decorated with dozens of portraits, antiquities, and Japanese vases. The garden, apparently still well tended, had a "sad and tender dreaminess" about it, the long alleys so shady they felt like tunnels.

After Alexander II freed the serfs in 1861, the economic foundation of the Russian country estate was shaken to the core. Many manors—Nadezhdino included—gradually fell into disrepair, mirroring the fate of Southern plantations after the American Civil War. In her excellent book *Life on the Russian Country Estate*, Priscilla Roosevelt pointed out that the 1905 revolution—a dress rehearsal for 1917—greatly accelerated this decay. Angry peasants looted and vandalized manor houses. A special commission in one province, Novgorod, reported that the nobility's desertion of their estates went into high gear in the wake of the 1905 uprising.

"There were few cases of murder, but houses were burned down rather frequently with everything in them . . . [and] many estates were sold, passing into the hands of other classes," wrote Roosevelt.

Nadezhdino was no exception. In 1907, the Kurakin family sold the estate to the Aseyev brothers, textile merchants from nearby Penza. In 1910, the scribe from *Bygone Days*, A. Golombievski, and a photographer visited Nadezhdino. Judging from the pictures in the journal, the manor house was in decent shape. The exterior was completely intact, with only the yellow paint on the bricks fading. Some of the rooms were empty, but the marble columns and walls were undamaged, and a sizable amount of furniture was still scattered around the palace—Prince Kurakin's canopied bed, some chairs, marble pedestals and statuary.

But the author was overcome by the degeneration he found there. "Now there stands before us the sad duty of describing ruins," he wrote. On the first floor, "gloom rules," with some windows boarded up, an old, metal Kurakin family crest lying on the floor, and the smell of mold, trash, and decaying books permeating the air. He found clocks, tables, quite a few pictures, an icon, and a bust of Paul I. But on the third floor, once home to the girls who pleasured the prince, "our eyes witnessed not only the vileness of neglect, but also a picture of complete pogrom and destruction." Wallpaper hung in tatters. Partitions that had separated the small rooms lay in pieces on the floor.

Outside, Prince Kurakin's beloved English garden was overgrown and neglected. Golombievski concluded his article with the following words:

"Life at Nadezhdino will not return to what it was before. Who knows what awaits the palace? Maybe soon the words of Prince A. B. Kurakin will become an anachronism: 'If I'm not able to use the family estate and live in it, let it remain in this place as a lasting ornament and memory of me.' "

The Bolshevik commissars were not about to oblige. After the Revolution, the estate was nationalized and put in the hands of a committee of "workers and people's deputies." What was left in the house was apparently destroyed or carted away by vandals, although the immediate fate of Nadezhdino was far kinder than that which befell many other Russian country houses.

"In 1917 and 1918, in a riot of vandalistic, spiteful destruction of luxury," wrote Roosevelt, "young peasants swarmed through the gates and then the doors of countless manors, slashing paintings, decapitating statues, gleefully destroying orangeries, barns, and estate offices and their records, and finally either vandalizing or burning the house so the owner could never return."

A 1922 drawing of a large hall at Nadezhdino shows it stripped of all furniture and art objects, and a door hanging by its hinges. In 1927, the manor house was gutted by a fire, its cause unknown.

The outbuildings were untouched and in 1931 were opened as a regional Communist Party institute where collective-farm workers, newspaper editors, Young Communist League activists, and party hacks were taught the gospel according to Stalin. In 1939, what remained of Nadezhdino was turned into an agricultural institute. Finally, in 1959, Nadezhdino became an *internat*, as asylum for the insane and crippled. Many former palaces met a similar fate, converted into hospitals, sanitoriums, or institutes.

In 1932, on the Solovetsky Islands, a prisoner named A. Grech wrote an ode, entitled "A Wreath for the Estates," to the vanished world of the Russian nobility in the countryside. "In ten years," he wrote, "a grandiose necropolis has been created. In it lie two centuries of culture. The monuments of art and daily life, the thoughts and forms of Russian poetry, literature, and music lie buried here."

Priscilla Roosevelt neatly summed up the results:

"When Russia's landowners fled, they took with them the vitality that their presence, support and commerce had lent provincial cities and towns. In comparison to the pre-Revolutionary elite's endowments for orphanages, schools, charitable societies, churches and monasteries, their patronage of theaters, shops and restaurants, the contributions of the impoverished Soviet state and its new elite to town life was inevitably pallid. And so the life of these towns withered, grayed, and has never recovered."

I handed the history of Nadezhdino to Anatoly Ustinov, the director of the asylum. It was a fine, sunny day, the temperature near ninety degrees. We sat in his plaster-walled office, the leaves outside his window trembling in a gentle breeze, the room filled with a soft, foliage-tinged light. I had briefly met Ustinov five years before when he was chairman of a local collective farm and recalled only that he seemed a pleasant, progressive fellow eager to help Viktor Chumak launch his farm.

Ustinov—a handsome man of forty-six with curly, brown hair and brown eyes—told me that the asylum had between 200 and 250 patients, suffering from a variety of psychiatric disorders. There was enough money to feed the patients and workers, but that was it. Repair of the dilapidated outbuildings would have to wait for better times.

I asked Ustinov why, after eleven years as chairman of the collective farm, he had decided in 1995 to turn his back on agriculture and take charge of a shabby mental institution.

"It became impossible to work at the collective farm," he replied. "I thought and thought about whether I should take full responsibility for the complete disintegration of the collective farm, and I decided I would not do that. And so I left."

Beneath his placid exterior, Ustinov was simmering with resentment over the breakdown of the old system. He said he believed that the Yeltsin government and its corrupt associates had purposely, for unspecified economic gain, destroyed socialist agriculture. I held my tongue and asked whether the real problem in the countryside wasn't the continued lack of private property and private farmers.

"That's a controversial question," he replied. "Earlier, we had production in many spheres at or above world level. We spent a lot of money to raise the standard of living in villages like this and in many ways succeeded. Never say that the past was all bad, that we didn't accomplish a lot. We did. We built roads, schools, hospitals, houses, and telephone systems in many rural areas. I am not convinced private property is the answer. I'm really not. You have your own experience. We have ours."

In 1991, Ustinov had seemed like a fairly liberal man, a reformer in the Gorbachev mold. In the ensuing five years, however, the ground had shifted so totally that Ustinov now looked like a dinosaur, nostalgic for a system that he firmly believed had uplifted rural Russia. In his opinion, Communism had taken a feudalistic, peasant society and, in a few decades, brought it into the modern world. In this, he was half-right. What he couldn't see was what might have been, how much further life might have progressed in rural Russia had Stalin not exterminated the best farmers during collectivization, then saddled the survivors with the inefficient, initiative-deadening ziggurat of state farms.

"Our people were protected under the old Soviet system," he continued, "and now from you we have imported racketeers and corruption and prostitution. At least the Communists fought for a clean culture, a clear ideology. Of course there were mistakes. But what do we have now? Complete disintegration."

He suggested a tour of the prince's park, and I readily agreed. Kurakin's English garden still had some majesty to it—the seven alleys were discernible, and great groves of oak and linden rose high into the hot, azure sky. Ustinov's small, well-tended house bordered the old garden, and after a lunch of fried fish he showed off his prized pigs, chickens, and ducks. On the way back to Chumak's, Ustinov pointed out his accomplishments during his tenure as chairman of the Lenin Farm—new wood-frame houses, modern cattle barns, a footbridge just below Nadezhdino. At the peak of his reign, the farm had nine hundred cows. Now it had three hundred. Still, Ustinov said he was confident the countryside would rise again.

"Gorbachev turned on the tap and now a lot of rust is coming out. But eventually the water will run clear."

I was dozing on Viktor's couch around midnight when I heard the rumble of trucks and the screeching of air brakes. Peering out the window, I saw three trailer-loads of hay attached to Chumak's Kamaz. He lumbered in the door, exhausted, smelly, coated with dust. I followed him into the kitchen, where he gulped down a cup of coffee, spooned cold macaroni and ground beef out of a skillet, and poured us both a shot of berry brandy. He still had to return that night and fetch his two young workers, Andrei and Sergei, and wouldn't be back until 3 A.M. He had been up since five that morning.

"I don't know, Victor," I joked. "Maybe you'd be better off just working for a collective farm?"

"They wouldn't be able to produce enough vodka to console me if I were stuck on a collective farm."

Shortly after 3 A.M., I heard Viktor, Andrei, and Sergei in the kitchen. At 5 A.M., my alarm sounded; I had a train to catch at six-thirty in Serdobsk. Viktor was asleep in his second-floor, atticlike room—Olga had gone to Moscow—and I hollered up to him. A few minutes later, I saw, descending the wooden ladder, his dirty bare feet, followed by his shirtless potbelly. He had a cigarette in his mouth. *"Vsyoh OK"*—"Everything's okay," he announced.

Outside, the sky was growing light, and his son-in-law, Andrei, and Sergei were already in motion. Viktor and I hopped in his Zil truck and roared, in fourth gear, to Serdobsk, slowing down only once when a chicken ran across the road and nearly paid for the mistake with its life. Chumak had been fulminating about Olga's taking the car to Moscow instead of the train. "A chicken is not a bird, and a broad is not a person," said Chumak, which I took to mean that the second sex was scatterbrained, or worse.

It was a pleasant, clear morning, with a few clouds building to the north. "We'll be all right with the harvest today if this weather doesn't go to the dick."

As we rumbled down rutted dirt roads through still-sleeping villages, I asked Viktor how he'd changed in the five years since I last saw him. "Earlier, when you first met me, I'd say I looked upon things with a certain optimism, perhaps you could even say with a little fantasy. Now I look upon all this only soberly, with reality. After all this crap, I can look upon life in no other way."

We hit Serdobsk at 6 A.M. The sun was up, casting clean shadows on the town's concrete apartment blocks.

"Remember what I said about the collective farm eating the last dick without salt? Well, now I've got a little salt left. But there may come a time when I'll be forced to eat the dick with no salt at all."

Viktor drove past the small, concrete station, cruised up to the platform, and helped me haul my bags onto a green bench. A few people waited for the train, headed from Odessa to Ufa in the Ural Mountains. Viktor and I shook hands and promised to keep in touch, which was, I knew, a lie. I would see him if ever I came through Serdobsk again. Or perhaps one day I might pick up the phone and be greeted by Chumak's booming voice, informing me that he was in Minnesota to clinch the deal on his new $5.5 million "American agricultural complex." With Viktor, anything was possible.

Inserting a Prima between his lips, he lit up and clambered into his cab. Then he jammed the blue truck into first gear and roared out of the station with a wave. The last I heard from Chumak was the sound of the Zil's flatbed rattling and crashing as he flew down the deserted, cratered streets of Serdobsk.

4.

Distance

 Russia's vastness had always been an abstraction. Intellectually, I grasped the concept and could recite the same statistics as every other scribe in the Moscow press corps: Largest country on earth. Twice the size of the United States. Spanned ten time zones. Very, *very*, big place. Twice I had flown from Moscow to Vladivostok, spending eight torturous hours in the air wedged into the broken seats of a malodorous Aeroflot jet, terrified that at any moment the battered Ilyushin 62 was going to fall out of the sky. And all that while we never left Russian territory. That's nearly the same flying time between New York and Moscow, every hour of it spent hurtling through the sovereign airspace of the Russian Federation.

But it wasn't until I began creeping overland across Russia, by train, bus, and car, that I appreciated just how enormous a country it is. And there came a moment—after saying good-bye to Chumak and settling onto the eastbound Bashkortostan express—when I opened up my map of the former Soviet Union and was overcome by something akin to panic. It was early August, I had been in Russia more than a month, and although I had covered some fairly impressive chunks of territory north to south, I had barely begun the long march east. By late September, I was supposed to join an expedition on the Kamchatka Peninsula, more than five thousand miles away. That deadline aside, I knew that six weeks hence, in the remote regions of northeastern Siberia where I was bound, it would already be autumn, which in that part of the world meant snow, hard frosts, and—worst of all—the end of fishing. I had dallied in European Russia long enough. It was time to move swiftly into the Asian domains of the country, which beckoned with the gauzy promise of undefiled waters and untamed territory.

Far on the horizon was Lake Baikal, my first major stop in Siberia. But that was a continent ahead, and along the way I wanted to get off the train and test the waters. I had to fish the Volga—not a rational decision, since angling along much of the Volga, particularly fly-fishing, was not especially good. But it seemed indecent to fish one's way across Russia and not make a few casts on the storied Volga. Besides, the last fly-fishing contact I had before Kamchatka was in Samara. Having been badly burned by Artur Turkin on the Kola Peninsula, I was wary of calling up another alleged member of Russia's fly-fishing brotherhood. But curiosity overcame doubt, and when I phoned my angling contact from Chumak's house, the fellow on the other end of the static-fouled line sounded normal. Sure, he said, we'll take you out on the Volga for a day.

The Bashkortostan, bound for the Urals, made a one-minute stop at 7 A.M. in Serdobsk. Weighed down by an absurd quantity of baggage, I trotted desperately alongside the train, then hopped aboard.

My bunkmate for the all-day ride to Samara was a plump, mustachioed fellow of about fifty, Valery M. Kechin. His very ordinariness made him unusual in Russia. He was a middle-aged, friendly, successful businessman unencumbered by feelings of inferiority, paranoia, bitterness, or wounded national pride. You didn't meet such people every day in Russia, where seventy years of state terror, twisted ideology, and other indignities too numerous to mention had left many people with some bizarre ideas about the world and how it worked.

Kechin was a car dealer, running shops near Odessa and in Togliatti, the Volga River town where Fiat had long ago built a plant to make the boxy Zhigulis that ruled the road in much of Russia. He exuded a jaded optimism, stating in one breath that it would be at least twenty years before the situation "normalized in Russia," while averring in the next that "Russia will rise again. It has a lot of hardworking people."

The conductress interrupted us. Two railway inspectors had boarded the train, were raising hell in the first two cars as they checked to see who held legitimate tickets, and were headed our way. Westerners accustomed to buying a ticket and getting on a train might have trouble grasping the Russian way, as practiced by my companion and our conductress. Kechin traveled this route frequently and knew her well. He rarely bought a ticket, but merely boarded her wagon, paid her about half the price of a regular fare, and occupied one of the usually empty berths. Everyone was a winner: Kechin got a discount ticket, and the conductress pocketed the money. Of course, the Russian Railways got screwed, but cheating the state was a national pastime. This practice—known as earning money *nalevo*, "on the left"—was widespread. Indeed, conductors sometimes earned more selling berths on the side than they did from their regular salaries. After shuttling Kechin to a neighboring wagon, the conductress told me she was a single mother with three daughters to support. "What else can I do?" she asked. "I've got to make a living."

She got up and returned with another passenger, a dour man of about forty who had just lost his job at a factory in the Urals city of Ufa. He wasted no time telling me how bad things were at his old plant, which bottled oxygen. "You can't imagine the scale of theft. It is enormous. Everyone is swiping whatever they can get their hands on, from the very bottom to the very top. They are plundering the factory. It's unbelievable."

As he left, he said, "We wanted to become like you, but then we realized we had as much chance of doing that as going from here to the moon on foot."

The conductress returned with Kechin in tow. Apparently the inspectors had called off their search for illicit passengers after the train director slipped them some money.

Kechin explained that the inspectors were merely going through the motions until they got their payola. "In Russia we have a saying: 'First you shake them up, then you shake them down.' Everyone has their place in the food chain—the conductors, the head of the train, the inspectors. They're all looking for bribes and money on the side, and they know what they've got to do to get it."

A striking view of the Volga opened up near the historic city of Syzran. The river was wide, about two miles across, its meandering course broken by dozens of islands. High, white cliffs flanked one bank. The day was sunny and breezy, and whitecaps stirred up the dirty green surface of the river. A long blue-and-white cruise ship steamed downstream. The Volga's grandeur, its central place in national lore, its wooded shores backed by miles of fields, all led inevitably—and rightly so—to comparisons with the Mississippi.

My fly-fishing contact, Mikhail Furashov, met me at the train. My first reaction was relief that I was not slipping again into the maw of another operator. Furashov, a slender man of twenty-eight with thinning, blond hair, had a quiet decency about him. He and a partner owned Samara's only Western-style tackle shop, the Angler, and he'd arranged for a friend to take us fishing downstream of Samara. Over dinner in his claustrophobic apartment—he shared three tiny rooms with his wife, infant son, mother, ninety-three-year-old grandmother, sister, and brother-in-law—Furashov said he had worked at the giant Tupolev aircraft factory in Samara. Seeing that layoffs were coming, he quit and, with his small savings, opened his shop eighteen months ago. It had recently turned a profit, meeting a demand for decent, imported fishing gear in a town where all that had been available for decades were a couple brands of cheesy rods and reels that looked vintage nineteenth century.

Another shoot of the free market had taken root in the hinterland.

Samara, known as Kuybyshev under the Soviets, was a sprawling town of about 1.3 million and the sixth-largest city in Russia. It had the usual agglomeration of deadening Soviet high-rises, but it also boasted an extensive downtown of handsome, nineteenth-century brick and stone buildings. Set on tree-lined streets, these pre-Revolutionary structures were in a sorry state of repair, but their scale was good for the soul.

The Angler was located in a small room on the first floor of a solid, Stalin-era building. Any Red Man–chewing, monster truck–loving, bass-fishing good ol' boy from the American South would have felt right at home in Furashov's shop. Its walls were lined with hundreds of brilliantly colored lures from Finland, Japan, and America, shimmering baitfish imitations with names like Moss Masters Shakin' Shad, neatly encapsulated in hard plastic packages. Furashov also sold the latest spinning reels and lightweight, graphite spinning rods from manufacturers such as Daiwa and Abu Garcia. Some of the rods cost 1 million rubles, about $200. I wondered who in this city would pay that kind of money for a fishing pole.

Then I found out. In walked a good-looking, slightly overweight man of about thirty-five, casually dressed in the latest threads from Milan. He wore dark gray pants, a gray cashmere cardigan sweater, a white cotton shirt with blue stripes, and sleek black loafers. In one hand he held a set of BMW keys. In the other was a cell phone. Furashov and his two assistants came to attention.

The jaunty Russian strolled around the shop, selecting the most expensive items and instructing Furashov's partner, an attractive brunette, to ring them up. He bought a $450 sonar fish-finder, nets, lures, a $200 reel, and a Cortland fly-fishing kit for kids. In less than ten minutes he purchased nearly 5 million rubles—around $1,000—of fishing paraphernalia, about what the average pensioner received in nine months. He reminded me of the nouveau riche Russians I'd heard about who went to three-star Paris restaurants, ordered $600 bottles of vintage Romanee-Conti, then tossed back glasses of this rare wine in great gulps. If it was pricey, the man in the Angler wanted it. He said he was going on vacation. I asked where.

"The Volga, of course," said the man, who was rumored to have some connection with the Zhiguli factory in Togliatti. "What? Do you think you can really catch decent fish abroad? I was in Switzerland recently and the only fish there were in the stores."

Extracting a clump of fresh, one-hundred-thousand-ruble notes from his pants pocket, he counted them off and strolled out of the store.

"Now there," said Furashov, "is a New Russian."

Lev Bobolev was on the east bank of the Volga, hunched over his troubled outboard motor. For the next twenty-four hours, Bobolev—a strapping, irrepressible man who reminded me more of a garrulous American cowboy than the Russian security guard he was—would assume this position time and again. What would remain with me long after this fishing trip ended was not the fishing. It was Mr. Bobolev, and his engines.

The evening was overcast and windy. Furashov, his coworker Aleksei Kharitonov, Bobolev, and I were heading thirty miles downstream to a cluster of islands, where the fishing was reported to be hot. Bobolev's boat was beached on a sandy, litter-strewn bank just below some bluffs north of Samara. The vessel was a sixteen-foot, light blue, steel number that looked like one of those amusement-park boats that go round and round in a little pool. The Russians had a good nickname for such a craft. They called it a soap dish.

Affixed to the back were two dented, aluminum-covered outboard motors that looked like overgrown 1940s Waring blenders. One of these motors was out of commission, which meant we were going nowhere; with a one-engined soap dish, we would be at the mercy of the Volga's powerful currents. Lev tinkered with the stricken motor for nearly half an hour. It was past six, and just as I was beginning to wonder whether we'd be going anywhere, the engine came to life with a rattle, a cough, and a feeble puttering. He slapped on the cover and pulled the cord on the second motor, which had been in fine working order. Now it, too, was dead. Lev—dressed somewhat incongruously in black pants, a camouflage shirt, and a white pith helmet—went back to work.

"This equipment," announced Furashov, "borders on the fantastic."

Lev looked up, exposing four enormous gold front teeth in a radiant smile, and said, "It's a process, boys."

Within five minutes, the second motor was running.

"*Yes!*" hollered Lev in English, and we were on our way. Sort of. Lev was in good spirits; like many Russians, he had learned to take satisfaction in surmounting the obstacles—bad engines, bad consumer goods, bad service—that a dysfunctional system flung in his path every day.

We buzzed downriver. On our left was Samara, with its apartment blocks, waterfront park, arbored historic district, brick cathedral, and obligatory, absurd Soviet monument—a concrete shaft, atop of which was a socialist-realism figure born aloft on silver wings. The statue represented no one in particular, but was merely the fevered hallucination of a pack of inebriated Party hacks who decided their lasting legacy would be to erect this phallic evocation of Communism's "shining future" on the banks of the Volga.

"We call it the Monument to the Age of Stagnation," said Bobolev, referring to the golden epoch of Leonid Ilyich Brezhnev.

Lev pulled into a tributary of the river, zoomed under a bridge, and beached the boat on the shore of a dirty little cove. It was time to get gas. Hauling canisters out of the boat, the three of them hiked to a station, unseen behind a row of trees. What would have taken five minutes in America, where there are actually fuel docks on rivers, took us forty-five minutes, as Bobolev and company made two trips for gas. It turned out the petrol was being sold off a truck manned by enterprising workers from a nearby army base. They had stolen the gas and were hawking it at a discount. Again, everyone profited—except the state.

"Well, we saved two thousand rubles a canister—not a lot of money, but all the same it's pleasant," said Bobolev.

We had gone only a few hundred yards before one of the engines died. As he worked on the machine, Bobolev said there was no way he could afford to replace the twenty-year-old motors. "A good, new engine would cost half my annual salary," he said. "I have no choice but to stick with these."

At last, as overcast skies cleared and the sun poked through, we made it back to the Volga. Winds were light, and Bobolev throttled up both engines. We fell silent, enjoying the feel of being on the broad river. Passing cruise ships and oil tankers, we quickly put Samara behind us, entering a scenic landscape of high limestone cliffs, forests, islands studded with willows and poplar, and clusters of small dacha colonies. Campers in elaborate summer shantytowns of tents and plastic lean-tos cooked dinner on the shore. Poachers dragged bays with nets. In one village of wooden cottages, an old brick church with leaning cupolas sat in splendid decay. Above the village were meadows and haystacks touched at sunset with a golden light.

Shortly after nine, with darkness descending, we arrived at our destination, the houseboat of a fisherman named Volodya Pankov. There were four of us, uninvited and unexpected, yet Pankov and his son—who were friends of Bobolev's—welcomed us warmly to their already cramped quarters. Russians nearly always extended such hospitality, and their displays brought home how atomized, regimented, and—by comparison—inhospitable we in America had become. Somehow, the more you get, the less you seem to want to share it.

The Pankovs and two others from his crew served us fish soup, sausage, bread, and vodka. Pankov, a short, solidly built man of about fifty who had fished commercially on the Volga for thirteen years, was a teetotaler—a rarity in Russia—and as the rest of us tossed back vodka, he talked about the river. On the Volga, as almost everywhere else in Russia, poaching was epidemic. He said people killed fish without regard to legal limits, seasons, or prohibited species. Even licensed commercial boats fished with abandon, dredging the bottom of the river in the manner of high-seas trawlers. The great fish of the Volga—the sturgeon and its smaller cousin, the sterlet—were rapidly disappearing. Farther downstream, where the Volga emptied into the Caspian Sea, caviar poachers were slaughtering sturgeon by the ton.

"I take a little and try to preserve what there is," said Pankov.

Bobolev was downing vodka at a heroic pace, the spirits bringing out the poet in him. He rhapsodized about the legendary *ukha*—fish soup—made from sterlet, saying it was a miracle cure for hangovers. Remembering one particularly bad morning and the relief the sterlet *ukha* had brought, Bobolev said, "It was fantastic, as if Jesus Christ was walking barefoot over my very soul."

After five hours' sleep, we awoke at eight to a screaming wind that promised to make fishing—particularly fly-fishing—difficult. Bobolev was subdued and hungover, and there was no fish soup, much less the miraculous sterlet *ukha*, to ease his suffering. The houseboat was tied to the bank of a small creek, about fifty yards from the Volga. I walked onto the deck and discovered, in the daylight, that we were all urinating off the houseboat next to the spot where Pankov and company were fetching water for cooking. One of the fishermen assured me there was no need to worry.

A front had moved through, with the temperature dropping to about seventy and thick, white clouds moving swiftly across a sparkling blue sky. Pankov said the wind would make fishing in the Volga nearly impossible and suggested we try the creek, where voracious pike were said to lurk.

I always associated pike with Russia, perhaps because of Slavic fairy tales in which talking pike promise the moon to lazy peasant fishermen if they release them. Pike, common in most of Russia, are sleek, fierce predators, their duckbill mouths bristling with dozens of sharp teeth. In North America, they are sometimes known as water wolves for their propensity to gobble up not only fish, but also rats, frogs, and ducks. Sergei Aksakov, a nineteenth-century Russian author and angler, wrote in his classic work, *Notes on Fishing*, that large pike were known as "duck eaters." He said he saw a man catch a pike weighing forty-nine and a half pounds and once witnessed a fully fledged duck squawking with pain and lifting itself nearly out of the water, a pike clamped to its hindquarters.

"The greediness of pike," wrote Aksakov, "knows no bounds."

Armed with a box of big, colorful flies designed to appeal to the pike's worst predatory instincts, I stepped into Bobolev's cursed boat with high hopes.

Things went well for five minutes. We cut the engines and drifted down the creek as I cast to the grassy bank. Sheltered from the wind by a small woods, I found the casting easy, and I had that sixth sense—often unreliable—that a fish was going to assault my fly. When the time came to move farther down the creek, Bobolev yanked the rope attached to his Tonka-toy engine. It was, predictably, dead. No amount of pulling could revive it. I continued to fish as he worked on the engine. Finally, Pankov's son towed us back to the houseboat, where Lev, cursing mildly, began dismantling the motor.

Mikhail Furashov and I rode with Pankov's son to a nearby lake. It turned out that Furashov rarely fly-fished, but he was handy with a spinning rod and soon caught two small perch. We circled the lake, connected to the Volga by a channel, as I cast to the grassy banks. Stripping in my fly, I felt resistance and thought that my minnow imitation was hung up in the weeds. I yanked the rod and discovered a pike on the end of my line. A small one, about sixteen inches, it was a disappointing catch, since I had expected pike to hit my fly with the force of a sucker punch. But at least it was a pike, and it proved to be the only one caught that day.

Back at the houseboat, Bobolev's engine was no more. The motor of two hours before was now a heap of screws, springs, and doodads scattered over the boat and the dock. He had taken apart the engine completely, forcing me to entertain visions of spending days on the Volga with Mr. Pankov's fishing crew. That afternoon, as we caught a dozen perch, we would return from time to time to find Lev Bobolev hunched quietly over his motor. I would long ago have heaved the thing into the creek, but Lev just kept on cleaning, assembling, and aligning. Slowly, by late afternoon, the jumble of parts began to look once more like a motor. Shortly after five o'clock, he wrapped the rope around his little engine and yanked twice. It started. Lev Bobolev was a deeply satisfied man.

We rode back to Samara in the lee of the western shore, stopping once to fish and catching nothing. Mainly we traveled in silence, the evening air bracing, the sky cloudless. Once, Bobolev turned to me and said with a big, golden grin, "I love this boat, but it's an iron carriage."

Thereafter, all summer, I noticed burly, patient Russian men hunched over cheap engines, trying to coax them to life. I found myself wishing that as capitalism rolled over Russia, its sweet benefits trickling down from big cities to little Volga villages, that Johnson or Evinrude would set up a factory and make reliable, cheap engines for the legions of Russian fishermen tortured by shoddy motors. From a purely humanitarian point of view, it would be a nice move.

The next morning, Furashov saw me off as I boarded a train whose route began in Adler on the Black Sea and ended at Novosibirsk in central Siberia. As I shook hands with Furashov, I was saying good-bye to my last contact in Russia. From here to the Pacific Ocean, I didn't know a soul. It was a good feeling.

A woman of about sixty, dressed in a robe, lay across from me on the bottom bunk. Next to me was a former Communist Party official blathering about how much better things were in the old days. Tuning them out, I opened my map and considered my next move. I had bought a ticket to Ufa, in the Urals, and planned to visit the Belaya River. A fly fisherman in Moscow had told me that the Belaya, a mountain stream popular with white-water rafters, held both trout and grayling. But Lev Bobolev said a recent chemical spill had wiped out many fish in the river. I looked at my map, daunted by the territory that remained. The decision was easy; I would skip the Belaya and ride the train to its final destination, Novosibirsk, about fifteen hundred miles ahead. From there, I would travel south to Gorno-Altai, a mountainous region bordering Mongolia, where the rivers reportedly contained many grayling, as well as vestiges of the legendary Siberian fish, the taimen.

The director of the train said seats were available to Novosibirsk and moved me to another four-berth compartment. That afternoon, clouds moved in as we rolled over the steppe toward the Urals. We passed fields of golden sunflowers and recently mown hay. Strung out along the rail line were villages with log huts and wooden cottages. Toward evening, as we neared the Urals, a line of hills materialized to the north. I watched and dozed, still plagued by diarrhea, stomach cramps, and fatigue.

We reached Ufa at six forty-five that evening, stopping—theoretically—for half an hour. As I stood on the platform, the conductor told me to walk four cars ahead and buy a new ticket from the train director. We weren't supposed to leave for another five minutes, but the train was late and the engineer impatient. I had walked just two cars forward when a whistle blew and the train lurched ahead. It was leaving. I trotted to the next car, where a stout conductress stood on the steps, coolly surveying the handful of passengers—myself included—scrambling to hop aboard. Just as I reached her, the train began to pick up speed. I started to jump on the steps. She stiff-armed me.

"Get on your own wagon!" she yelled. "This is not your car."

"But my conductor told me to go see the director of the train," I pleaded.

"Then walk up to him," she sneered.

Looming before me was the clichéd Russian, female nightmare with the swinish face, linebacker build, withering stare, and control over your destiny. Jogging next to the train, I quickly weighed my options: (1) Barrel through this battle-ax. (2) Sprint and try to reach the car of the train director. (3) Drop back two wagons and attempt to leap aboard my car. All I had with me were my diaries. The rest of my gear, including thousands of dollars of fly-fishing paraphernalia, was in my compartment. By the time I caught up with my luggage in Novosibirsk, I knew it would be picked clean.

I had only one option.

I went for the conductress.

Lowering my shoulder, I jumped onto the bottom step and felt her pushing me back onto the platform. Now I was pissed. I slammed into her, my left arm and shoulder sinking into a quivering mass of belly and bosom. She pushed back. Grunting, I elbowed her. The blow loosened her death grip on a bar that ran along the door. The next thing I knew, she was bouncing backward against the door, and I was on the train.

"What the hell are you doing!" I hollered as I scrambled up the steps. "Are you out of your mind! You could have—"

Smack! I felt a stinging pain between my shoulder blades. Wheeling around, I saw the Crazed Bolshevik Conductress standing with an eighteen-inch wooden baton in her raised right hand. I couldn't believe this was happening.

"You goat!" she sputtered.

I braced myself for another blow, but none came. She stood, her weapon at the ready, just in case I might try to bounce her prodigious derriere onto the platform. The thought crossed my mind. Muttering curses, exchanging poisonous glances with the nastiest Russian train conductor I had ever come across, I slowly backed up, opened the door to the next wagon, and—never taking my eye off her—headed in the direction of the train boss.

Three men had joined me in my compartment. Two of them, a father and son from a small town near Chelyabinsk, sat opposite me on the lower bunk. They were Muslim Tatars—earnest, dark-eyed, and friendly. In the West, you might break the ice with a stranger on a train by chatting about the weather. In Russia, your traveling companions tend to launch right into a discussion of the upheaval in the country and the travails in their lives. The father was a detective, which afforded him a particularly nasty view of the current situation. In his village, crime and drunkenness were on the rise, to say nothing of bribery. It seemed that everyone, including many of his fellow policemen, was on the take.

"The honest people pull one way and the dishonest people pull another, and as a result we stand still and go nowhere. It really upsets me as an honest policeman to see my dishonest colleagues getting rich while I'm earning eight hundred thousand rubles [$165] a month."

I had scarcely eaten all day and pulled out some sardines and bread, offering them to my companions. Not wanting to take food from a traveler, the father excused himself and walked into the corridor. The eighteen-year-old son, who had been sitting quietly, took a chunk of bread and fixed me with large, brown eyes.

"You can see my father is a Communist. He thinks that so much of what is happening now is bad and that things were better then. We actually have some very intense arguments about this."

I asked him what he thought of the Communist era.

"There was a lot that was very bad about that time. I'm glad it's over."

The sun set as we moved higher into the Urals, traveling through a landscape of steep, wooded hillsides and cabins with sharply pitched roofs. I drifted off to sleep around 10 P.M. We seemed to stop every hour, and at each station women screamed announcements through tinny loudspeakers on the platforms. At dawn, the detective and his son disembarked.

Saturday morning I awoke in Siberia and celebrated by taking a pill designed to wipe out the parasites that I suspected had taken up residence in my bowels. Flagyl is a powerful drug that can make you feel worse than the disease, but a week of diarrhea and profound fatigue had left me no choice. You can't drink alcohol during the two-week course of the medicine, a drawback that I feared might put a crimp in my socializing. Less than a week later, however, my teetotalism would be my salvation.

The train had crossed the Urals, entering Asia, but I felt no romance. We chugged through the flat, dust-blown steppe of southern Siberia and northern Kazakhstan, past grim towns with blighted, four-story concrete apartment blocks. At 2 P.M., as we stopped for fifteen minutes in the Kazakh town of Petropavlovsk, a dismal scene played itself out in the station. In a steady rain, more than one hundred locals hustled up and down the platform hawking everything imaginable—bicycle-tire pumps, luggage carts, radios, socks, fried fish, chicken, boiled potatoes, salted fish. The conductor told me the peddlers were part of the growing ranks of the unemployed, now living off what they could sell to train passengers. We assembled by the doors of our wagons, surveying the platoons of vendors standing there with soaked, stringy hair, dressed in seedy clothes. No one bought much, but the plaintive hawkers stayed with the train until it pulled out of the station.

I had the compartment to myself. A dark, sad-looking man with a prodigious nose came in and sat down. He was a Turk and seemed as depressed as I was. A computer technician working near Samara, the man was not fond of Russians, finding them "cold." I couldn't agree, but was not surprised his impression of Russia and mine should be so divergent. I was a tall, white-skinned, mustachioed man from a country many Russians still held in awe. Take away my clothes and my accent and I could have passed for a Russian. The Turk was a swarthy, alien-looking Muslim, working in a land where many people had an abiding prejudice against what they termed *chyornenkiye*—"darkies"—from the Caucasus or the Middle East.

We crossed the muddy Irtysh River and pulled into Omsk at 7 P.M. in a pouring rain. Walking into the imposing stone station in search of food—I had lived off sardines and cucumbers for two days—I found scores of people milling miserably about inside. Nearly one hundred soggy souls stood in line at two ticket windows. There were a pair of "buffets," both selling rancid-looking sausage and putrescent chicken that I dared not buy.

The Turk, also searching for food, sidled up to me. My face must have betrayed my disgust.

"One reason the Russians live this way," he said, "is that they're willing to put up with all this. They have patience for this. They let it happen to them. In Turkey, people wouldn't put up with this for one minute. The Russians bring it on themselves."

Back on the train, we stood in the corridor and watched as the flat landscape of western Siberia rolled past. Shaking his head, he marveled that such a big country, with so many riches, was such a mess.

"Oh, but they can talk so well, these Russians. They talk and talk. Everyone's a poet, a philosopher. All this 'la, la, la,' and look at the country. They talk beautifully, but look how they work and what they put up with. It's a lack of self-respect. A lack of respect toward oneself and one's work."

Rain drummed all night on the roof of the train. At 5 A.M. Sunday, in keeping with the annoying habit of the Russian Railways, the conductors woke us with jarring radio music ninety minutes before the end of the line. At 6:30 A.M., nearly forty-eight hours after leaving Samara, the train lumbered over the wide, murky Ob River and pulled into Novosibirsk. The station was dingy, cavernous, and possessed some of the most ludicrous Lenin art I had seen in Russia. In a corner of the main hall hung a large oil painting showing the bloody dictator in his kindest *dedushka Lenin*—"grandfather Lenin"—guise, kneeling in a snowy park, fur *shapka* on his head, talking sweetly with a couple of kids. I agreed with Russians who opposed erasing monuments and vestiges of the Communist past, but purely on aesthetic grounds it would have been nice to thin out some of the Lenin detritus that still littered the countryside.

I was too tired to fight with the taxi driver, meekly submitting when he charged me about $10—three times the going rate—for the short ride from the train station to the bus depot. At the bus terminal, two tables of hustlers, working with several blatant shills, fleeced the gullible in fast-moving card games. The skies cleared, and thick clouds scudded low over the concrete office and apartment buildings near the bus station. As I waited for the southbound bus, I noticed a fellow traveler, a short, well-groomed man with olive green fatigues and a towering backpack. He, too, seemed headed for Gorno-Altai.

The bus was clean and fairly modern, and as we drove south out of Novosibirsk over a gently rolling plain, I found myself thinking that this might be a pleasant ride. Then the sirocco hit. The temperature had been in the sixties, the air washed clean by the storm, when suddenly—about an hour out of Novosibirsk—a wind rose out of the Kazakhstan desert to the west and struck us with brutal intensity. You could see the wall of scorching air moving in from miles away, stirring up clouds of dust. In a matter of minutes, the temperature rose thirty degrees. By noon, the interior of the bus was pushing one hundred. The windows barely opened. Resting their heads on the backs of their seats and keeping movement to a minimum, the passengers settled in for a long, miserable ride.

After several hours we pulled into a great dusty lot, lined on one side with about twenty-five kiosks and food stalls. Helixes of dirt and litter skittered across the rest area, settling on the dumplings and shashlik proffered by the gauntlet of peddlers. Passengers devoured enormous, greasy, meat-filled pastries and tore chunks of pork off aluminum skewers with their teeth. I saw men heading for a low-slung concrete building, evidently the bathroom. The odor hit me from fifty yards away. As I approached, I could see piles of feces and puddles of urine ringing the building. Conditions were so appalling in the bathroom itself that travelers had taken to relieving themselves all around it. Joining a few other men, I peed in the open air. Recalling the words of the Turk the night before, I wondered: Why *do* Russians tolerate such squalor?

The outdoorsman was standing near the bus. He was trim, about five feet nine inches tall, and had a full head of dark brown hair combed straight back. He wore sunglasses and an inscrutable expression. I asked if he was heading to Gorno-Altai. He took off his glasses, revealing hazel eyes, and said he was. In a deep, clipped voice, he informed me he was going to Teletskoye Lake, one of the most famous in Siberia, for ten days of camping. He suggested that we share a cab from Biysk, where the bus was heading, to Gorno-Altaisk, the capital.

Arriving in Biysk in late afternoon, we found a cab and pushed south. The rolling plain gave way to the foothills of the Altai Mountains, and in the distance I could see green ridges. Our taxi sped down a scenic, two-lane asphalt road, miles of which were mercifully shaded by overhanging poplar trees, their dusty, silver-green leaves buffeted by the sweltering wind. On the roadside, babushkas stood in front of wood-framed cottages and sold tomatoes, cucumbers, berries, melons, and green onions. I caught glimpses of Altai natives, cousins of the Mongolians to the south.

Along the way, my companion and I became acquainted. His name was Vladimir Avdoshkin, and he was thirty-five. When I asked him where he worked, he replied cryptically that he did "scientific work near Moscow." I didn't pursue it. His voice was absurdly deep.

Gorno-Altai is a mountainous region of two hundred thousand

people in southern Siberia, sandwiched between Mongolia and Kazakhstan. Originally populated by a Mongol-like people, it was for centuries ruled by various khans. Then, in the early 1600s, Cossacks and Russian adventurers began streaming in, forcing local tribes to pay tribute. By the mid–nineteenth century, the region was under Russian control. Ever-larger numbers of "old believers"—Russian Orthodox faithful who had broken off from the main church, were persecuted, and fled to Siberia—quietly moved into Gorno-Altai.

The region was a natural paradise, with scores of undefiled rivers and streams; large forests of Siberian pine; one of Russia's tallest mountains, 4,500-meter Mount Belukha; and Lake Teletskoye, considered by many to be the second most beautiful lake in Russia, after Baikal. This setting gave rise to an apocryphal tale that hidden within Gorno-Altai was a land rich beyond measure, where gold could be found in abundance and crops grew ten times as quickly as in the rest of Siberia. The land was known as Belovodye—"whitewater"— and thousands came in search of this Shangri-la.

Much of the beauty that gave rise to the Belovodye legend remains today, although logging has despoiled some of the landscape, and Gorno-Altai's major river, the Katun, is polluted downstream and the target of engineers eager to build dams. I had heard that several of Gorno-Altai's rivers—including the Biya—still had populations of taimen, a salmonlike fish that is increasingly rare in Siberia.

Pulling into Gorno-Altaisk, a picturesque town of about fifty thousand nestled amid lush, green hills, I felt for the first time that I was in Asia. The Altaians had round, copper-colored faces, and their listing, wooden homes adorned the terraced hillsides outside the capital. Soviet planners had torn down most of the wooden architecture in the center of town, replacing it with five-story buildings of brick and concrete. But despite their efforts, Gorno-Altaisk still had a pleasantly rural feel to it, with cows grazing in pastures not far from the main thoroughfare.

The Hotel Tourist was a squalid, five-story eyesore in the heart of town. Many of the windows on the first two floors were broken, which may explain why guests were relegated to the top three stories. After waiting vainly for a receptionist on the ground floor, we trudged up to the fourth and located an employee. The corridors were long and dingy. A receptionist said she could give us one of the few rooms with a "shower." The chamber was a narrow affair with two beds, a ripped, brown linoleum floor, and mint green walls. The bathroom was the size of a small closet, the "shower" a handheld nozzle that splatted water over the filthy sink and the toilet, which lacked a seat. The floor was brown, coated with scum and missing half its tiles. I didn't care. The heat, coupled with ongoing nausea and diarrhea, had left me feeling utterly debilitated. I stripped, tiptoed into the cruddy bathroom, and hosed myself down with ice-cold water for five minutes. Then I collapsed on the springy bed. Lying there, I sensed that this infernal day might turn out to be the nadir of my trip. I was almost right.

Avdoshkin counseled me to consume herb tea, honey, and walnuts until my stomach was on the mend. He was a romantic Russian naturalist, a lover of Siberia who came often to Altai to hike and live alone in the mountains for a couple of weeks, subsisting on pasta, raisins, walnuts, berries, mushrooms, and wild grasses. His demeanor was serious, and he did not often crack a smile. But he was friendly and sympathetic, and his rectitude, formal bearing, and handsome, clean-cut features brought to mind a member of the nineteenth-century Russian nobility.

We ate, then lay on our beds, relishing the cool breezes that began to stir around sunset. We were chatting about the fiendish bus ride when Avdoshkin casually mentioned that he was a lieutenant colonel in the Russian army. A few minutes later, he explained that he was an instructor at a military-space institute near Moscow. I tried not to show my astonishment, but was enough a product of the old Soviet days to be amazed that I was sharing a hotel room with a Russian officer employed at a once-secret military facility.

"Five years ago you certainly wouldn't have been traveling with an American journalist," I said.

"Earlier, I wouldn't have run away from you, but I wouldn't have spoken to you, either," replied Avdoshkin.

He seemed to loosen up after his revelation. Pulling out a detailed topographic map of 2,500-meter Lake Teletskoye and a surrounding nature preserve, he showed me his hiking route.

"It's a very high energy place, from the point of view of cosmic energy," said Avdoshkin. "A compass there can all of a sudden have a swing of sixty degrees from magnetic north. Once, debris from the

stages of a rocket that blasted off at Baikonur Cosmodrome [in Ka-
zakhstan] fell into the hills around Teletskoye. Some of the locals
picked them up and used them as roofs for their barns."

I remarked that he was quite a nature lover. In his basso voice,
he replied, "What else is there to love if not nature."

Without warning, out of the mouth of this appealing character
came hard-line rhetoric echoing the most reactionary politicians in
Russia. At first it was unsettling. Avdoshkin subscribed to some of
the cardinal—and highly paranoid—doctrines of the Communist/
nationalist coalition in Russia. There never was a real coup in August
1991; the whole affair was part of a Gorbachev-inspired plot to kill
off the Soviet Union. Under this conspiracy theory, the CIA master-
minded the demise of the USSR.

"It seems that this was all thought out and planned in advance.
But our leaders are to blame for letting it happen."

He decried the rampant corruption in his homeland, the idiocy of
trying to bring capitalism to Russia overnight, the depths to which
the country had sunk as institutions crumbled, people lost their jobs,
and salaries went unpaid. He hadn't received his salary in nearly
three months. "Now why," he asked, "do we need that kind of
government?"

No doubt, many American officers would have reacted with similar
dismay had they lived through a decade of upheaval that had left
their country impoverished and its armed forces humiliated and in
disarray. What Avdoshkin—and many others—objected to was the
recklessness of reforms, the way in which the country's leaders demolished the old structure without building something in its place.
This heedlessness was a national trait, noted by foreign travelers over
the centuries.

"Russia advances on the road of progress not in that smooth,
gradual, prosaic way to which we are accustomed, but by a series of
unconnected, frantic efforts, each of which is naturally followed by
a period of temporary exhaustion," Sir Donald Mackenzie Wallace, a
British journalist who traveled in Russia in the late nineteenth and
early twentieth centuries, wrote in his book *Russia*.

More recently, American scholar James Billington wrote in *The Icon
and the Axe*, "Repeatedly, Russians have sought to acquire the end

products of other civilizations without the intervening process of slow growth and inner understanding."

Avdoshkin's aspirations were not so different from those of his American counterparts: he planned to marry a twenty-six-year-old woman from his hometown of Tomsk, retire from the army at age thirty-nine, and then go into business, perhaps something involving aerospace. He wanted a house, a little land, a few kids. And an airplane.

"Someday I would love to have my own small plane and fly to different parts of the country. It would be expensive, but perhaps I could eventually save that kind of money."

The following morning we tried to board a helicopter that would take us to a mountain village near Teletskoye Lake, but the flight was canceled. I wondered aloud if I shouldn't just return to Novosibirsk. Ever the soldier, Avdoshkin replied, "Not one step backward."

Instead, we got on a bus bound for Teletskoye Lake. Avdoshkin planned to head to his retreat in the mountains, and I would fish a nearby river, the Biya. The thirty-seat bus was ancient and filled to overflowing with Russian kayakers and vacationers. We climbed slowly into the high country, traveling through a verdant, hilly landscape. Two men scythed hay in a field, and farther down the road, in front of a log cabin, a gypsy woman in a brightly colored dress sold cloth to a Russian family. Clouds moved in, the bus becoming so cool that passengers shut their windows. The road was mainly dirt and gravel, and a fine dust seeped into the rickety bus, coating tourists and luggage alike.

I first saw the Biya around 2 P.M. It was a striking river, about 150 yards wide and containing long, emerald green pools and extended riffles. Flowing out of Lake Teletskoye, the Biya eventually joined the Katun, a wider, more polluted river that flowed into the Ob.

Our bus pulled into the regional center of Turochak, located on the banks of the Biya, around 3 P.M. It looked like as good a place as any to stop. Avdoshkin helped me with my bags, and I pulled out pictures of my family as we waited for the bus to leave. He said his fiancée was already making wedding plans. Then he wrote down his address and told me to get in touch when I was in Moscow. I gave him my card, gripped his hand with both of mine, and said good-bye.

Turochak was a drowsy town of about five thousand hacked out of the taiga and ringed by low mountains. When I inquired about a place to stay, a passerby suggested I ask at the Rural Soviet, or council, a hub of activity in the Communist era. Walking down dusty streets, I came upon a two-story wooden building. There was no sign of life in the cool, wood-floored corridors on the ground level. Trudging upstairs, I stood at the end of the hall and listened. It, too, was quiet as a crypt. Then I caught a faint voice coming from a room halfway down the corridor. On the door was a sign that read Agricultural Reform. I walked in, laden with luggage.

Three men sat behind desks in the gloomy room. Swiveling my way, their faces assumed expressions of stupefaction, and alarm. One of the men was about fifty with a scruffy brown beard. He had a remotely intellectual air about him, and an angry countenance.

"Good afternoon," I said. "I'm an American writer and fisherman passing through your area. You wouldn't happen to know if there's a little hotel here where I might spend the night?"

The bearded one took charge. "Let me see your documents."

I handed him my press pass from the Russian Foreign Ministry. A second man—slender, hawk-nosed, bespectacled, about sixty—piped up. He slurred his words.

"Who the hell did you say you are? Where are you from? Do you speak English?"

The bearded one waved off the drunk. "Where did you come from?" he demanded. "Why are you visiting here? With what goal in mind?"

I was close enough to the bearded one to detect a whiff of vodka. His eyes were bloodshot. Standing in a moribund office, I was confronted with three tipsy hacks playing KGB. A few years before I might have had the patience for such fools. I no longer did.

"I can see I came to the wrong place," I said. "I didn't come here to be interrogated. I came here to ask about a place to spend the night."

Handing me back my press card, the bearded one changed his tune. "No, no. Stay. You came to the right place. You can stay at my house if you want. I'll give you my bed."

Now I was in trouble. Instead of being merely boorish, the bearded one wanted to treat me to some of his aggressive hospitality. I should have bolted. Instead I stood there, looking for a graceful exit.

The older, drunker man crossed his legs, leaned forward, and continued his inquiry. "I don't understand. Why did you come to Turochak? Hey, in Russia, before we talk, we share a bottle? Do you drink?"

"Not right now I don't."

"What are you *really* doing here? Are you really an American? Where do you live in America?"

"Near New York City."

The bearded one jumped up. "Don't go anywhere," he said. "I'll be right back."

Three minutes later he returned with a bottle of Russkaya vodka. He set it down on his desk. "Come on. Let's drink fifty grams."

I was overcome with depression. "Look, excuse me, but I don't want to sit here in the middle of the day and drink vodka. I want to go fishing. Perhaps you could suggest someone who knows something about fishing around here?"

"Uh, there aren't many fish left anymore," replied the bearded one.

"Look," said the drunk, "I still don't understand what you're doing here."

"Okay," I said. "You guessed it. I'm a KGB agent, posing as an American, and I was sent from Moscow to investigate you and your work here. I know your full name, date of birth, everything about you."

There was a moment of befuddled silence. Then the drunk laughed awkwardly and shut up.

"Okay," said the bearded one, who I imagined lived in some grim bachelor hovel, "if you don't want to stay at my house, that's your right."

Thanking him, I backed out and fled.

I wound up in a small, wooden guesthouse run by the regional trade organization. That evening, grabbing my waders, fishing vest, and fly rods, I walked a block to the low bluffs overlooking the Biya, scurried down a steep bank, and was delighted to see a wide, scenic river flowing past town. I knew the Biya held grayling, a troutlike fish—with a sail-shaped dorsal fin—that had virtually been wiped out in the lower forty-eight states of America by rampant market fishing a century ago. But what had brought me all this way was taimen, a celebrated creature considered by many to be the greatest angling prize in Siberia.

Once, taimen were found in abundance from the Danube to the Pacific. Members of the salmonid—or trout and salmon—family, they were famed for their enormous size and delectable taste. With the exception of one species, they were river-dwelling fish, inhabiting many of the major basins in Eastern Europe and Russia. No salmonid in Europe was bigger; the world record, caught in a net on Russia's Taymyr Peninsula, weighed 240 pounds. Their enormity gave rise to an odd tradition in Russia, as anglers took to shooting them, either in their spawning beds or when they rose to the surface after being hooked.

In his *Notes on Fishing*, published in 1847, Sergei Aksakov called taimen an "utterly splendid fish" and noted they were common in his home province of Orenburg, in the southern Urals. But the combination of their prodigious size and delicious flesh made them so prized that taimen gradually began to disappear in Europe and western Russia. No fish was a better indicator of the incursion of civilization.

Today, five species of taimen remain on earth, most of them in Siberia. A small number still inhabit the Danube. The Siberian taimen, *Hucho hucho taimen*, is under increasing pressure from fishing and pollution. In the Russian Far East, there is an anadromous taimen, the only taimen species that—like salmon—spawns in rivers then migrates to the sea. Two other species exist in small numbers in Asia—one in the Yalu River, bordering North Korea, and one in the Upper Yangtze in eastern Tibet.

The Biya was the sort of large, fast-moving river favored by taimen. A darker, more streamlined version of a salmon or a trout, taimen were voracious predators, devouring small animals as well as fish. In parts of Siberia, some fishermen still caught taimen by threading a large hook through the skin of a live squirrel or a lemming, tossing the animal in the water, and letting it paddle furiously across the current, attracting the attention of the taimen. I had an arsenal that should have been only slightly less effective—three-inch mouse imitations, and other large, furry flies that would throw off a sizable wake as I dragged them across the surface.

I stood on the wide shore of the Biya, the wooden homes of Turochak to my back, and surveyed the river. It executed a sweeping turn as it flowed past the village, and shallow riffles ran down the near bank. A few hundred yards downstream, at a sharp bend in the river, I could see a deep pool flanked by a smooth rock ledge. The hills opposite were covered with pine, cedar, and birch. A half dozen fishermen were strung along a mile of riverbank, angling for grayling with *udochki*, twelve-foot poles with a slightly longer length of line, at the end of which were a half dozen artificial flies. It was about 7 P.M., the air cool and clear. I still had two more hours of daylight.

Wading into the river, I maneuvered around an automobile tire and other debris. I could make out a deeper stretch of water about fifty feet away and cast my mouse imitation at a forty-five-degree angle downstream, then let it swing across the current. The mouse skittered on the surface, throwing off a wake that should have attracted the attention of any taimen in the vicinity.

Slowly moving downstream, I kept this up for half an hour with no sign of the fabled Siberian fish. Then I noticed, all around me, hundreds of small, white mayflies. Grayling were rising, sipping the flies off the clear, green surface of the Biya. Returning to shore, I scooped a few of the mayflies off the water, found a reasonable imitation in my fly box, and tied it on my trout line. For the next hour, I underwent a humiliating but fascinating lesson in how *not* to catch grayling. More than twenty times, small fish struck my fly, but never took the hook. They batted the fly, teased it, once even jumped over it, but I couldn't get them to swallow it. In dozens of trout-fishing excursions, I had never experienced such a problem. Later—too late, I'm afraid—I figured it out: most of the grayling were tiny, less than eight inches, and I should have used flies with smaller hooks.

Around nine, with a vivid orange sunset glowing through the trees on the opposite hills, I retired to my room. As I was fiddling with my angling gear in the reception room adjoining mine, wondering where I would fish tomorrow, I heard footsteps in the hallway of the deserted guesthouse. The door opened. A policeman in gray uniform entered. Immediately I wondered what I had done wrong. Then I remembered; I hadn't registered with the local authorities.

"Sorry I haven't registered, but the woman who runs the guesthouse said she'd take care of it tomorrow."

"I'm not worried about that," said the man, a tanned, well-built fellow with short, brown hair and handsome, hawklike features. "I heard there was an American fisherman here and I wanted to meet him."

I showed him my graphite rods, and he was astonished at their delicacy and strength. But what really convinced him that the right side had won the Cold War was my fly collection. As he studied the hundreds of intricately tied deceptions, he marveled at the quality of the materials, the sharpness of the hooks, the sheer artistry of some of the creations. When I told him that more than a dozen U.S. companies were locked in intense competition to produce all manner of high-quality fly-fishing equipment, he could only shake his head in awe.

His name was Pavel Chernichenko, forty-one, and he had lived in Gorno-Altai for twenty years. Chernichenko, a captain in Turochak's police, had the wild gleam in his eyes of the zealous outdoorsman. He spent a month every winter in small cabins in the taiga, hunting deer, wolves, mink, and sable. The angling was still good on the Biya, he said, although the taimen were under heavy pressure and becoming increasingly scarce.

"I've been adding a room on to my house all summer and have hardly been fishing," he said. "I was planning to go tomorrow. Come with me."

Pavel's friend, a man named Volodya, waited for us on the riverbank with his twelve-foot metal boat. We headed downstream, quickly leaving the village behind. The Biya was a picturesque river, a limpid, green stream surrounded by hills thick with cedar, aspen, birch, and Siberian pine. There was no source of pollution upstream, save for a village or two, and Pavel and Volodya drank freely from the river. I declined, pleading microbe overload. Volodya—a stocky, ruddy-faced, unshaven man—claimed to have caught 150 grayling yesterday, a number that I assumed to be an exaggeration but which nevertheless instilled in me a certain optimism about the day's prospects.

We came to a straight stretch of the river, killed the engine, and fished for grayling by drifting with the current. The Russians used a string of nymphs—the underwater stage of insects such as mayflies—with their spinning rods, and I fished with a nymph and my fly rod. But I should have been there yesterday. We had a few strikes, but no one landed a fish for the first hour. Volodya blamed it on the midday sun, which he claimed was too bright. He also said, however, that the level of poaching on the river was intense. Some people strung nets across the Biya's tributaries, snaring grayling—and taimen—as they migrated up the branches to spawn. Others, Volodya said, even poured chlorine into the tributaries, driving the fish into nets downstream.

Volodya was an ethnic German, a descendant of the Teutonic farmers Catherine the Great had persuaded to come to Siberia two centuries before. He had decided to return to his roots and, in a few weeks, after four years of paperwork, was emigrating with his wife and three children to Germany. Close relatives had already relocated there, and were doing well.

"We're tired of all this here," said Volodya.

At 4 P.M. we came to a spot of unsurpassed beauty. Two small islands rose from the river near midcurrent. One was composed of several massive gray boulders that gave way to a long gravel bar. A stone's throw away was a second island, a twenty-foot granite outcropping covered partially in moss. From the rock pile sprouted a lone cedar. Between the two islands was a short, surging rapid that flowed into a deep pool about fifty yards long. The pool was mysterious and serene, colored a shade of green so pure that I stood mesmerized by its intensity. Behind it was a granite cliff. All around were rugged, verdant, cedar-covered hills. A few white clouds drifted across the sky. Save for our presence, there was no hint of civilization.

Pavel and Volodya stood on rounded boulders and caught six-inch grayling feasting on insects in an eddy above the first island. I cared only about the pool. Wading onto the gravel bar, I tossed a fluffy, brown mouse imitation two-thirds of the way across the gently flowing body of water. As the fake mouse skated across the current, a V-shaped wake forming behind it, I don't think I'd ever been so certain that an enormous fish was about to streak up from the depths and devour my fly. The mouse looked so good, the water so pristine, the location so prime, I was certain I was about to experience the angling thrill of my life. I could feel the fish under the water, eyeing the mouse with dim, bloodthirsty instinct. At any moment, I expected the river to be churned by a terrible thrashing as the taimen assaulted my fly.

It never happened. I cast up and down the pool numerous times, lingering at the bottom, or tail-out, where fish were likely to be holding. I dragged that mouse through every inch of water, but there was no sign of taimen. Pavel said the area, although a dozen miles from the village, was visited often by men with rods and—worse yet—nets. My taimen had probably disappeared long ago.

There still were grayling, and I amused myself for an hour by standing on the gravel bar trying to catch the tiny fish toying with my mayfly imitation. I caught one the length of my hand. We moved a short distance to another spot, where we stood on tall granite boulders along the shore. Bigger grayling were rising to a mayfly hatch, but like their smaller brothers they merely darted at my fly, batting it, and I never hooked a single one.

Pavel and Volodya had patiently watched me employ my dilettante methods for taimen. With evening upon us—it was now six—it was time to get down to business. From the bottom of the boat, they produced an item known in America as a planer board. It was wooden, about two feet long, and looked like the hull of a sailboat. Attached to it were long strands of monofilament line, and affixed to the line were eight treble hooks. Pavel—wearing an olive green jacket, old gray police pants, and white cap—pulled out eight small grayling from his creel and ran hooks through them. We began cruising slowly downriver, Volodya driving as Pavel let out fifty yards of line. The board knifed through the water, parallel to the boat, the dead grayling twitching and dancing on the surface of the Biya. No taimen could resist this line of flapping bait.

"Now we're going to get these underwater gangsters," said Pavel.

To me, the method looked unsporting in the extreme. But I was not a meat fisherman and held my tongue. As we trolled along, the sun dropped below the western hills, leaving us in cool shade and casting a radiant light on the opposite hillside. We passed a few meadows, a small collection of huts, and sheer cliffs.

For a long time, there was no sign of taimen, prompting Pavel or Volodya to blurt out occasionally, "We almost always catch taimen here. . . . Taimen are in this place all the time."

Rounding a wide curve, Pavel called my attention to a jagged wall of rock about 150 yards high. Halfway up the cliff, someone had painstakingly carved a five-foot silhouette of Lenin. On a likeness of the Soviet flag, the sculptor had painted these words:

"The name of Lenin, his accomplishments, his work, will live eternally."

Looking at me, Pavel said, "The guy"—meaning the artist, not Lenin—"was mentally ill, I think."

Just downstream, we hit a broad, deep stretch of water. As we trolled through it, a large fish splashed out of reach of our planer board. Volodya turned the boat around, directing the dancing grayling over the spot where the fish had surfaced. The three of us held our breath as the rig passed over the fish. Suddenly, there was a furious splash, and the line jerked Pavel's arm.

"There he is!" screamed Volodya.

I saw a silver-green blur, perhaps two feet long. Pavel furiously hauled in the line. Just as suddenly, the planer-board rig went slack. The taimen had thrown the hook.

Volodya put Pavel and me ashore, and as darkness fell and a brilliant orange sunset faded on the horizon, we tried once again—and in vain—to hook a taimen.

Motoring at full throttle back to Turochak, we saw three men just below the Lenin cliff. They were poachers, known to Chernichenko, and were preparing to step into their boat and drag the river for taimen and grayling. "Life forces them to do it," said Chernichenko.

We rode back in silence, the temperature dropping sharply as the sky filled with stars.

· · ·

Pavel and I walked down the darkened dirt streets of Turochak. Behind wobbly, wooden fences, dogs snarled at us, straining at their chains. Returning to the guesthouse at 11 P.M., we discovered that it had undergone an ugly transformation. A group of policemen from Gorno-Altaisk had showed up for a special assignment in Turochak and had occupied the little hotel. Walking into the antechamber next to my room, Chernichenko and I were confronted with a scene of squalor and debauchery. One policeman was passed out on a foldout couch. Another cop weaved our way, scarcely able to stand. A woman with oriental features—probably an Altai—was only slightly less inebriated. The room was filled with smoke and littered with vodka bottles and food.

Chernichenko, who rarely drinks, was not amused. He informed them he was a captain of the local police force—the headquarters was just across the street—and told them to clean up and go to bed. We locked my gear in my room and hitched a ride with a local policeman to Chernichenko's neat log home.

His wife was a warm, outgoing woman, curious about life in America. We talked and ate fried grayling and vegetables from their garden until past midnight. I asked him his opinion of the current upheaval, and he replied, "I welcome it. At last there is movement. Now people have to use their brains a little to make a living. That's good."

He was leaving town the next day, and we said good-bye after dinner. He invited me back in the winter to go hunting.

Approaching my lodgings, I noticed that the lights in the antechamber had been extinguished. I was relieved, for I no longer had the captain to keep the drunken policemen at bay. Apparently the trio were unconscious.

Carefully I opened the door, the light from the hallway casting a beam on the foldout couch. The room was still strewn with bottles and garbage, and two people were asleep—the woman and the man who had been unconscious earlier. As I tiptoed into the room, the drunk on the couch stirred, then came to life. Staring into the hall light, seeing only my silhouette, he yelled, "What the fuck! Get the fuck out of here! Who are you? Where the fuck are you going!"

"I'm a guest here, I'm going to my room."

"Then go. Get the fuck out of here, or I'll—"

"Take it easy. I'm an American, and a guest of the captain."

"Get the fuck out of here!"

No sooner had I entered my room and flipped on the light than I heard the rustling of covers and a great thud. The woman was weeping. For a moment I was paralyzed. Then, overcoming strong, cowardly instincts, I opened the door.

The woman was on the floor, wailing and holding her side, after evidently having been kicked or knocked out of bed by the policeman.

I looked at him. He wore an expression of utter derangement. I had no idea if he had a gun, but was hoping he was too drunk to do much harm.

"What are you doing?" I demanded.

"Nothing. It's none of your fucking business!"

"The woman's crying. I want to see what's going on."

"Fuck off!" he bellowed, weaving even as he sat up in bed. He was a big, blond man, his eyes grotesquely bloodshot.

"Look, I'm a guest of the captain. And either you cut this out right now or I'm going across the street and getting the police and you're going to wind up in jail."

"Ahhh," he bleated, softer now. "Fuck you."

I was bluffing. I had no idea how he'd react, or even if there were policemen still working across the street. But I sensed he was becoming slightly less rabid and decided to assume the high-handed tone I had seen other Russians take when dealing with drunks. Most of the time, it worked.

"You're with the Ministry of Internal Affairs," I said. "I am a guest of the captain of police in Turochak. If you don't settle down, there will be consequences."

"Ahhhh, fuck," he mumbled, then turned on the light, struggled with his shoes, and walked out. The woman was whimpering, and I asked if she was all right. She looked cowed, miserable, and hungover. Nodding that she was okay, she got into bed.

I returned to my room and locked the door. A few minutes later I heard the man walk back in and snarl at the woman. I had no idea of their relationship.

She began crying. Once more I opened the door. The man was standing in the middle of the room. He was about five feet eleven and solidly built.

"Give me one hundred grams, will you," he said, looking in my direction. "I got to beat this hangover."

"I don't have any vodka."

"Come on, give me one hundred grams. I got a hangover. I'll give you back a bottle tomorrow. I promise."

"I don't have any vodka."

"Come on, you're lying! Give me one hundred grams. I'll give you a bottle tomorrow."

I retreated for the final time to my room. The woman cried for five more minutes, then the antechamber fell silent.

Many times in Russia I had passed battered women in the streets, their eyes blackened from blows apparently inflicted by abusive, drunken husbands. This was, I knew, a universal problem, but there were an unusual number of women with bruised faces on Russia's streets. The West was coming to grips with the abuse of women, but in Russia—particularly rural Russia—the problem was scarcely even recognized.

It was an old one. A century before, in his story *Peasants*, Chekhov described the squalor, drunkenness, and wife-beating common in Russian villages:

"Going up to his wife, [Kiryak] swung his arm and punched her in the face; stunned by the blow, she did not utter a sound, but sank down, and her nose instantly began bleeding. . . . Marya was afraid of Kiryak, and whenever he stayed with her she shook with fear, and always got a headache from the fumes of vodka and tobacco of which he reeked."

I had considered staying in Turochak a third day, but the scene at the guesthouse convinced me it was time to move on. Waking up the next morning at five forty-five, I walked through the antechamber on my way to the outhouse. At opposite ends of the foldout couch, the drunk and the woman lay in poses of miserable slumber. A glimmer of doubt about departing flickered inside me, but was extinguished when I entered the outhouse and saw that one of the drunken policemen had defecated on the floor of the crapper. I urinated in the grass, packed my bags, and headed for the six-thirty bus to Biysk.

It was a cool, clear morning, and a small crowd had gathered in front of an old, yellow bus. Someone had smashed out a large window the night before, and the two dozen passengers—who filled every seat—bundled up against the morning chill. Luggage and spillover passengers crammed the aisles as we jounced down dirt roads. From time to time, I could see the Biya to our left, cloaked in heavy mist. Dust poured through the open window, and soon everyone and everything in the bus was coated in a fine, brick-colored powder. A young mother from the city, returning home after visiting her parents, grew increasingly annoyed as she tried in vain to shield her daughters from the wind. Babushkas wrapped their faces in scarves. For many of the passengers, the ride was a nightmare; Russians fear a draft the way Americans fear cholesterol.

Nearly two hours into the trip, we stopped in a village to pick up passengers. The young mother could stand it no longer.

"Can't you do something about the broken window?" she shouted to the driver, a grizzled figure of about fifty-five.

Across from me, a babushka removed the scarf from her mouth and said to no one in particular, "Oh, we Russians are so patient. It's awful!"

"What do you want me to do!" hollered the driver. "The window was just knocked out last night and there was nothing to fix it with. There's no garage in Turochak."

But the women were already in motion. Clambering over bags to the front of the bus, two women shamed the driver into helping them and returned a few minutes later with pieces of wood and a sheet of greenhouse plastic. The driver—muttering, defensive, yet sympathetic—jerry-rigged the plastic, and we resumed our ride, the breeze diminished but far from gone.

An hour later, we hit, at last, a stretch of asphalt, ending the torment of bouncing through potholes in a bus that seemed to lack completely a suspension and shock absorbers. At a stop a few minutes later at another village, the passengers chatted animatedly, pleased with their triumph over the window. I joined in the atmosphere of good cheer, yelling to the driver, "Well, the worst part of the road is behind us, anyway."

"No," he shot back, "the worst part of the road is still ahead."

This seemed to me a tidy metaphor for the difference in outlook between Americans and Russians—me chirpily optimistic, the driver bluntly pessimistic. With time, I learned to heed his words. "The worst . . . is still ahead." It made a nice mantra.

He was right. A few miles farther, the asphalt turned once again to dirt, and the holes were deeper than ever.

Six hours after setting off from Turochak, we arrived, shortly after noon, in Biysk. Transferring to a long, red Icarus bus, I rode six more hours north to Novosibirsk, where I planned to board a train on the Trans-Siberian rail line and travel to Irkutsk and Lake Baikal.

Novosibirsk looked tidy and tranquil on a clear, sixty-five-degree summer evening. The city's avenues were wide, its opera house handsome, even its black Lenin statue in the main square a cut above the rest. The train station, a green-and-white stone building that dated to Stalin's time, was covered in scaffolding. Inside, I looked at the schedule board, a puzzling roster of train numbers and times, of expresses and slow trains, rolling into this crucial rail juncture on various odd and even days. The Number 8, Siberia, caught my eye, an express from Novosibirsk to Vladivostok, stopping in Irkutsk. It was due to leave that evening at 8:10 P.M., forty minutes hence. I stood in line for fifteen minutes, only to be told by the woman behind the glass window that there were no tickets on the Siberia, and that the earliest I'd be able to leave eastbound would be in two nights. Anyway, she told me, you're a foreigner and have to buy your ticket at the Intourist window. I protested and groveled unsuccessfully for a berth on that night's Siberia.

Predictably, the Intourist window was closed for the day. Returning to the ticket seller, I jumped to the head of the line and informed the woman that Intourist was shuttered.

"I know that," she said.

"So what can I do?"

"Go see the station administrator, right over there."

She pointed across the expansive room to another line of windows. People behind me were grumbling, so I marched over to the administrator's office. All the windows were curtained. I rapped loudly. There was no response. Another man waiting nearby shrugged. I read the fine print on the window and fathomed why no one was home. The administrator was on break. She wouldn't be back until 8:30

P.M., twenty minutes after the Siberia would have pulled out of the station.

It's odd that *nyet* is the word most closely associated in Americans' minds with Russians. The truth is that in no other country does *no* mean less than in Russia—at least, that is, if you're a Westerner, or someone willing to shamelessly parcel out bribes. It was seven-fifty. The Siberia was scheduled to leave in twenty minutes. The thought of spending the night at some overpriced Intourist hotel in Novosibirsk was intolerable. I would have to talk my way—or buy my way—onto the Siberia.

The train was on platform five. I needed the train boss, who, I soon learned, held court at car No. 8. Shuffling up to her wagon, I engaged a conductor in conversation, and he told me she would be back shortly. Arriving, at last, at 8 P.M., she was immediately accosted by six other people pleading to get on the train, some with fantastic tales of why they *absolutely* had to be on the Siberia. I was dismayed. Not only did she look incorruptible—she was a trim, grandmotherly figure of about fifty-five with short brown hair—but she also sent one of the prevaricators on his way, saying, "It's not possible."

As she meted out justice to the others, she glanced at me, and I flashed her my warmest Yankee smile. After dispatching the other supplicants, she turned my way. It was five minutes before departure.

"What can I do for you?" she asked. I sensed possibilities.

"Well, I'm an American writer traveling across Russia and I've had a terribly hard time getting a ticket to Irkutsk. . . ."

I was polite, obsequious, a touch pitiful. I even lowered my Russian language a notch to elicit empathy. She looked me over. Dust-coated and haggard after three hours' sleep and fourteen hours on the road, I must have looked pathetic.

"One moment," she said, walking a few steps to a man in a railway uniform. They conferred, and she returned.

"Okay," she said, "hop on."

My spirits soared. I thanked her—nearly hugged her—and tossed my soiled black backpack onto wagon No. 8.

"Just leave your bags there, next to the door, and we'll find you a place to sleep in a little while," said the train director.

The Siberia left at 8:15, five minutes late. As we rolled out of

Novosibirsk and into the countryside, I experienced undiluted traveler's euphoria. What a fine feeling to close the book on a grueling leg of a journey, to put people—decent and otherwise—behind you, to be heading east on a train through Siberia at sunset. On that cool, still evening, Russia possessed the primitive radiance I loved. A woman picked berries in a clearing. A man scythed hay near a log-cabin village. Forests of straight, tall, white-barked birch trees passed before my eyes. How pleased I was with myself! What a swell traveler I fancied myself to be, arriving in Novosibirsk at 7 P.M. and then, quite seamlessly, managing to charm my way onto an eastbound express leaving at 8:15! Quite a feat! I told myself.

What fun!

What hubris!

What a fool to forget the words uttered by the bus driver that morning: "The worst is still ahead."

I was about to experience the grimmest train trip of my life.

At first, all went well. The director gave me a berth in the night conductor's compartment. He was a lanky, blond twenty-one-year-old, friendly but unfazed that an American was sharing his room. In the thirty-six-hour ride to Irkutsk, I would sleep in the compartment at night, and he would bunk there during the day.

The trouble began around two the following afternoon. I opened the door to my compartment to find the conductor and a friend sitting on the bottom bunk. The room was thick with smoke. Two vodka bottles stood on the table. The second man, whose name was Slava, looked like a hired assassin—about forty, a pockmarked face, blond hair, gold teeth, and hard, blue eyes. Sergei didn't begin his night shift until 8 P.M. He and Slava, a cargo handler on the train, were getting drunk.

"Sit down," commanded Slava. He wasn't bombed yet, but he and Sergei had gone through half a bottle, and his engines were revving.

"Have a drink," he ordered. I explained I couldn't because of my stomach medicine. He laughed, poured four ounces into a plastic cup, and shoved it my way.

"Sergei tells me you're a writer. What the fuck are you doing on this trip?"

I explained. He stared at me for about ten seconds. I had the feeling he'd just as soon kill me as talk to me.

"You'll get a fucking Nobel Prize for such a book, because no one will ever understand the mind of Russia. You, as an outsider, will never understand Russia. You can only understand it from the inside."

"You're probably right," I said.

"Pour!" he ordered Sergei, and Sergei obliged. It was clear who was the alpha male in this pack.

"Everyone's stealing now, from top to bottom," Slava told me. "How else can you live? Our whole life the system stole from us, and now we're stealing back."

He explained that he earned seven hundred thousand rubles a month, about $150, as a cargo handler. "But that money means nothing to me. Pooofff! I can give that much away each month to charity."

"So how do you make money?" I asked.

"Steal, of course," he replied, explaining that his job in the cargo section of the train offered unparalleled opportunities to pilfer, as well as providing a means to transport goods for side businesses. He was heading to Vladivostok, for example, to buy food and booze for the two street kiosks he owned.

"I could go to America and in one month easily figure out how to operate there—illegally, of course."

Slava began to display the peculiarly obnoxious mix of inferiority and aggressive chauvinism common to some Russians, one minute telling me his country was a corrupt mess, the next saying it was the greatest nation on earth. "When Russia gets on its feet, the ruble will destroy the dollar," said Slava.

I gave him a noncommittal look. He was like a werewolf, transmogrifying before my very eyes into a dangerous, venom-spewing monster.

"Pour!" he said to Sergei. You had to give Slava his due. He went about his drinking with true determination.

"I get along fine with whites," he said. "But I hate black-assed bastards, and darkies from the Caucasus. And the Chinese—they're cockroaches."

He noticed I wasn't drinking. I explained again why I couldn't.

145

My teetotaling seemed to arouse in him suspicions that I was on an espionage mission in his homeland.

"I don't understand what you're doing here. What are you doing? You're lying. You're not telling the truth."

I started to explain the joys of travel, but poetic justifications of the peripatetic life held no interest for this chauvinist, convinced that his sordid little life was as good as it gets. His eyes were profoundly bloodshot, and they narrowed to evil slits as he spoke.

"Why would I want to go to America? To see how people cook kabobs, just like here? To see that some people live better than here, and that some live worse? Why do I need that?"

He downed another four-ounce shot, shuddered, and drank a beer. This produced in him another temporary change of character. He called me his "golden friend" and complimented me on how well I understood Russia. He asked me about my family, marveling that I would leave my wife for such a long time. "I pray to God—I honestly do—that she's not screwing around on you, and that you won't go back and find some other man in your bed."

"Thank you," I said.

"I have four kids from three wives," he said, launching into a speech about how he sleeps with whomever he pleases, including prostitutes.

"You're not worried about your wife leaving you?"

"What? I have the apartment, the car, the dacha. Where can she go?"

The train came to a stop. Slava struggled to his feet. I stood also, realizing I was far too close to him in the narrow compartment. His breath was a nauseating blast of vodka fumes, cheap tobacco, and garlic.

"Sick to your stomach? Hah! You can't be poisoned in Russia. It's clean here."

I didn't respond.

"Russians are honest!" he yelled, spraying my face with spittle. Then he jabbed me hard in the chest with his finger. "Russians are honest!"

He weaved down the corridor and onto the platform, accompanied by Sergei, who was slightly less drunk. I looked out the window and saw Slava haggling with a babushka over the price of meat dumplings. Gathering up my books, I fled to the dining car.

An overweight man with the blood-vessel-blasted face of an alcoholic was sitting in one of the booths, opposite a young man in uniform. Otherwise, the dining car was empty. Earlier, I had heard the fat man in the dining car warning of impending civil war—just the kind of Russian I strove to avoid. I walked past him, heading for another booth.

"Hey, brother, where are you from?" asked the man, a jowly picture of ill health.

"America," I replied. When would I learn to shut up?

"Sit down. Let's talk a bit."

Not wanting to offend a second Russian in as many minutes, I plopped down next to him, figuring a little polite chatter might do wonders for world peace. He asked me what I did. I told him I was a journalist.

"So, do you have some kind of permission, some kind of documents, that allow you to travel all over Russia?"

I could have been nice. But Slava had set me on edge, and I was weary of belligerent fellow travelers.

"Maybe you haven't heard, but this is a free country now."

"So you can come over here and write what you want about us, write all the lies you want, heh? Americans think they can come over here and take over this country. You think you can buy us and take us over, huh? You never will! If you try and take over Russia, we'll rip your heads off! You hear me! *We'll rip your heads off!*"

The soldier was embarrassed and tried to quiet him.

"Fucking Americans!" said the man, an off-duty train engineer. "Think they own the world!"

When I had first set foot in Russia seven years before, I rarely was on the receiving end of such vitriol. Occasionally, I'd wind up in a debate over the merits of Communism versus capitalism. But during perestroika, most Russians seemed euphoric that their country had at last opened itself to the world. Americans were greeted more as heroes than enemies. But a lot had changed. Or, perhaps more accurately, had gone back to the way it had always been; for centuries, Slavophiles in Russia had reviled the venal influence of the West on Mother Russia. Now, with their nation no longer a superpower, with economic ruination and humiliation all around, more Russians than I cared to imagine had become profoundly resentful of America and the West.

I returned to my compartment. Slava and Sergei were there, greasy meat dumplings spread out on the table between the two beds. So I caromed back to the restaurant car, sitting in the back where the engineer couldn't see me. Things went smoothly for about five minutes. Then Slava lurched into the restaurant, slumped into a seat, slowly looked around, and caught sight of me.

"Come have a drink with me!" he hollered.

"No thanks," I said.

He hauled himself up and stood over me, swaying wildly. "You don't do this in Russia," he said, his words nearly indecipherable, his face contorted with drunken rage. "A Russian has offered to treat you! Do not refuse!"

Apparently taking pity on me, the head waitress walked over and promised Slava a free bottle of vodka. Slowly, she led him away. I picked up my things and returned to my compartment, fed up with this confederacy of inebriated dunces. I hid there reading, cracking my door a few inches.

All was quiet until the next stop. Suddenly, a hideous wailing came from the end of the wagon.

"Pleeeeeease, men, pleeeeeease let me go! I beg you. Pleeeeeeease!"

It was a man's voice, hysterical, sobbing. The hairs rose on the back of my neck.

"Ohhhhhh, God! Pleeeeease, men, pleeeease let me go!"

Half the passengers, including myself, were in the corridor, looking for the source of the howling. At the end of the wagon, I saw a policeman bent over a heap on the floor.

"Men! Men! Pleeeeease let me go!"

A half dozen plainclothes policemen drove a dirty, disheveled man of about thirty down the corridor, the passengers scattering for their bunks. The man's face was contorted with terror and exhaustion and streaked with tears. The policemen slammed him into the compartment at the end of our wagon. Later, I walked past and saw the man sitting up, dozing, handcuffed to a bed.

Soon, the rumor mill had doped out the situation: the wailer was a heroin user and dealer, snared in a plainclothes narcotics investigation.

It was an evening of unparalleled loveliness—cool, clear, long summer shadows—but something undeniably sinister was in the air. I should have locked my door and drifted off to sleep reading Chekhov. But I longed for some greasy fried eggs and headed to the dining car.

The worst was still ahead.

The dining car was deserted. All the drunks, Slava included, had been carried to their berths. The waitress and the cook sat in their booth, reading the paper. It was nearly 8 P.M., and a serene light flooded the car. The waitress knew me by now, and she shook her head and smiled as she approached. "I bet you're glad you're alone in here at last," she said.

I ordered salad, fried eggs, buckwheat kasha, and an orange soda. I was just polishing off my salad, studying my Russian road atlas, when three middle-aged women walked into the car. They stood and stared at me. One asked, "You looking at a map of the world?"

"No, Russia."

Another woman told the waitress they'd like something to drink. A second said, "We'll drink with him."

In a flash, they were in my booth—two opposite me, and one at my side. The woman next to me was about forty-five, heavyset, with a great pile of dead, bleached-blond hair on her head. Opposite me were a dark-haired woman of fifty, and a modestly attractive woman of about forty with shoulder-length, peroxide-blond hair. At first, I thought they were merely bored travelers looking for a diversion. They asked me what I was doing and told me they were "shuttle traders" who had been buying clothes for their business in Ulan Ude. Soon, however, I sensed something was awry. They weren't prostitutes, of that I was certain. But they were brassier than any other women I had met in Russia. And they kept up a steady patter, peppering me with questions, yet seeming to have absolutely no interest in my answers.

The waitress brought four vodkas. I told them I couldn't drink because of my stomach medicine. Meanwhile, the blonde opposite me pulled out a bottle of contact lens solution. She began looking at her eyes in a compact mirror. I never saw her remove her contact lenses.

They were sorely disappointed I wouldn't drink with them and insisted several times before giving up. Then they ordered Fanta. The waitress brought four glasses, placing one in front of me. The blonde next to me reached over and downed my glass. I found this strange, but still couldn't fathom what was going on. The blonde opposite me began reciting a creepy poem about a woman and roses and death. The dark-haired woman blurted out, "Oh, my, look at that beautiful woods." I looked out the window. The other two were moving around glasses of Fanta like pieces in a shell game. The pretty blonde had the bottle of contact lens solution in her hand, and out of the corner of my eye, I saw it pass over a glass. I turned back to the table, and the big blonde next to me was still shuffling glasses.

"Here," she said, extending a glass with a small portion of Fanta. "Cheers. Let's drink a toast to you."

The women raised their vodka and Fanta glasses. I looked at mine. Finally, it began to dawn on me: these women were trying to drug me. The contact lens bottle, the shuffling glasses, the insistence I drink the vodka. Starting to sweat, I remembered the case of an English correspondent for the *Moscow Times*. Two diners in western Siberia had slipped a Mickey into his drink, but they had overdone it. The poor fellow had nearly stopped breathing. They stripped him clean.

"No, thanks, ladies, I'm not thirsty."

They were not pleased. Forcing smiles, they cajoled, flattered, implored. The woman next to me picked up the glass and put it in my hand. But I refused to drink.

"Oh, come on," she said, plainly exasperated. "Are we not good enough to share a drink with you?"

"Sure, you are, but my stomach's a little upset, and I'm not thirsty."

I saw the two blondes exchange a look. The one next to me backed off. I began to wonder if I was merely being paranoid.

"Okay, then, you'll have to have some cucumber fresh from our garden," said the blonde next to me. She cut a half dozen slices. Again, the dark-haired woman insisted I look at something out the window. The two blondes shuffled the cucumber slices back and forth. The pretty one held the lens solution bottle in her hand, and a blue lens container rested on the table. The bottle went under the table, the dark-haired woman said, "Look!" and pointed to a field. The blonde next to me was offering a cucumber slice.

"Try this," she said.

I wasn't thinking clearly enough to realize that if, as they said, they were returning from a long business trip, they were unlikely to have cucumbers from their garden. I still had a strong feeling that something was awry. But a tiny, imbecilic portion of my Boy Scout soul didn't want to offend these ladies, who in all likelihood were trying to knock me out and rob me.

I took a bite of the cucumber. It had a sweet, almost chemical taste, and I quickly spit it into my napkin. I looked into the eyes of the blonde at my side, and it chilled me. For perhaps the second time in my life, a sense that I was in the company of pure evil ran through me like a charge from a socket. I was scared now, trying to figure out a way to bolt without making a scene.

The next two minutes were a blur. I remember experiencing that feeling you get when you first take a hit of pot, that sense of reality shifting, as if the ground itself has moved. I was in full-blown panic, and it's unclear to me now whether the disorientation I felt at the table was the result of terror, or the effect of a tiny dose of whatever was in the contact lens bottle and on the cucumber. The woman next to me kept insisting I eat her cucumber and drink the Fanta, but I was way beyond that. At one point she grabbed her prodigious breasts and asked me if I'd like to feel them. The dark-haired woman across the table said something, but the big blonde waved her off. Then the big blonde started firing questions my way, asking where I had just been, where I was going. I felt as if I were at the bottom of a tunnel, her words drifting down to me in weird, tinny slow motion. She looked grotesque—gold teeth, cold eyes. I couldn't think straight. I couldn't recall where I had just been or even where I was going.

Now I was experiencing pure fear. My only thought was to get away from these hags and make my way to the train director as quickly as possible.

"I'm not feeling well. I've got to go."

"Oh, what do you feel like?" asked the blonde next to me. She looked as if she weighed about 175 pounds.

"I've got to go."

Grabbing my knapsack—I learned later I left my road atlas on the table—I pushed against the blonde.

She didn't budge. "No, you stay with us."

I pushed her, and she pushed back. She was not letting me out. Her two companions were staring at us.

"I've got to go *now*." With that I smashed against her and knocked her to the floor on her ass. Exclamations flew from the mouths of the three women. Not even glancing at the waitress, I charged out of the car.

I wasn't aware that the train had stopped. Hustling to my wagon, one car ahead, I hurried outside. Standing near the train director, I drew deep lungfuls of cool Siberian air. My heart was still racing, my mouth dry. Before reboarding the train, I told the director about the three women and what I thought had happened. She looked at me as if I might be mad. Then she said she had heard of such occurrences on Russian trains, but never on hers. A few minutes later we went together to the dining car. The three women had disappeared. The waitress said the women had acted strangely, but she assumed they were merely drunk.

"This poor man," said the waitress. "Every time he came in this car today, no one would leave him alone."

After traveling cavalierly across half of Russia, confident that my fluency in Russian and knowledge of the country had rendered me untouchable, I was thoroughly shaken, afflicted—at least for now—with raging paranoia. Later, when I recounted the details of this episode to Russian friends, they were certain it had been an attempt to drug and rob me. Several Russian papers had written stories about the increased druggings on trains. One article had said that a popular method of delivering the drugs was from bottles used for contact lens solution. I was merely grateful that I was taking antiparasite medicine, and not drinking. Had I downed the first shot of vodka offered by these angels of doom, it might have meant the end of the trip.

Back in my compartment, Sergei the conductor was passed out on a bottom berth. I figured it wasn't the wisest of career moves for this new conductor to get blind drunk, just before his shift, in plain sight of the train director. But then, what did I know of the path to success in Russia? For several hours, he slumbered, and I read, delighted to be conscious and in possession of my faculties, wallet, and passport. Around midnight, the day conductor, a young woman, succeeded in rousing Sergei. He slouched off to his duties with a killer hangover.

From 2 A.M. to 5 A.M., I dozed fitfully. Every time I surrendered to sleep, I would wake with a start, half-expecting to see the Trinity of Bleached-Blond Mayhem standing over me, the one with the big breasts wielding a foot-long syringe filled with enough anesthesia to kill me or put me under for a week.

The nightmarish ride on the Siberia ended as we pulled into Irkutsk at six o'clock on a Friday morning. Stepping off the train into a thick fog, I felt exhausted and unhinged.

5.

BAIKAL

How couth my fellow Westerners looked, breakfasting in the vast dining room of the overpriced Intourist hotel, none of them tossing back tumblers of vodka to banish a hangover, none of them sucking the gristle off a chicken bone, none of them chain-smoking acrid Bulgarian cigarettes. After six weeks of unspeakable outhouses, bad beds, and restless nights on trains, I took some comfort in a quiet hotel room and the well-pressed, decorous presence of English, French, and German tourists. But not much. The Intourist hotel made me feel as if I were in a third-world country, with the foreign swells and a tiny minority of Russian tycoons at the top, and the unwashed masses somewhere on the bottom, rummaging through our leftovers. Although this yawning gap between rich and poor was undeniably a part of the new Russia, it was not the Russia I had come to see.

In Irkutsk it was impossible to avoid, for this was a city reclaiming its nineteenth-century status of freewheeling boomtown. Since its founding by Cossacks in 1661, Irkutsk had been a Siberian center of transportation and commerce, a crucial link between East and West. Harmon Tupper, in *To the Great Ocean*—his superb account of the building of the Trans-Siberian Railway—described the Wild West atmosphere of Irkutsk in the late nineteenth century. Gold miners, mine owners, nefarious businessmen, Chinese smugglers, exiles, and convicts all converged on the city. Crime was horrendous, with a murder a day and robbers routinely garroting victims. The police, according to one American writer at the turn of the century, "seem

154

to amount to nothing at all, and to be of the most corrupt order." In many ways, little had changed, with 1990s organized-crime bosses disbursing payoffs many policemen found impossible to resist.

In the old days, nouveau riche mine owners and fur barons ostentatiously displayed their wealth, building palatial homes and freely dispensing money to charities. Many of these magnates were crude Russian *muzhiks*, or peasants, a bit unsure of how to handle themselves in high society. A century ago, a French traveler visited the home of a Siberian millionaire, who pointed out a lavish, canopied bed with an ebony frame and a Gobelin tapestry. The Siberian told the Frenchman, "This is my bed. But I sleep *under* it, you know. It is too good to use."

The spiritual descendants of such men could be found in Irkutsk during my visit, roaring around the city in black Mercedes sedans and Toyota Land Cruisers. Crew-cutted, stocky, dressed in Italian suits, these men acted as if they owned the roads—which they did—cursing at anyone who failed to leap quickly out of their way. I had only a vague inkling of the world of the Russian mobster and the New Russian ruble billionaires. But their instant wealth was often the result of larceny on a grand scale, including underhanded trading in timber, fish, minerals, and other Siberian resources. In a decade, Russia had moved from an ossified, state-run economic system to a gross parody of capitalism. Observing the crooks who led this charge, I was reminded of a wonderful line from the Marquis de Custine, written two centuries before: "The Russians have rotted before they have ripened."

Irkutsk, population six hundred thousand, was one of Russia's prettier cities, blessed with hundreds of pre-Revolutionary buildings. Most were of brick and stone. But there were still scores of old wooden structures, decorated with gingerbread trim, the survivors of an 1879 conflagration that swept through the city, destroying three-quarters of its buildings.

The town's new robber barons and the vanguard of the emerging middle class could be found on Karl Marx Street, a thoroughfare sorely in need of a name change. Comrade Marx would not have sanctioned the activity on this picturesque, tree-lined avenue of czarist-era buildings. Shoppers streamed in and out of a Reebok store, a Lancôme perfume shop, and a boutique featuring in its window a

Giorgio Armani poster showing the naked backside of a model marching into the sea.

I stopped at a purveyor of fine meats and chatted with a sixty-nine-year-old salesclerk. Sitting on a stool, dressed in the white coat worn by Russian shopkeepers, she recounted the deprivations of the Stalin era, World War II, Brezhnev's Communism, and the current regime.

"Son," she told me, "there has not been one period in my entire life when we lived well. Not one. . . . These days, a lot of us are just waiting to slip into the grave."

Irkutsk's shops sold everything imaginable, but many of the young people behind the counters were as rude and clueless as their Soviet predecessors. In a soap shop, a young woman waited on me with a mix of grunts and scowls. In a pharmacy on Karl Marx Street, five minutes before closing for lunch, a woman rudely ordered all customers out of the store. When I went to one of the two banks that cashed traveler's checks, the teller handled my American Express checks as if they were radioactive, carrying out the transaction with such painstaking caution that what should have taken ten minutes took fifty. At breakfast in the Intourist hotel, even when only a dozen tourists were eating at the buffet, the gaggle of young waitresses huddled in a corner, gossiping, rarely venturing out to do their main job—pouring tea and coffee. Even to many young Russians, service still seemed an alien concept, to which they were almost genetically indisposed.

In the evenings, hundreds of people—many of them striking women in miniskirts—strolled along the Angara River promenade. In a large square, residents bought imported beer from kiosks and drank it at plastic tables. At an open-air pavilion that served as a disco, a few dozen teenagers danced to George Michael and lousy, throbbing Russian pop music. Just up Karl Marx Street, residents played tennis and basketball in a quiet park.

You'd need a dozen summers to fish Lake Baikal. I had less than two weeks, hoping to make it by boat to the lake's northern shores by the end of August. Randomness was the key.

My first stop would be the Barguzin River, halfway up the lake on the eastern shore. There was boat service to Ust Barguzin, the town at the mouth of the river, and several fishermen had told me the upper Barguzin basin offered excellent angling. Two species of fish interested me, above all. The first, which existed only in Siberia, Mongolia, and northern China, was the *lenok*, a troutlike fish rumored to voraciously attack large flies skated across the surface of a river. The second species was Baikal grayling, a relative of the arctic grayling found in Alaska and Canada, only bigger and prettier.

Cruising down the Angara River, our hydrofoil emerged onto the lake around 10 A.M. At first, Baikal was covered in fog. But soon the sun emerged, revealing a striking panorama of the vast lake and a wall of six-thousand-foot, snow-covered mountains on the opposite shore, twenty miles distant. Never had I seen water so clear, a translucent turquoise in which a silver coin could be spotted 120 feet below the surface. "You can see through the water as if looking through air," wrote Anton Chekhov, who visited Baikal in the late nineteenth century.

Formed about 20 million years ago, Baikal is a natural wonder. It is the deepest lake in the world, with a maximum depth of more than a mile—5,712 feet. Nearly four hundred miles long and fifty miles wide in some places, Baikal holds 20 percent of the earth's aboveground freshwater supplies. About three hundred rivers and streams flow into Baikal, but only one river—the Angara—flows out of it.

More than twenty-five hundred species of plants and animals live in Baikal and on its shores; two-thirds of these are found nowhere else in the world. Among the more remarkable endemic species is a large population of Baikal seals; a delicious whitefish, known as the omul; the Baikal oilfish, a bizarre, semitransparent creature that customarily hangs out at a depth of fifteen hundred feet, is 50 percent fat, and gives birth to young instead of laying eggs; and a tiny crustacean, the *epischura*, which exists in the millions and is believed to help keep Baikal pure by filtering huge quantities of water through its system.

Despite a gigantic pulp mill at the southern end of the lake and pollutants flowing in from the Selenga River on the eastern shore, Baikal is still remarkably clean. In the middle and upper reaches of the lake you can drink the water without fear. Though still

bounteous, fish populations—including omul and Baikal sturgeon—
have declined in recent years. Overfishing, and the destruction—by
logging—of spawning beds in adjacent rivers are the main culprits.

One of the first Russian visitors to Baikal was Archpriest Av-
vakum, in 1662. He had this to say of the "sacred sea":

"Exceedingly many birds, geese, and swans swim upon the sea,
covering it like snow. It hath fishes—sturgeon, and salmon, sterlet,
and omul, and whitefish, and many other kinds. . . . And the fishes
are plentiful; the sturgeon and salmon are surpassingly fat—thou
canst not fry them in a pan, for there will be nought but oil."

In addition to boundless supplies of fish, Baikal was famed for
something else—its storms. They arose quickly and with great intensity, generating waves as high as fifteen feet. "It is upon the Baikal
in autumn," wrote Dr. Henry Lansdell, an American traveler at the
turn of the century, "that a man learns to pray from his heart."

On my last night on Baikal, I would silently mouth a few prayers
myself.

For most of the ten-hour, 225-mile run to Ust Barguzin, the hydrofoil hugged the western shore, passing craggy cliffs, low, forested
mountains, and a village or two with weatherworn huts. Halfway
through our trip we came to Olkhon, an island considered by many
to be the loveliest spot on Baikal. The sun shone brilliantly, revealing
white cliffs, wooded hills rising to three thousand feet, and expanses
of olive-covered heath. At the northern end of the island, sheer, five-
hundred-foot cliffs—partially clothed in moss, lichen, and pine
trees—dropped dramatically into the green waters.

The last leg of our trip took us across the widest and deepest
section of Baikal. We cruised past Holy Nose Peninsula, a jagged,
six-thousand-foot mountain chain running down its spine. Behind it
were the peaks of the Barguzin Range, some rising to nearly nine
thousand feet and blanketed already by the first snows of the season.
Brown bears, snow sheep, moose, and the famed Barguzin sable inhabited the mountains. Just beyond them was the valley of the Barguzin River, where I planned to fish.

I was cruising on the most beautiful lake in Russia, just past the
peak of the summer season, yet we saw almost no one all day—
twenty residents of a dacha colony, a handful of villagers, two yachts,

and as many motorboats. Along the shore, much of which is a nature preserve, there were few signs of man, only the mountains, heaths, and cliffs framing the magnificent lake.

The hydrofoil arrived in Ust Barguzin at 8 P.M. Along the way I had met an affable Irkutsk businessman, Volodya Pashichev, who knew his way around the town of nine thousand and suggested I stay with him. After throwing my gear into his friend's car, we drove down dirt streets, through neighborhoods of one-story wooden cottages. Soon, we arrived at the dark brown, wood-frame home of Pyotr Chirkov, one of Ust Barguzin's most successful businessmen and an occasional partner of Pashichev's. Chirkov—a powerfully built man with curly, brown hair, blue eyes, full lips, and the richly timbred voice of the cigarette smoker—seemed pleased to see two more guests, in addition to the two already encamped in his house. Within thirty minutes, his wife and another woman had covered the table in the summer kitchen—a shed next to the main house—with smoked pork, sausage, salted fish, fried omul cutlets, potatoes, chicken, and fresh vegetables from the garden.

For the next four hours, we engaged in a marathon dinner-table conversation, chewing over the country's ills until two in the morning. Chirkov, who was about forty-five, was a shrewd businessman who had worked for years in the high-paying arctic town of Norilsk, and then, just before Yeltsin's economic reforms and astronomical inflation, invested his savings in a boat, a store, and several other buildings in Ust Barguzin. Now he ran a grocery store and a bakery and was thinking of opening a gas station. He wanted to get into manufacturing, but punitive taxes and red tape discouraged him. "The only thing that's profitable now is trade," Chirkov said.

"We're floating in a zone of half-lawlessness, half-law," he said, stabbing fish cutlets and proposing an occasional toast. "We destroyed the old system but replaced it with nothing. There is a vacuum."

Still, the vacuum was better than what was, and he professed immense relief that Yeltsin had won the presidential elections the month before.

"Yeltsin—for all his faults, and there are many—at least is a reformer," said Chirkov. "That's why the election was so important.

That mass of thirty-two million people, a lot of them old people, who voted in July for the Communists will simply die out. Many will be dead by the next election. There's no way back now."

Altering the thinking of people tainted by seven decades of Communism would take a few generations, however. Chirkov cited the example of one of his best shop workers.

"We know from our books that for every fifteen days she works, she steals about one million rubles [$225]," said Chirkov. "She isn't stealing it from us, she's stealing it by short-weighting customers and other little tricks. She earns five hundred thousand rubles legally every month and about one and a half million illegally. But she's not stealing from me. There are no complaints from the customers. She's polite and she works well. We know she steals, so we pay her a wage that takes that into account. So what would you do in this situation? Well, she's still working for me."

I retired at 2 A.M. Walking through the vegetable patch to the outhouse, I looked up into a sky brimming with stars. The temperature was near freezing when I slipped into bedding on the floor of the winter kitchen. Two hours later, Volodya came into the kitchen, crawled under the blanket next to me, and within a minute was expelling vodka-fumed puffs of breath into my face. I turned my back to him and drifted off to sleep, grateful for the warmth his body provided on the frigid floor.

The road to Ulyunkhan was long and torturous. It ran northeast from Ust Barguzin, more than one hundred miles up the valley of the Barguzin River. My plan was simple: to stay on the bus until the end of the line, find a place to sleep, and fish. From experience, I already knew that the chances of catching popular species near towns and villages were slim. The higher up the Barguzin valley, the better.

The dirt road became rougher and the scenery more spectacular as we rode along. At the town of Barguzin, the bus emerged from thick forest into a broad valley, perhaps eight miles wide, the floodplain a patchwork of swamps, marshy pasture, and meandering, willow-lined streams. The day was sunny, and hawks rode the currents of warm air. To the northwest, looming over us, was the rugged, granite wall of the Barguzin Range. Pine and larch covered the slopes to about six thousand feet, above which were flanks of battleship-gray scree. Snow filled the high valleys and had buried the peaks. It was August 21. Autumn was approaching.

About two-thirds of the way up the valley, the last Russian passenger got off the old, twenty-five-seat bus. After that it was all Buryats, a Mongol-like people who inhabited the upper reaches of the Barguzin. The driver was Russian, and as we rode along, he gave elderly passengers the bad news: the Buryat Republic had ended free bus rides for old folks.

"You're joking, right?" a smiling, seventy-year-old Buryat woman said to the driver. "So you're taking away our last hope, are you? . . . Well, okay. Just as long as there is no war. The rest we can live through."

At 7 P.M. we bounced into Ulyunkhan, a seedy, somnolent hamlet of about one thousand people tucked in the shadow of the Barguzin Range. It was the end of the line, and when the driver pulled out, I was greeted with profound silence and a spectacular view. I hadn't a clue where I would sleep, but figured someone would be eager to take in an American angler for a few dollars. Seeing the open door of a store, I walked in. The shopkeeper scarcely looked up as she said she had no idea where I could sleep. I asked who was the mayor of the village. She told me his name—Vitaly Vibe (pronounced *Vee-bee*), an ethnic German—and gave rough directions to his house. Outside, cows grazed along the street. As I was putting on my knapsack, two young boys wandered up and stared. I sensed that few foreigners had made it to Ulyunkhan.

I was marching down the dusty main road when I heard a whistle. Looking to my left, I saw three men huddled conspiratorially on the side of a decrepit cabin.

"Come here," someone said in English.

There were two younger men, both of whom looked slightly drunk and had the ruddy faces of vodka junkies. The older man—the English speaker—looked slightly nervous, but his face put me at ease; the serene, moonlike visage brought to mind a Buddhist monk. He was thin, with close-cropped, graying hair and high cheekbones. I judged him to be about fifty.

In Russian, the men asked me where I was headed. I replied that I was looking for the mayor.

"I have hotel," the older one said in English.

I was skeptical.

"Me, hotel. You—come."

A combination of profound fatigue and curiosity persuaded me to accept his invitation. Grabbing my gear bag and rod case, the older man led the way at a brisk clip down the main road and through meandering side streets. Along the way, he informed me that his name was Alexander Sedenov, that he was forty-eight, and that he had worked for twenty years at various collective farms in the region, rising to the position of head technician. But with the disintegration of most state-run farms he had lost his job and now lived mainly on earnings from chopping firewood.

We scaled a fence, then headed for a wooden warehouse faded to a weather-beaten gray. Putting a key into an ancient padlock, he said, "Please come in."

I entered a spartan, crepuscular realm. In the kitchen were a scarred wooden table, a couple of chairs, and a dirty, whitewashed stove built into a wall. The adjoining room had a table or two and a boarded-up window. Finally, the man led me into his bedroom, a large, nearly empty chamber with a wooden platform, where he slept. A sack of flour sat on the floor, out of which protruded a vodka bottle. On the wall, a Buddhist prayer was typed in Buryat and Russian on a yellowing piece of paper.

"I live like a monk," said the man, switching back to Russian. "This is my cell. . . . You can have any room you like. Perhaps this one would be most comfortable for you."

It smelled like a grain warehouse, and I wondered about the rat situation. But something about this man's gentle demeanor put me at ease. I told him I'd be happy to stay with him.

The two young men walked in, accompanied by a pair of women and a teenaged girl. All but the girl looked badly in need of a drink.

"We'd like to celebrate your arrival—drink, drink!" one of the men said nervously.

"Fine," I said. "But I'm afraid I can't join you."

"No money," he said. "No money."

"How much do you need?"

"Fourteen thousand."

I handed him twenty thousand rubles—about $5—and he returned a few minutes later with a third of a bottle of grain alcohol, which he mixed with water from a tin bucket. The man filled glasses, then engaged in a Buryat ritual—pouring a drop of spirits on the stove, wetting his fingers, and flicking a few drops on the table. This offering was for ancestors and the gods. It did not inhibit robust drinking.

One of the younger men wanted to know if my family kept chickens, cows, and pigs, as they did in Buryatia. I told him it was against the law where I lived, which perplexed him. The group soon broke up, and Alexander and I went to talk to the mayor about angling possibilities.

The sun had set behind the Barguzin Range, and a half-moon hung in a cool blue sky. Walking down dusty streets, we soon came to the wooden home of the mayor, a rangy man with a big-boned, blue-eyed, blond-haired Teutonic look. He said he'd help me find a jeep to take me farther upstream, where there was a hot springs resort named Umkhey, and decent fishing. Alexander smiled at me and said, "I can be your guide. I have free time."

We ran into one of Alexander's friends, Valery Songolov, a professional trapper and hunter who took to the Barguzin hills in winter and snared sable, squirrel, fox, and other animals. The most prized animal, he said, was the dark-coated Barguzin sable, which fetched $100 apiece. He trapped about fifteen sable a year on lands he leased from the Evenk nation. He used to catch more, but poaching of all animals—sable, deer, bear, and others—was heavier than before.

"I am just one person—what can I do about it?" asked Songolov, a trim, forty-two-year-old with reddish brown skin and short, black hair. "We used to have six hundred workers employed in this area with the forest industry. Now they're all unemployed. They've got to live, so they head to the woods and kill what they can."

Songolov, a passionate angler, knew the upper Barguzin well. Alexander asked him to join us at the hot springs, and he agreed.

Back at his house, Alexander pulled out a tattered, blue *English Primer*. He read a few sentences and asked if I could practice with him tomorrow.

"Now, please rest," he said. "Do not be afraid if your door opens in the middle of the night. It happens a lot. The old building is settling. Maybe there are ghosts here, I don't know. I am not afraid. I hang these prayer papers on the wall to counteract them."

That night, I was plagued with a high fever and stomach cramps and was unsure whether this was a continuation of the pestilence I had picked up at Viktor Chumak's or was some altogether new scourge I had acquired near Lake Baikal. I slept terribly. At 1:30 A.M., in the midst of a febrile dream, a group of drunken, young Buryats strolled up to Alexander's house, singing. They asked for a bottle of vodka, but he sent them away empty-handed. I awoke again at 4 A.M., soaked in sweat. Turning over and over on the hard, wooden plank, my mood was black, and my overheated imagination conjured up visions of my journey coming to a pitiful end as I succumbed in this remote valley to fever and dysentery. The entire trip looked like idiotic self-indulgence, a ridiculous lark that was depriving my children of a father, my wife of a husband, and me of the most rudimentary comforts.

Alexander and I had overslept, and the mayor was leaning on the horn of his jeep. I wanted to sleep all day, but had lofty hopes for fishing the upper reaches of the Barguzin and hauled myself out of bed. Alexander and I quickly breakfasted on raisins, tea, and stale bread— a subsistence diet typical for him. He had mentioned the previous night that he ate little meat. The village stores were among the barest I had seen in Russia. It was dawning on me that Ulyunkhan was a dirt-poor place.

"Come on!" yelled the mayor as we trudged up to his jeep. "You're like a bunch of old ladies getting ready. It's almost eleven o'clock."

The mayor—also the chairman of the local collective farm—had decided to drive us to Umkhey. He was a maniac behind the wheel, zooming over the rutted track that ran through the Barguzin's floodplain as he filled me in on the facts of life in Ulyunkhan. It was another warm, glorious day.

"To me, it's all the same, the old system or the new," said Mayor Vibe, flashing a gold-toothed smile. "If you have a head, good hands, strong shoulders, you work and you do okay. That's what counts. Just don't be lazy."

Whipping the wheel, he avoided stumps and holes.

"The taxes are what kill us. So the government is deceiving and cheating us and we deceive them. That's the way it works these days. You pay a tax inspector five hundred thousand rubles a month [about $120] and you expect him not to take bribes? Of course he takes bribes. There's no other way for him to live."

Rattling down a sandy road in a pine grove, the mayor slammed on the brakes. To our right was a tree, and tied to its branches were hundreds of shreds of colored cloth. Beneath the tree was a pile of about one hundred empty vodka bottles and a mound of cigarettes and matches. This was a *burkhan*, a Buryat shrine. Valery crawled out of the jeep, announced he was hungover—to me he still looked drunk—and extracted a bottle of vodka. He splashed some on the tree, flicked a few drops in all directions, then took a mighty swig. Alexander and the mayor followed suit.

Valery, already feeling better, said the revival of Buddhism in Buryatia was a good thing.

"You have to believe in something," he said.

"Yeah, shit," retorted the mayor. "Before you believed in Stalin and Lenin, and as soon as perestroika started, you began to pray. What the fuck is that?"

We jumped in the jeep, and hizzoner floored it.

"We used to have two hundred and sixty workers at the farm," he said. "Now we have fifty-two. People are getting by with their garden plots and the cattle they've accumulated. But they're gradually eating their cattle. Things could be bad in a couple of years."

I asked him how much he earned as mayor and as head of the farm.

"Very little. The government doesn't pay me and I work for them. What do expect me to do?"

"Steal?"

He smiled. "If I tried to live on what I made as mayor, I would have dropped dead of hunger a long time ago."

He hit the brakes. Another shrine. This one they dispatched drive-in style, remaining seated while the mayor dumped the vodka out the window, then passed the bottle.

Mayor Vibe sped off on the last leg to the hot springs. Fording a tributary of the Barguzin, we arrived on the tiny island known as Umkhey. It was paradise—a half dozen wooden cabins set in a grove of towering pines, and a series of hot springs bubbling into tiny bathhouses. The Barguzin flowed past the spa. It was a narrow, swiftly running stream, its water an inviting, translucent green. Several deep pools were in sight of the island and a high cliff rose from the bank on the opposite side. A wooden teahouse, resting on stilts, was perched over the river.

After offering another toast at the spa's *burkhan*, Valery and I headed for the hot springs. We undressed in a hot antechamber, stooped, and entered the bath. It was a tiny, enchanting room. In the center was a pool of scalding water—six feet square and three feet deep—with a gray sand bottom. Gas bubbled up from the sand and was released on the surface, permeating the bath with a sulfurous odor. A narrow wooden sluice carrying frigid springwater ran alongside the bath. Valery lifted a wooden gate in the sluice, and the springwater flowed into the pool, cooling it. We eased in, sat on the sandy bottom, and acclimated to the heat. Valery showed me how to wash by grabbing handfuls of the sulfurous sand and scrubbing. A half hour later, I emerged feeling vastly improved.

The caretaker's wife, a comely young woman with high cheekbones, light brown skin, and black eyes, served us tea and fried bread. The spa, she said, had far fewer customers than in the Soviet era, when workers were guaranteed an annual visit to a place such as Umkhey. She said her family often had no meat and sometimes had to walk eleven miles into Ulyunkhan for bread.

Shortly before 4 P.M., Valery, Alexander, and I set off downstream in search of fish. The chasteness of the upper Barguzin filled me with hope. Just one hundred yards below the hot springs, we came upon a lovely, fishy-looking spot. A tributary joined the main branch of the Barguzin at a gravel bar, and just below it was a long, deep, jade-colored pool. Standing on the bar, I threw everything I had at the fish I knew to be lurking there—big flies that I skated across the surface, smaller mayfly imitations, several underwater doodads posing as baitfish. I carefully covered every inch of that pool. Valery came after me and dredged it with his heavy spinning gear.

No luck.

166

Then Valery noticed piles of stones used to hold nets. Someone was poaching the river's upper reaches.

Valery could sense my dismay. "Five or ten years ago, there were a lot more fish. I could come to the river in the morning, right by the village, and catch seven or eight grayling in a short time, no problem. Now it's hard to find fish. There are a lot less. I think it's because so many people are unemployed, and now they're fishing to feed their families."

He suggested a stroll downstream. After walking nearly a mile, we stumbled upon a reminder of the rigors involved in taming the Siberian wilderness. In the late 1970s and early 1980s, the Soviet government was completing its last, great public works project, the Baikal–Amur Mainline railway—BAM, in Russian—essentially a northern spur of the Trans-Siberian. Engineers hoped to link the Buryat capital, Ulan Ude, to the BAM by road. A road existed from the capital, through Ust Barguzin, to Ulyunkhan. Intrepid crews wanted to extend the track through the wilds of the Barguzin Range to the BAM.

Emerging from a forest trail onto a sandy floodplain, I saw the results of their efforts. A half dozen sections of a long, steel bridge were strewn like driftwood along the riverbank. A powerful spring flood had swept it away, and other remnants of the failed project— rotting boots, chunks of machinery, pots and pans—littered the shore.

Five hundred yards below the ruined bridge was another sublime pool—a long, slow run, with sheer cliffs rising on the opposite bank. I fished hard. So did Valery. Neither of us got a bite.

That night, lying in a metal bed whose springs nearly sagged to the floor, I fell asleep to the whisper of the Barguzin.

Valery was not easily disheartened. We were at it again the next morning, this time walking upstream to another pool sandwiched between two rapids. A four-hundred-foot cliff rose dramatically above this hole from the opposite shore. Unfortunately, we were not alone. Two Russians had arrived on a motorcycle and were working over the pool with their spinning rods, chucking great, weighted bobbers, from which were suspended nymph imitations. They had caught two small grayling. Valery and I caught nothing. Over a cup of black tea, the two Russians agreed that the fishing had gone to hell lately, thanks to hungry poachers.

The mayor was scheduled to pick us up that afternoon. But Valery concocted a plan: we would hop in his little rubber raft and float downstream to Ulyunkhan. Clearly, wherever there was a road, the locals had hounded fish populations into near oblivion. The float trip would take us along sections of the Barguzin where few people fished. Alexander would ride home with the mayor and send a jeep to meet us near Ulyunkhan that evening.

Shoving off at 2:30 P.M., we floated through a landscape showing the first signs of autumn. A barely discernible shade of yellow had appeared on the birch leaves. Along the foothills, the larches—pine trees whose needles turn color and shed—were starting to fade to gold. We moved soundlessly around bends with deep, slow-moving pools, and over long, wide, shallow runs where my ass bounced off stones in the riverbed. From time to time, Valery hopped into the frigid river in pants and sneakers to dislodge us from a boulder. He seemed unfazed by the cold.

The breakthrough came an hour into our trip. Stopping at a curving, emerald pool, I cast cross-stream and let my fly—a two-inch, buoyant, gray-and-yellow foam number—skate with the current toward shore. I had fished nearly the entire length of the pool, and my attention was flagging. I glanced at scattered, cottony clouds bumping over the Barguzin Range. Looking back at my fly, I saw it zipping sweetly across the surface. Then, with a great splash, a fish attacked. I watched in amazement as my fly disappeared in a swirl of water, my fly-line went taut, and my rod bent with the weight of a powerful fish.

The creature ran upstream, pulling line from my reel, and in a few minutes it was at my feet. I dragged the fish onto the pebbly shore. It was about eighteen inches, perhaps one and a half pounds, with silver-green hues, dark spots, and a rose-colored stripe running the length of its flank. Its lips were pursed. It was a *lenok*, the first I had caught in my life. Knowing that fish populations in the river were besieged, I released it. The spell was broken.

At the next pool, on my first cast, a fish rose and gently sucked in my fly. It was an eighteen-inch "black" grayling, a charcoal-colored fish with a graceful dorsal fin. I released it, too. Valery was having no luck with his spinning rod, so I gave him one of my fly rods with a large mayfly imitation and offered two minutes of casting instructions. On the fourth or fifth cast, he caught a twenty-inch "white" grayling, a rarer species found around Baikal. He, too, released his fish, something he had rarely, if ever, done. A few minutes later I caught a white grayling, perhaps the same one released by Valery. Apparently, no one with a fly rod had ever fished these waters, and the *lenok* and grayling responded to artificial flies with heedless greed.

I caught two more *lenok* that afternoon and evening, one grabbing my fly with a wild thrashing, the other gently pulling it beneath the surface. Valery was delighted at having caught a grayling on a dry fly and pleased, too, with the American habit of catch-and-release.

"I think this is a sign of a very civilized society," he said as we floated toward Ulyunkhan at dusk. "We haven't reached that point yet."

Beaching the boat, I felt like a child who had just gotten off an amusement park ride and wanted more. We had failed to explore numerous pools, and I asked Valery if we could float the river the next day. He agreed.

I began the day in moon-faced Alexander's roofless outhouse, where his toilet paper consisted of pages from a tenth-grade primer entitled *History of the USSR*. The deputy chairman of the collective farm, a disagreeable Buryat, drove us upstream. Alexander had told the deputy chairman I'd be paying for the ride. On the way upriver, I mentioned how much I appreciated his help.

"You don't sew furs with thank-yous," he said.

We began our float just below the ruined BAM bridge, stopping at the pool that produced the two big grayling the day before. This time, we fished Russian style, killing a pair of two-pound fish—a *lenok* and a black grayling. Zhora, a young man accompanying us, cleaned the fish, butterflied them, impaled them on forked sticks, and grilled them over a campfire. Their flesh was delicious, but the pleasure of consuming it was dimmed by the knowledge that we had removed two healthy specimens from a river already sorely stressed from overfishing.

Low, gray clouds vaulted over the Barguzin Range at midafternoon, and the wind rose. We bobbed down the river and at five-thirty hit the mother lode, a hundred-yard-long elbow-bend where the water was deep and wildly green. I cast from the inside of the bend toward the far bank, about one hundred feet away. On my first effort, the biggest *lenok* of the day—about two and a half pounds—walloped the fly and fought tenaciously for two minutes before quickly tiring. I let it go. Slowly moving down the pool, I hooked a *lenok* every few minutes. Once, near the tail-out of the pool, I saw the silver flash of a *lenok* as it streaked up from the bottom to eat my fly. Later, gray sheets of rain descended from the mountains, and a rainbow arched across the sky from the Barguzin peaks to the foothills at my back. At the end of an hour, I had landed four fish and hooked and lost an equal number, attaining the state of focused angling bliss that had eluded me for two months.

Unfortunately, things deteriorated once the fishing was over. Everyone, it seemed, had his hand out. Driving us from the river to Valery's home, the deputy farm director dropped a few strong hints about wanting to be paid. I gave him two hundred thousand rubles, about $40, which silenced him. Alexander, my monklike host, began to talk of nothing but money, telling me how poor everyone was and how offended Valery and Zhora would be if I didn't compensate them handsomely. "Oh, yes, if you don't pay for those three days, everyone will think, 'Oh, that greedy American.' "

Eating salted mushrooms and fried potatoes at Valery's house, an awkward silence descended upon the table. The dollar had driven a wedge between us. I had given Valery a dozen flies and some other presents, and he had invited me to return in winter and go trapping in the taiga. I wanted to pay him for his time, yet did not want to offend him by offering money. In the end, I gave him about $60— half the local monthly wage—and he took it sheepishly. I paid Alexander slightly less for several nights' lodging in his hovel. I didn't mind parting with the money, but I did object to the constant hints that I ought to pay.

We returned to Alexander's warehouse. His solicitousness seemed to me now more like obsequiousness. Sitting in his kitchen drinking tea, he cut a forlorn figure in his soiled, pinstripe suit, vest, and white, threadbare dress shirt. Recently divorced, out of work, stuck in this impoverished village, dreaming of the larger world I represented, he seemed to me a far sadder fellow than the man I had met a few days before.

Roosters crowed and cows mooed as Alexander escorted me to the bus at seven the following morning. Changing buses at Kurumkan, I walked into an outhouse so coated with excrement that I was immediately forced to retreat. Eight Buryats pulled up in an old gray Volga sedan, the men dressed in suits and ties and looking like former apparatchiks. One man wandered over to a fence next to the tiny, wooden bus station, vomited, wiped his mouth, straightened his tie, and announced to his friends, "Everything's okay." The group crammed back into the car and roared off.

The driver of our dilapidated blue bus started the engine by crawling under the hood and touching two wires together. We set off for Barguzin, passing Buryat families walking along the dusty road, buckets in hand for berry picking. At one point, the bus came to a stop and a mother hurried her young son toward the door. He threw up in the bushes, returning sweaty and pale. I imagined the entire region stricken with food poisoning. My own guts churned with diarrhea.

I wanted out of Buryatia.

The relics of the old system flanked the bumpy road—rusting machinery from a collective farm, sheep grazing in a neglected soccer field, crumbling Lenin statues, peeling, stucco schools with washed-out socialist-realism murals showing Soviet scientific achievements. In Barguzin, I met a wayward soul with a fantastic but plausible tale. He was a forty-five-year-old Azerbaijani arrested in the late 1980s in a major corruption scandal that involved siphoning funds from his hard-currency store in Baku and the gift of a bejeweled Turkish sword to former Soviet leader Leonid Brezhnev. The Azerbaijani was first sentenced to be shot, then to life imprisonment, then given a break and merely exiled to Barguzin.

"Oh, this is an old place of exile, dating back to czarist days," said the man, a stocky, olive-skinned fellow with dark, curly hair. "Most of the Russian inhabitants here are descendants of exiles."

He married a local Russian woman, raised two children, and decided to stay in Barguzin even after his sentence was commuted following the collapse of the Soviet Union. Now, he was running a grocery. I told him that local inhabitants had struck me as more money hungry than any others I had seen in rural Russia.

"Well, people have gotten very greedy now," he said. "They have no money. They're desperate to get it."

The Azerbaijani gave me a ride to the main highway, where I hitchhiked to Ust Barguzin, on Lake Baikal. Arriving in late afternoon, I wound up in a two-story, gray stone hotel that belonged to the local lumber mill. The dour receptionist gave me a cell-like room with flickering fluorescent lights and filthy towels that resembled gas station rags. Depressed and drained of energy, I ate a handful of walnuts and took a nap.

In the evening, I prowled Ust Barguzin's docks—a string of rickety piers, in the center of which was a mountain of coal—in search of a boat that might take me to a lakeside hamlet with good fishing. I didn't find a boat, but did find an employee of the Barguzin Wildlife Preserve, who subjected me to a nationalist diatribe, during which he professed his admiration for Stalin.

"Look," he said, "you can raise up a country using the conscience of the people, or you can use fear. Russians need fear."

Walking the town's dusty streets at dusk, I was overcome with homesickness.

"In the evening hush, when you saw before you one dull window behind which the natural scene softly fades away, when the hoarse barking of strange dogs and the muffled squeaking of a strange accordion reaches your ear, it is difficult not to think of home," Anton Chekhov wrote in his story *An Encounter*, exactly a century before. "He who has been a wanderer, whom necessity or Fate or whim has separated from his kin, knows how long and wearisome an evening in the country among strangers can be."

. . .

My prayers for a boat were answered the next morning in the form of a craft from the Trans-Baikal National Park. The ship was steaming to Chivirkuisky Bay to pick up a group of young German hikers; along the way, the captain and his son—who also was the first mate—intended to scout out berry-picking possibilities on the western shore of Holy Nose Peninsula.

The weeklong stretch of warm, clear weather continued as we cruised west out of Barguzin Bay and close to Holy Nose Peninsula, the eastern flank of which was steep, rugged, and cut by dozens of wooded ravines. Steaming in the boat to the middle of the lake, we made a quick stop at Big Ushkanny Island, a heavily forested, rocky outcropping. In the surrounding waters, Baikal seals basked on boulders.

About 5 P.M., the captain gently ran his boat aground on the smooth-stone beach of Holy Nose. Walking down a flimsy wooden gangplank, we charged over a bluff and into the forest primeval in search of red and black currants. Russians take their berry and mushroom picking seriously, in large part because many people rely on their foraging for food. I followed the captain's son, Zhenya, a short, wiry twenty-four-year-old who moved swiftly up a sharp, densely wooded incline. For thirty minutes, we bushwhacked the mountainside in search of currants, finding almost none. What the peninsula did have was a healthy supply of brown bears, which made me highly uneasy as we crashed through underbrush, scarcely able to see twenty feet ahead.

We entered Chivirkuisky Bay around 7 P.M. It was a stunning body of water about twenty miles long, scalloped with sandy coves and rocky points and surrounded by the snow-covered mountains of the Barguzin Range and Holy Nose Peninsula. The water in the shallow bay was the warmest in Baikal, reaching seventy degrees in the summer—twenty degrees warmer than in the center of the lake. Our destination that night was the settlement of Chivirkui, a collection of several wooden shacks inhabited by two game wardens in the summer and one stalwart man in the winter.

Chugging into the Chivirkui cove, we passed the German girls camped out on a spit of land and dropped anchor at the mouth of the Chivirkui River. The first thing I noticed were the grayling.

More than a dozen eighteen-inch fish were plainly visible in the crystalline water, dimpling the surface as they ate mayflies. Never in my life had I been treated to such a clear view of my angling quarry. It was a little unnerving.

Three wardens in dirty green uniforms boarded our boat, and we retired to the mess for dinner. For the first time in more than two weeks I drank vodka, and went ashore mildly inebriated to fish for grayling. Gnats swarmed over me, and they, along with the effects of the vodka, led to a highly frustrating half hour of fishing as I tangled my line on every rock and branch in the vicinity. By the time the gnats drove me back to the boat, I had caught only one, fourteen-inch grayling, which—at the captain's request—I killed.

A three-quarter moon rose over the white crest of the Barguzin Range, and the last of the sunset colored the sky over Baikal a radiant indigo. The half dozen German girls sat around a campfire on the opposite side of the cove, taking in the sublime evening. But the Russians had seen it all before. They lounged in the smoke-filled aft cabin, drinking tea and watching a mayhem-filled Dolph Lundgren video.

I was up early to redeem my angling performance of the night before. The morning was still, clear, and cool, the surface of the cove a green mirror. I could see large grayling cruising. Tying on a yellow humpy, I cast into the middle of several rising fish, twitched the fly once, and watched as a fat, eighteen-inch grayling gulped down my artificial. In short order, I landed three large grayling, dispatching them with a rock, as the captain wanted fresh fish for lunch.

Later, standing with my trout rod on the stern of the boat, I spotted the biggest grayling of the day—a twenty-inch monster, weighing more than two pounds. He was a dozen feet below the surface, lazily patrolling the bottom of the cove. I cast above him, twitching my yellow humpy. He ignored the fly, and I retrieved it. Then he rose in the water column, swimming about six feet below the surface and no more than twenty feet from the boat. The next moment was a slow-motion angler's fantasy. I cast the fly about six feet in front of his nose. It landed softly, and I let it sit. Then I tweaked it. The grayling looked at the fly. I gave it a short pull, the grayling locked on, and I watched spellbound as the fish shot like a torpedo toward the yellow humpy. Its mouth opened, the fly disappeared, and my lightweight rod bent sharply as the grayling bolted toward open water. After a brief fight, I muscled it toward the deck, but the fat fish—too heavy for my tippet—snapped the line and splashed back into the cove.

The German girls bathed naked in the bay, prompting one of the wardens to grab some binoculars. It had been nearly a week since my last bath, and after the Germans had finished, I walked a few hundred yards beyond their camp, stripped, and waded into the sandy shallows. The water was in the low sixties, and I swam, then washed from head to toe. Lacking a towel, I stood on the beach in the sun and drip-dried. I shut my eyes, listening to the lapping of waves on the shore. Behind my closed eyelids, I sensed golden heat. Weeks of fatigue ebbed away.

High winds arrived that night. I bedded down in the hamlet of Kurbulik on the floor of a park office. The moon, nearly full, was rising over Chivirkuisky Bay as I walked out on a small pier, crouched down, and washed my face in Baikal.

August was at an end. It was time to find a northbound boat, then board the Baikal-Amur railway, the BAM, and head east.

For two days, with winds intensifying on the lake, I walked Ust Barguzin's piers in search of a ship. All was quiet on the docks, forcing me to contemplate a long, circuitous journey by bus and train to get to the BAM. On the third morning, my host—park official Nikolai Tyulkin—drove me one last time to the docks. There, in a berth that had been empty the night before, sat a gray, eighty-foot ship, the *Khakusi*. I knocked on the above-deck cabin door. A stocky, blond man opened it. The boat was leaving that afternoon for Nizhneangarsk, at the northern end of the lake. Yes, said the man, there was room for me.

Grabbing my gear, I returned to the docks and waited until evening for the boat to leave. The blond man was Yuri Usynin, one of the ship's two captains. The second skipper, a swarthy man of forty-four who looked to be in his late fifties, had been drinking vodka since docking at 1 A.M. By the time I saw him at eight, he was beyond redemption, mumbling incoherently as he shoveled food out of a skillet.

The boat belonged to a hospital, which used the vessel to transport patients to a hot springs on Baikal. But Captain Usynin and crew also transported cargo and made money on the side by taking passengers. More than a dozen had boarded our boat. One of them was a pudgy, baby-faced blond man in a suit, who that morning had seemed a model of sobriety and rectitude. As I sat belowdecks at 4:30 P.M., the man reappeared, so drunk he could scarcely navigate his way down the steep steel stairs. Caroming off the walls of the cramped cabin, he made his way to a bunk and collapsed. His eyes rolled back in their sockets, and he expelled shallow breaths that filled the cabin with vodka vapors.

The skies were clear, and the wind was roaring in from the west, roiling the waters of Barguzin Bay. I had taken a seat in the cabin with Captain Usynin, who suggested that I might get a taste of Baikal's fury when we rounded the point of Holy Nose Peninsula. Passing a shrine at the tip of Holy Nose, five of us in the cabin each took a hit of vodka and mumbled hopes for a safe passage. I popped a Dramamine and held on.

The moment we entered the open lake, the waves smashed head-on into the boat. As high as six feet, they pummeled the bow and sent spray flying onto the cabin window. It was a moderate blow for Baikal, but it wasn't long before several of the passengers came down with mal de mer from the yawing of the ship. Usynin immediately canceled plans to pick up a load of cargo on the eastern shore, since we'd be forced to turn broadside to the waves. Instead, he headed straight into the gale, setting a course for the western shore, about thirty-five miles away. Darkness came quickly, the mountains on the opposite shore a black line against a lead gray horizon. A full moon rose to the east, throwing a bright yellow beam on the stormy waters.

We pitched along in silence for an hour. Abruptly, the cabin door flew open. Standing there, drenched, was the baby-faced drunk from below, threatening at any moment to let go of the door handle and slip over the side into oblivion. Struggling mightily, he scrabbled his way into the cabin.

"With light steam!" hollered Captain Usynin, employing the traditional greeting used when a person emerges from a Russian bath. The men in the cabin burst into laughter. The drunk—suffering a killer hangover—stood there in brain-addled silence, water trickling down his beet-red face.

A few minutes later, the boat's number two drunk, Capt. Nikolai Kotsiyenko, emerged from the forward bunk hatch. He weaved his way to the cabin, absorbing a bucket or two of water along the way, and joined us. Haggard and hollow-eyed, he threw down a shot of vodka to restart his engines. Slowly he came to life. But even after a few cups of tea this man was an incoherent raconteur, the words leaking from his mouth in meandering, nonsensical dribs and drabs.

"You know this girl . . . Uh . . . Big boobs . . . On an island . . . Oh, I lost the point."

Usynin was a powerfully built man with thinning, blond hair, blue eyes, and an air of absolute reliability. With him at the helm, I didn't fret about the gale. As he gripped the wheel with one hand and puffed on a cigarette with the other, he recounted how he had worked as a merchant seaman in the Russian Far East. Twenty years ago, tired of long absences from his family, he moved to Baikal and had been working on ships there ever since.

Shortly before midnight, Usynin announced he was ready for sleep. The other captain, Kotsiyenko, was at best hungover and at worst still a little drunk. The thought of the groggy second captain at the tiller did not fill me with confidence. Usynin departed, and for half an hour I watched Kotsiyenko. Convinced he wasn't about to turn us broadside into the swells, I followed Usynin into the front cabin and fell fast asleep in a wildly rocking bunk.

When I awoke the next morning, the engines were dead and the water was slapping the side of the hull. Climbing out of the forward cabin, I saw we were at anchor in a cove on the western shore. The wind had dropped slightly, and a drizzle fell as heavy, gray clouds soared low to the east. Captain Usynin took the wheel again, and we cruised north. At Severobaikalsk, the main city at the northern end of the lake, I got my first view of the Baikal-Amur railway. Clinging to the mountainside, it snaked along the lakeshore, passing through long tunnels blasted out of granite. A green passenger train moved slowly along the tracks. Misty clouds veiled the peaks above.

Nizhneangarsk was a port town of tightly packed wooden homes and log cabins, hemmed in by the BAM. Chugging into the harbor on a cool, dreary morning, I felt the elation of entering a new world, far from the foreign tourists in Irkutsk. The BAM was the pipeline into northeastern Siberia, as wild a region as existed in all of Russia. I was about to travel two thousand miles to the Pacific Ocean, without once laying eyes on another Westerner.

The captains invited me to share a pot of meat stew. I was famished before the meal and yawning furiously after it, prompting Usynin to quote from the never-ending fount of Russian proverbs.

"Life is a struggle," he said. "A struggle against hunger before lunch, and a struggle against sleep after lunch."

Usynin drove me home in his red Niva jeep. He and his wife lived in half of a one-story, wooden house, the other half occupied by a neighbor as handy as Usynin. The captain had labored mightily on his homestead, building a fence, a garage, a toolshed, a workshop, a Russian bathhouse, and a greenhouse where large tomatoes had failed to ripen in the short Siberian summer. To the house itself, he had attached a glassed-in front porch. Inside, the place was tidy and spacious, with a couple of bedrooms and a large living room.

Pulling out two photo albums, he recounted his seafaring life. The pictures captured a strikingly handsome, blond-haired cadet at the Leningrad Maritime Academy, a young sailor celebrating as he crossed the equator on a voyage from the Kamchatka Peninsula to Morocco, a family man standing with his wife in port cities of the Russian Far East. The album conjured up an era, in the 1960s and 1970s, when Russia was a great power, its navy and merchant-marine fleet confidently roaming the world.

Repairing to an outhouse at the back of his large garden, I chuckled when I saw his toilet paper—a hardback edition of *Lenin: A Biography*. When I returned to the kitchen, I asked him when he stopped believing in Communism.

"From a very young age, sixteen or seventeen, I had my doubts. But there was no glasnost then, there was no other information I had with which I could argue against all our state propaganda."

We jumped in his car and drove to the train station to buy my ticket for the BAM. Along the way, we passed his old house, a tiny wooden structure where he and his wife, his parents, and other relatives had lived in close quarters. Pointing to the dilapidated structure, Usynin said, "I got tired of a system that treated people like that, put them in houses like that, related to people as if they were cattle. I knew this life was no good."

He resigned from the Communist Party in 1989 and since then had gradually built a middle-class life, enjoying space and comforts he had never dreamed would be his. Despite the current hardships, he danced on the grave of *uravnilovka*, or "leveling," when *Homo sovieticus* was happy if he could enjoy the same impoverished existence as all the other comrades.

"I like the freedom now. I don't have to wag my tail in front of some boss because that's the only place to work. Now at least there's the freedom of finding work where we want."

Yuri's wife, Natasha, had prepared a meal of fried pork, cabbage, cheese, salad, and Bulgarian wine. She was a lively, intelligent, and curious woman, with short, dark hair. She and Yuri had two boys— one married with a son, the other a university student.

Shortly before midnight, in a light rain, Yuri drove me to the tiny station. The train stopped for two minutes at Nizhneangarsk, and we had to sprint for my wagon, about 150 feet off the short platform. I tossed my luggage on board as an ill-tempered conductress peppered me with commands and questions. Firmly grabbing Yuri's hand, I bid him thanks and farewell and clambered aboard the BAM.

The train was a madhouse, jammed with people returning from summer vacation. Fifteen passengers were camped out in the aisle of my wagon, sitting and reclining on heaps of baggage. Climbing over suitcases and burlap sacks, knocking into weary travelers—some of whom had been on trains for six days—I made my way to the last compartment, where I stowed my bags and clambered into a top bunk. A half dozen people had taken up residence in the four-person compartment, but I paid them no mind. Undressing to my underwear—the wagon was stifling and redolent of body odor—I slipped under a sheet and slept restlessly until nine the following morning.

When I awoke, the mob was gone, many people having disembarked during the night. There was another change, as well. Summer was over. I looked out on a raw, somber mountainous landscape already well into fall. It was the last day of August. The leaves on the birch saplings were yellow, and the scrub covering the rocky ground was a mixture of oranges, golds, and rust reds. It was drizzling, and low clouds hovered just overhead. As we rolled along that morning, climbing into the Stanovoi Plateau, the landscape became wilder. Snow covered the ground as we lumbered up ravines flanked by seven-thousand-foot mountains. Once, we passed three hunters and a dog huddled by a campfire along the tracks. Dressed in filthy brown clothes and framed by a broad river valley and snow-covered mountains, they were at the heart of a tableau from another century.

Settlements were scarce and forlorn. Several of the major BAM towns boasted garish blue and red concrete buildings that had fallen into disrepair. Not far away were the shantytowns inhabited by BAM workers in the 1970s. Now, the shacks and cabins were tilting helter-skelter in the shifting permafrost. Some of the old settlements had been burned, others razed.

The train was moving through the heart of the Baikal–Amur Mainline, the last of the Soviet public works extravaganzas. Conceived in the 1930s under Stalin, the BAM was supposed to unlock the vast, wild taiga of the Trans-Baikal and the Russian Far East, a region rich with minerals, timber, and oil and gas. Soviet planners foresaw that the BAM would transform the area north and east of Baikal the way the Trans-Siberian had opened up southern Siberia at the turn of the century.

Stalin began construction using gulag laborers, but scrapped the project during World War II. Revived in 1974 under Brezhnev, it was the last gasp of a decaying system. Siphoning off $25 billion in state reserves—mainly derived from oil—the Soviet government built a two-thousand-mile link through some of the most rugged territory on earth, blasting long tunnels through seven mountains. The BAM began in Taishet, northwest of Lake Baikal, and ran all the way though forest and swamp to Komsomolsk-on-the-Amur. From that city, there was a direct link via the Amur River to the Pacific Ocean.

In October 1984, track-laying crews met near the town of Kuanda, finally completing the line. In reality, the BAM didn't begin functioning for another five years due to repair work. By then, the party was over. With the Soviet Union and the centralized economy sliding toward oblivion, there was no money from Moscow to build the dozens of new cities, mining centers, and factories once envisioned for the BAM. While the railway was a remarkable feat of engineering and construction, there was little traffic moving along it in the waning days of the USSR. With the end of the Soviet Union in December 1991, any hopes of the state further developing industry along the BAM were dashed.

In recent years, the workers who had flocked to the Baikal–Amur Mainline had gradually drifted away. The towns they had built in a last gasp of enthusiasm for the Soviet state were steadily losing population. The hastily constructed infrastructure was decomposing in the harsh Siberian climate. Someday, no doubt, capitalist Russia would make use of the BAM. But as my train chugged along, I saw only a derailed Communist dream.

As we neared Kuanda, a stocky, energetic, dark-haired man sidled up to me in the corridor. His name was Georgy Baslik, and he had come to the BAM in 1981, a member of a crew clearing forest to make way for the rails.

"You should have been here in the 1980s when it was boiling with activity," said Baslik. "It was hopping then—trains, trucks on the roads, people everywhere. Now they're closing everything down. It's a gloomy picture. There are few people left."

Baslik had decided to stay and was earning good money working for a geological company. He was returning from a two-month vacation in his native Crimea.

We passed the spot where the two crews—one laying rails east from Severobaikalsk, the other working west from Tynda—had met in 1984 to complete the BAM. The site was marked by two railroad ties rising vertically out of the ground. The train continued to climb, passing through a long tunnel and emerging onto a plateau with a lake on one side of the tracks and a waterfall tumbling off a cliff on the other. Looking at this wintry landscape, rolling past mountainsides caked in gray scree, Baslik said, "It's hard to believe it was fifteen years ago that we built this. Then there was nothing here—wild taiga, that's it."

I wanted to fish in the mountains north of Baikal, for I had heard the rivers there still had sizable populations of taimen. The Chara was one such river, and all day I had wondered whether to disembark there. That afternoon, as the train climbed to a peak and then descended into the Chara River valley, my doubts disappeared. The river meandered through a striking landscape, bordered on two sides by nine-thousand-foot, snow-covered ranges reminiscent of the Montana Rockies. I was getting off the train.

A teacher in my compartment helped haul my bags to the taxi stand at the Chara station. I wanted nothing to do with Chara, a BAM creation, twelve miles from the river, deciding instead to head for Old Chara, a smaller river town founded by geologists in the 1930s. After ducking quickly into the train station, I emerged to find the teacher standing next to a short, middle-aged man. "Everything's arranged," said the teacher. "This fellow is a fisherman from Old Chara, and you can stay with him."

I squeezed into the backseat of a Lada with the man, a forty-eight-year-old named Sergei Sorokin. He was missing most of his teeth, and air whistled through the gaps when he spoke. By this time, I had the yips about winding up in the care of a boozer. While Sorokin talked about his life, I sized him up. He had a deeply lined face, blue eyes, tousled brown hair. He looked sober. As he described the travails of his professional life, a jaded half-smile came across his face.

Sorokin had worked two decades for the Udokon Geological Expedition, an exploration and mining company, hustling his way up to chief mechanic.

"They had twelve hundred employees, and two years ago they just liquidated the company, laid everyone off, sold and stole the equipment. . . . They left the town high and dry. . . . I'm unemployed now. . . . Nothing is stable anymore. It's a madhouse. The sooner all this uncertainty ends, the better. What idiots we have in the Kremlin."

"Sergei," a female friend from Old Chara chimed in from the front seat, "when have we ever had good leaders in the Kremlin?"

Sorokin went on to tell me the story of his sixteen-year-old son, killed in June 1995 in a car accident. He and two other boys were riding in a motorcycle and sidecar when they were run over by a speeding Volga. The other two boys were injured. The driver of the Volga was drunk. But he was the personal chauffeur of the local prosecutor, Sorokin said bitterly, and was never punished for his crime.

"My boy was so bright, top in his class, a really handsome kid.

We've gone to the cemetery so many times in the past year. My wife is still not over it and never will be."

In a cold rain, Old Chara was a doleful place, its muddy, cratered streets flanked by log cabins and beat-up wood-frame homes. The Kadar Mountains were only a few miles away, the peaks shrouded in clouds. Sorokin's small wooden home was built on swampy permafrost, and we had to tread on a narrow wooden boardwalk to stay out of the water.

I sat down in the living room, and Sergei showed me his photo albums. We flipped through pictures of his dead son, Evgeny, and of his surviving son, now living in Khabarovsk. There were dozens of shots of Sorokin on hunting and fishing trips. His wife, Alexandra, walked in as we paged through the albums. She was reserved and seemed always on the verge of a sigh.

At dusk, Sorokin and I drove to the cemetery on the outskirts of town. It was a gloomy evening—the temperature in the high thirties, rain falling, the clouds perched a few hundred yards above the trees. His son's graveyard was in a large pine grove. Surrounded by low, blue-and-white metal fences, hundreds of graves filled the grove, many of them marked with black stones, on the face of which were affixed black-and-white photographs of the deceased. Plastic flowers were piled against the headstones. We walked up to his son's grave, which had a black marble marker. The photograph on it was of a serious, good-looking, dark-haired boy. Raised two feet off the ground, the grave was bordered by black stones, some of which were sinking into the permafrost. Sorokin kneeled down, straightened a stone, then touched the mound of earth.

"Oh, my bright boy," he said. "My bright boy."

We stood there for a minute or two, after which we searched for the grave of a local boy killed in the Chechen war and awarded the Hero of Russia medal. Sorokin had a hard time finding the marker, and we wandered through most of the cemetery. After several minutes, I began to notice the ages of the dead. There were children aged one, and three, and eight. And there were scores of people—mostly men—who had died in their twenties, thirties, and forties. Sorokin knew many of them, and he rattled off their fates—heart attack, complications from drinking, suicide, died in the hospital during an operation. After ten minutes of this roll call, with all the young and middle-aged faces staring out at us in the twilight, I was overcome with melancholy and wanted to flee the cemetery. Looking at this array of graves, I more plainly understood how life expectancy for men in the country had dropped to the abysmally low age of fifty-eight.

As we got into his car, Sorokin said, "You see what a life we live."

On the way home, I asked him how he was getting by without a job. He said he occasionally worked for a gold-mining company, tended the family's two cows, and hunted and fished for meat.

After dinner that night, Sorokin's wife—a handsome woman with dark hair and pale, unblemished skin—grew more talkative.

"Look at my husband, and you'll see the toll life takes on people here. He's forty-eight and looks ten years older. He's lost all his teeth, his face has aged. . . . Five years of reform and things just keep getting worse and worse and worse. It's all falling apart, and I don't see it getting any better."

She was weary, too, of living a life that Americans had jettisoned early in the century—toting water from wells, tending cows, cutting firewood, relieving herself in stinking outhouses. "We're completely overloaded," she said.

I told her how much I missed my mother, who had died the previous year. Looking at me eagerly, she asked, "Do you believe in life after the grave?"

I replied that my mother's spirit lived on in me, my father, my children, and those who still remembered her. I wasn't sure, I said, but perhaps her spirit lived on in other ways, as well, and that one day we might be reunited.

"I would like to think that, too," she said. "I think I believe more in the afterlife than not believe in it."

Her eyes welled with tears, and she walked into the kitchen to wash her face. Sitting back down, she said, "We've thought of leaving Chara, but now with Evgeny buried here, I couldn't imagine going."

Heavy rains had swollen the Chara River, and Sergei was worried fishing would be lousy in the murky water. We decided to go anyway. Before driving to the river, Sorokin hauled something resembling a rabbit carcass out of his freezer. It was a *tabbagan*—a black-headed marmot—that he had recently shot in the mountains. They were increasingly rare, and listed in Russia's "Red Book" of threatened species, Sorokin said. But poaching this animal seemed of minor concern to him, for the flesh was delicious and the fat reputedly an excellent medicine for lung congestion and other ailments. From the refrigerator, Sergei extracted a jar of a viscous, yellow substance—the melted-down fat of the *tabbagan*. That night, we ate the *tabbagan*, and it proved a tough, but tasty, piece of meat.

Earlier, a friend of Sergei's had shown us the large, curled racks of two snow sheep he had shot, a creature also listed as threatened in the region.

As we rode to the settlement of Chara-Ologo to begin our fishing trip, Sorokin talked about a small mountain deer, the *kabarga*, which was relentlessly pursued for its fine flesh and musk-scented glands used in perfumes. He recounted how his brother and a friend had crawled into the den of a brown bear and killed the sow. She had four cubs, and rather than consigning them to suffering and almost certain death without their mother, the men killed them, too. Sorokin recalled these escapades in a matter-of-fact tone and seemed little bothered by them. Like many of the Russians I met, he and his friends shot, netted, and hooked just about everything that walked, swam, or flew, regardless of season. Their attitude was reminiscent of that of nineteenth-century Americans; like our forebears, many Siberians seemed confident that the bounties of nature were inexhaustible, or at least that their own killing sprees were inconsequential. Who wouldn't think such a thing in eastern Siberia, a land of almost incomprehensible immensity, with more wild territory than any other place in the Northern Hemisphere?

But with helicopters and all-terrain vehicles, nearly every inch of Siberia had become accessible. The arrival of the BAM was illustrative. Before the construction of the railroad, the vast region to the northeast of Lake Baikal—including Chara—was wilderness. Aboriginals, such as the Evenks, roamed the territory, but their numbers were small and their impact insignificant.

The BAM changed everything. The arrival of the rail line and the roads that accompanied it not only opened up a once inaccessible area. The BAM also brought in thousands of workers, men who had access to helicopters and off-road vehicles, and who loved to fish and hunt. Since construction of the BAM began, these workers ranged hundreds of miles north and south of the railway. In the 1970s and 1980s, fuel in the Soviet Union was so cheap and abundant as to be virtually free. Returning again and again to once remote rivers and lakes, the BAM workers netted and caught countless fish. Don Proebstel, an American ichthyologist who had traveled in the area, said the workers virtually eliminated a large form of char, known as a *davachan*, in many lakes.

Sergei agreed that the BAM had taken a heavy toll on fish stocks. The large taimen that once filled the rivers were rarely caught these days. Crossing a small river, the Ikabya, that had contained a healthy population of large grayling, he said, "Now they're a lot less. Civilization has wiped them out. There were many more fish here before the BAM."

The inclement weather of the previous day dispersed as we drove north in a wide valley, the Kadar Range on our left and the Udokan Range to the right. The tops of the summits were still obscured by clouds, but you could make out a snow line at about six thousand feet.

Chara-Ologo was a grim, unkempt settlement of about one hundred houses, mainly populated by Evenks. Listing log cabins stood behind ruined picket fences. The main dirt road was awash in mud. Stumbling down the middle of it at 1 P.M. were three Evenk men and a woman.

"Oh, they're drunk—they drink an ungodly amount here," said Sorokin. "Ten years ago, there were dozens of Evenk herders here and thousands of reindeer. With perestroika it all fell apart. Now the herding has mainly gone to hell. The Evenks have drunk everything up."

Sergei borrowed a small, metal boat from a friend, attached his own outboard motor, and we headed upstream. The Chara was as wide as a football field, the water high and murky from the rains. Sorokin knew the river well and maneuvered us skillfully around riffles and snags. It was about forty degrees and windy, and as we motored twenty miles upstream, patches of vivid blue sky appeared amid the retreating cloud cover. Low, wooded hills bordered the river, the yellow and chartreuse leaves of the birch and aspen quivering in the breeze.

Around 2 P.M. we came to a spot where the mountains closed in and the placid river turned into surging white water. Sorokin hitched his boat to a tree, and we scrambled up a bank to a clearing, where several old campfires blackened the earth. After eating, we set off on foot upriver. At the start of the hike, we fished with no results. Then we cut inland, walking on a hillside covered in pine bush—twelve-foot shrubs heavy with cones and nuts. This was a brown bear supermarket, and we passed mauled cones and bear scat. The pine bushes were thick, and at times I lost sight of Sorokin. Being from the East Coast of America, I had not yet come to terms with the feeling that there was a creature in the forest higher on the food chain than I was.

"Sergei," I asked at one point as we walked briskly along, "aren't you afraid of bears?"

"Let them be afraid of us," said the unarmed Sorokin.

The hillside was thick, too, with *brusnika*, a crimson berry known in English as a mountain cranberry, or cowberry. We took a rest in the midst of a sprawling patch of fat, ripe *brusnika*, gobbling handfuls of the succulent, slightly tart berries. Russians and Evenks said *brusnika* did wonders for the digestion, kidneys, and urinary tract. They also were a superb diuretic and were used as a cure for hypertension.

Continuing for two miles along the hillside, we crossed small brooks. With each step I became more convinced I was heading to an angling paradise; few people, I told myself, would make this trek just to go fishing.

And then I saw him, an unshaven character in green fatigues, with a steel box in his hand. Stooping, he raked the ground with a metal comb attached to his box. He was picking berries. Sergei knew the man, who looked as chagrined to see us as we were to see him. Accompanying us to a nearby clearing, he showed us crates of *brusnika* he had gathered.

I could have lived with a berry picker. But what depressed me beyond measure was to find, in the honey hole where Sergei and I were to fish, a second man pounding the water with his spinning rod. The fisherman was occupying the prime real estate—a gravel bar that jutted into a jade-colored pool at the confluence of the Chara and a fast-moving stream. Not about to relinquish his position, he informed us that he had been fishing there for two days, landing eighteen grayling and a *lenok*, which meant he had pretty much cleaned out the joint. He and his berry-picking partner had been driven here by a friend in an all-terrain vehicle (ATV), a tanklike monster built for the Soviet army. Not far away, I could see the muddy tread marks left by the vehicle. The men were camping here for a couple of weeks, picking a winter's supply of *brusnika* and killing every fish in sight.

I tried to work around the Russian. Staring at me as I fly-cast, he asked where I was from.

"New York."

"Well, let's see how your New York fishing methods work in Siberia."

"They work just fine."

"Hey, give me one of those flies as a gift."

"Later."

Several times, small grayling nipped at my fly, but never took the hook. Whenever the moron spotted some action near me, he would toss his big, weighted bobber at my rig. He had no shame. I moved over to the Chara, tied on a large dry fly, and searched for *lenok*. There was no action. Finally, at 7 P.M., Sergei said it was time to go.

A few remnant storm clouds sailed over the mountains, but otherwise the skies had cleared. As we rode home on the glassy river, a stunning vista opened up. In the distance, on all sides, were jagged white peaks. As the sun set, they lit up with hues of gold, orange, and pink. The temperature had dropped into the thirties. Huddled in the bow of the boat, I breathed the sweet air and watched night fall over the Chara valley.

Hopping in Sorokin's car, we sped toward Old Chara as the first stars appeared in the heavens. Sorokin and I carried on a subdued conversation, and I asked him what he planned to do next.

"I have two years to go until I get my government pension at fifty. Then I'll hunt, fish, tend my garden, and keep our cows. The pension will give me enough money for bread. Hopefully, some com panies will one day begin geological work here again. I don't know.

But I can tell you one thing—I'm not interested in doing business. I'd rather give money away than trade or do business."

An owl, visible against the last light of day, sprung off a roadside post and flew low over a field. To our right, on the BAM, a locomotive with two cars pulled alongside us, and the engineer blew his whistle. Sergei honked his horn and began racing the train. We were neck and neck for two minutes. Then, with a final toot, the locomotive pulled away and disappeared into the dark.

6

TRUCKERS

When a Russian says of the way ahead, "It's not so much a road as a direction," you can relax. The trip will not disappoint. Such was the case with the path that lay in front of me on the penultimate leg of my journey. No one seemed quite sure if there even *was* a passable summer road from the BAM—the Baikal–Amur Mainline railway—to the Pacific Ocean. All I knew was that my outdated Russian-language map of the Soviet Union showed a squiggly black line running from the BAM town of Tynda about fifteen hundred miles north and east to Magadan, on the Sea of Okhotsk. This track would take me through some of the coldest, least populous regions of Russia, an area crisscrossed with rivers that were once undefiled and filled with fish. It also would lead to Kolyma, a harsh, remote territory that became the deadliest island in the gulag archipelago.

When I got off the BAM at Tynda—a grim rail and road junction I remember chiefly for the swarthy North Korean guest workers who stood at bus stops clad in dark green—my plans were hazy. I could see on my map that a half dozen rivers intersected the road from Tynda to Yakutsk, the capital of the enormous Sakha-Yakutia republic in northeastern Siberia. I wanted to stop along one of these rivers, fish for a few days, then push north to Kolyma.

I traveled the first 250-mile stretch of the punishing gravel road in buses and communal taxis, riding through a misty landscape of high, sparsely forested plateaus, the scrubby ground covered with patches of snow. On the second day, my cab drove through terrain gouged with quarries, crossing numerous murky, green streams whose beds had been scoured by gold mining. A deserted mining village—little more than a pile of collapsing stucco-and-log buildings—sat on a riverbank. The driver remarked that mining had ruined many rivers, and that the fishing was lousy. It would be the first of a nearly unbroken series of despoiled streams that would stretch all the way to the Pacific.

I arrived at noon in Aldan, the end of the line for public transportation. From there to Magadan, a distance of about twelve hundred miles, I would have to hitchhike or hire drivers, assuming the road was even open. The initial news at the Aldan bus depot was not good. The bridge over the Aldan River near Tommot, forty-five miles north, was closed for repairs. But I found a taxi driver willing to take me to the river, where I could walk across the bridge, then hitch a ride on trucks that were fording the Aldan near the span.

The landscape changed to classic, wooded taiga of golden birches, aspens, and larches. My driver, a tall, thirty-year-old blond named Yevgeny, explained that the road was once used by horse and camel caravans that transported gold to China and returned with pure grain-alcohol spirits from the Orient. Some Chinese traveled more than five hundred miles on foot from the Sino-Russian border, hauling barrels of alcohol on their backs, then returning with gold. Banditry was rife. The caravans continued into the 1920s.

Yevgeny was an enthusiastic, loquacious man who loved to hunt and fish, and he, too, rued what mining had done to local streams. He worked as a lineman for the power company, but hadn't been paid in six months and was surviving by ferrying passengers and doing odd jobs.

"We need a good, smart manager. Look at the wealth all around us, all this gold. Yet look at the condition of the roads, the houses, how poorly people live. These riches are sold off or wasted by our leaders, who are lining their pockets. We need an American to come here and run things."

I walked across the bridge over the rain-swollen Aldan River at 1 P.M. and traipsed through a tiny settlement. It was a cloudless day, the temperature near sixty degrees, and villagers were out in force harvesting potatoes. Placing my bags on a nearby bench, I waited for a ride. The first three drivers didn't stop. Then, after forty-five minutes, a brawny man rolled down the window of his baby blue Kamaz cab, listened to my spiel, and said, "Of course. Why not? Get in."

His name was Georgy, and he was my introduction to the brotherhood of long-haul Siberian truck drivers, a stalwart group of men who engendered more hope for the future of the Russian economy than any other I'd met. I settled into his wide cab, which sat high above the ground and bounced relentlessly over the highway. He was thirty-six with receding brown hair, rugged features, thick forearms, and a prodigious belly. He sat on an ersatz Oriental rug and had decorated his dashboard with stickers showing women in varying degrees of undress.

Georgy owned three trucks, driving one himself and leasing two to other drivers. For several years he had been carrying goods along the route we were traveling, the Tynda–Yakutsk highway, and was just returning from a three-day run transporting cabbage from Yakutsk to Aldan. After expenses, he had earned more than 7 million rubles—about $1,500—for his efforts. In a year, he could easily earn $50,000, a handsome sum in Russia.

Thinking big, Georgy was already planning to buy his fourth and fifth rig if the punitive federal tax structure was changed. He had five sons, aged nine to eighteen, some of whom he hoped would follow him into the business. Nostalgia for anything remotely resembling the Communist past, when Georgy drove for state-run enterprises, was not in his range of emotions.

"Before we just earned kopeks," he said, grappling with his thirty-inch wheel as the Kamaz jounced over the road. "Now I can earn real money. There's no comparison."

Averaging about twenty-five miles an hour, we rolled along under a blue sky, the taiga undulating to the horizon. Georgy pulled over and grabbed two sixteen-ounce Danish beers, a loaf of bread, and hunks of ham and sausage. Handing me a beer and popping one open for himself, he took a prodigious swig, sawed off chunks of ham, and revealed the family secrets: He had a girlfriend along the route, in Berkakit, and all had been going well until eighteen months ago when he brought his brother-in-law on one of his trips. The brother-in-law partied with Georgy, met his mistress, then returned to Yakutsk and sang to his sister.

"She's been cussing me out and crying for the past year and a half. She almost threw me out. . . . I have one woman waiting for me in Yakutsk and one in Berkakit. It gets difficult."

We drove two hours without seeing a settlement, and only occasionally passing a truck or a car. At 4:30 P.M., it was time for another break. Pulling into a long dirt lot at the crest of a hill, Georgy produced a portable South Korean propane stove, fixed me a cup of tea, then crawled into his cab for a nap. This was a Yakutian rest stop—one hundred yards of litter-strewn dirt where you shat in the woods, rustled up your own food, and fixed your truck yourself. The five-hundred-mile highway was one of the worst in the developed world, and completely without amenities. You could buy provisions in a couple of towns along the way. Otherwise it was you, your fellow truckers, and the taiga. Every one of these drivers knew how to take apart the engine of a Kamaz, Zil, or Ural truck.

As Georgy snoozed, I stood in the deserted lot, watching downy clouds drift across the sky and listening to mournful Russian folk music pouring softly out of his radio. Aspen leaves fluttered in the afternoon breeze. Looking down, the picture was less pretty—old beer cans, vodka bottles, South Korean cookie boxes, burned tires, puddles of oil, and off to the side, piles of human excrement.

My goal was to reach the village of Upper Amga on the Amga River by nightfall. Earlier in the day, the taxi drivers had told me that the Amga offered the best fishing on the way to Yakutsk, although with poaching and mining pollution, nothing was certain. With a slanting, evening light illuminating the landscape, Georgy and I rode on until, at seven-thirty, we rounded a bend and cruised down a hill to the Amga River. A community of twenty cabins was strung along the near bank. Not a soul was stirring, although smoke rose from a chimney or two. Georgy suggested that the best place to spend the night might be the meteorological station just across the river. As the truck rumbled over a long bridge, I looked down at a wide, tea-colored stream flowing swiftly past the village.

Stopping at the end of the bridge, Georgy pointed out a cluster of several wooden shacks. I offered to pay him for the ride, but he waved me off, extended his hand, and wished me luck.

· · ·

I knocked on the door of one of the shacks and, receiving no answer, pushed it open. It was a one-room hut, maybe twelve feet square, with a wooden platform for a bed, a table, and a dirty, planked floor. Overhead, necklaces of dried mushrooms were suspended from wires. *"Dobry vecher"*—"Good evening," I hollered, just then noticing a pale, unshaven young man fiddling with a window on the outside of the cabin. Walking out to talk to him, I explained I was an American journalist and angler and asked if he knew of anyone who might put me up for a night or two. He insisted I stay with him.

One of several meteorologists at the government-run station, Yuri Parfyonov was a slim twenty-nine-year-old with an archetypal Russian face—high cheekbones, blue eyes, and a long, slightly upturned nose. The walls of his shack were plastered with Soviet movie posters and adorned with clothes hanging on nails. Preparing for winter, he was sealing windows and repointing his large brick stove, which was the only thing that stood between him and Yakutia's sixty-below-zero temperatures.

"I was just going to fix some dinner," he said, leading me to the garden behind his cabin. There was a cluster of meteorological instruments, and a potato patch. Rummaging around in the black dirt, Yuri extracted a few handfuls of pitifully small potatoes, most no larger than a golf ball. There had been two hard frosts in July, wreaking havoc with the potato crop.

Yuri rinsed off the potatoes in a bucket of river water, sliced them into a small frying pan, added some oil, a handful of dried mushrooms, and made one of those unadorned but unforgettably delicious meals you get from time to time on the road. It had been days since I'd had hot food, and his little dish, chased with a shot of vodka and consumed as the northern sun set in a red blaze over the taiga, would have made a confirmed Russophile of even the hardest cynic.

Yuri came to the far north after fighting in the Afghanistan war in the mid-1980s. He had served mainly in Kabul and had seen little action, but, like Vietnam, a stint anywhere in the Afghan war zone was enough to turn a young man's head around and send him looking for truth in far-off places. Yuri's chosen method of rehab was to retreat to remote weather stations in the most beautiful corners of Siberia, including the Kamchatka Peninsula and several locations in the deep freeze of Yakutia. I could see the appeal of such outposts—one-room, well-heated cabins; eight-hour shifts measuring the absurd lengths to which Siberian weather could go; endless taiga, far from humanity. It was an orderly, secure, solitary existence, just the thing for a young man who had experienced the brutality of life in the Soviet army and had witnessed the debacle in Afghanistan.

A couple of years ago, Parfyonov had begun to emerge from his secluded life, falling in love with a Ukrainian woman he had met in Yakutia, marrying her, and producing a daughter. They lived as a family for only three months, about which time Yuri's superiors said they preferred that babies not live in distant weather stations. Should an emergency arise, there was no money to fly the child out in a helicopter.

Ten months before I arrived, Yuri had shipped his bride and infant daughter back to her parents in Ukraine. In the ensuing time, they had written to each other but not called, since connections were poor and a ten-minute phone conversation would eat up 10 percent of Yuri's 1-million-ruble—$225—monthly salary. The Upper Amga station, to which he had recently been transferred, was less remote than others, and he hoped to bring his wife and daughter there within six months.

I told him how much I missed my wife and daughters after only two months and asked how he could tolerate a yearlong separation.

"I don't know, we Russians just get used to conditions such as these," said Yuri, exhibiting the slight stutter that sometimes marred his speech. "We tolerate them."

One of the drawbacks of working in a lonely outpost was that you didn't have much control over the company you kept. That truth became evident after dinner when a hopped-up Azerbaijani and a plump Yakut woman—each with a bellyful of vodka—came barging into Yuri's abode. The Azerbaijani was a thirty-six-year-old named Alek, and he had the harrowed look and tightly wired demeanor of a man who had spent too many years pouring booze, drugs, and other mind-altering toxins into his system. Apparently, he had once been a handsome man, the vestiges of his good looks still evident in his dark, curly hair, brown eyes, and hollow-cheeked, olive-skinned face. Though you knew he was burning the candle furiously at both ends and were loathe to trust him, there was still something winning about Alek. He was a drunk, but a carefree, irrepressible one who kept his audience laughing.

The main thing on his mind when I met him was screwing the Yakut woman. Zoya—missing quite a few teeth—probably was sweet when sober, but drunk she was tedious.

Sitting on Yuri's bed, Alek lunged for her. Giggling, she shoved him away.

"Come on, let me screw you," begged Alek. "Just a little pussy. Just once. Come on. Be a human being."

Turning to me, Alek—his bloodshot eyes dancing—said, "I have only one interest in life—fucking. That's it. That's what I live for."

In the words of Yuri, Alek was a "small-time speculator," a man who would buy or sell just about anything, just the kind of person who could stay afloat in the anarchic bazaar that was the new Russia. He had come to Upper Amga with a load of vodka, which he sold to Yuri's boss, the head of the meteorological station, who would sell it in turn to the locals. There was a tiny store in the village, but it worked fitfully, and demand for vodka was a round-the-clock affair.

Brandishing one of his vodka bottles, Alek offered everyone a shot. He threw back four fingers of the stuff, grimaced, shuddered, and chomped off half a cucumber. Then he asked me if I was married, and how many mistresses I had.

"None," I replied.

"Ahhhh!" he moaned. "Why do you torture yourself with only one woman!"

Alek and Zoya left for gayer company, and Yuri prepared to head next door for the night shift at the station. Before leaving, he offered me his bed, a refuge from the mice scurrying across the floor. I walked down to the Amga, thirty yards away, and washed my face in the river. The temperature was near freezing, and the sky white with stars.

The next morning, Yuri and I went in search of a villager whom I could pay to take me fishing. Crossing the potholed bridge, we walked the muddy streets of Upper Amga. A man in his sixties, standing behind a weather-bleached picket fence, declined; he and his wife were harvesting potatoes and were in shock over the decimation of their crop from the summer frosts. Farther on, the man who ran the village's diesel-fired generator—Upper Amga's only source of power—was having a midmorning drink with five friends who were heading seventy-five miles downstream to go fishing. His name was Vitaly, a powerfully built bachelor of about sixty who had been in the village twenty-five years. He promised to take me fishing the following morning, but warned that populations of *lenok*, taimen, and grayling had been clobbered by unrelenting fishing pressure.

"Fishing was a lot better twenty-five years ago. There were no motors on the boats then and no fancy fishing gear. Now, all up and down the river nearly every place is accessible. And there are too many fishermen now. So there are a lot less fish. A lot less."

He said the area near the village had been fished out and that I would waste my time trying. "There are nets across the river all summer long."

But the day was warm and sunny, and the Amga so inviting, that I succumbed to the urge to fish. Just upstream of the village, a small, whiskey-colored river flowed into the Amga. The confluence was a likely spot to find grayling or *lenok* feeding on insects drifting down the tributary into the main river. But Vitaly was right. An hour of casting, tying on a half dozen different flies, produced nothing. There was no sign of fish.

Later in the afternoon, I walked downstream. Wading in a long pool, I cast large flies on the surface, using the technique that had been so effective on *lenok* near Baikal. There was no response. Then I cast several different streamers—underwater baitfish imitations. The results were the same. Just as I was getting ready to quit, a boy walked along the rocky shore, pointed at the Amga, and said, "You won't catch anything here. There's a net there, from the island to the shore. The net will get all the fish. It's my uncle Sasha's."

Returning to Yuri's, I blundered into a daylong vodka binge featuring the mad Azerbaijani, Alek; Zoya; a meteorological-station worker; and a truck driver who had stopped for a rest and wound up drinking himself into a stupor. They were gathered outside, about twenty yards from Yuri's, and Zoya invited me over for some chicken soup. Famished, I started their way, but the truck driver intercepted me, barely able to keep his feet. He was a huge brute—about five feet eleven, 225 pounds, with a misshapen face that looked as if every bone in it had been broken. I was dressed head to toe in fly-fishing gear—vest, waders, hat, the whole silly getup—and to this barely conscious imbecile must have looked like the biggest dandy within five thousand miles.

Lurching next to me, he pawed my vest, frowned, and mumbled, "Wha' the fuck is this crap?"

He grabbed my arm. I didn't know quite how to proceed, other than to try out what some Russians recommended in such cases: be stern.

"You're drunk," I said. "Sit down."

Swaying to and fro, he shot me an enraged look, cocked his fist, and bellowed, "I'll give you a taste of this!"

"That's enough," I said, turning away just as Zoya and Alek hustled up and called off the trucker.

The boozing went on all night. Yuri was filling in for his drunken colleague, who was prone to go on two-week benders. At 11:30 P.M., Upper Amga's generator switched off for the night, and I crawled into my sleeping bag. From time to time I heard the bleating and howling of the drunkards next door and thought to myself: the countryside is awash in an 80 proof sea, and there is no hope.

As promised, Vitaly was waiting at 7 A.M. in his small blue boat. The morning was overcast, drizzly, and cold. In contrast to my precious Gore-Tex duds, Vitaly was sporting serious Siberian outerwear, vintage 1960—a long, steel blue greatcoat over an olive drab jacket, black pants, and rubber boots. Atop his head was a pancake-shaped, brown wool cap. He was a quiet man with a large head, a firm set to his mouth, and blue eyes behind thick, plastic-rimmed glasses. In taking me twenty-five miles downstream, I think he was as much interested in earning some money as he was in watching an American fish with this long, skinny "buggy whip."

The Amga was dark, glassy, and about two hundred yards wide. We chugged past tan dolomite cliffs, hills thick with golden larches, and steep slopes littered with gray scree. What most surprised me was the number of fishermen who had set up camp on the riverbank. A track paralleled the northern shore, and on it we saw a half dozen cars and fifteen or twenty fishermen living in tents and lean-tos, many drying nets on wooden racks. Determined to take me to a deserted fishing hole, Vitaly pushed on until—more than two hours after our departure—the riverbank road ended and we had the Amga to ourselves. It was one of his favorite spots, a scenic bend in the river with an island in midstream. When we arrived, I was so frozen I could barely open my clenched fists.

Walking along the grassy bank and casting a metal-spoon lure with his spinning rod, Vitaly quickly caught a pike and a *lenok*. He hooked and lost two more *lenok*. I was getting nowhere with my fly rod, and Vitaly suggested we pile back in the boat and head downstream to the opposite shore.

Fishing a side channel near the island, I cast a long, silver streamer—a baitfish imitation—into a dark vein of water. All was quiet. Then I tied on a two-inch, purple-and-black, evil-looking creation that appeared to have been fashioned from a bad hairpiece. It was called a bunny leech. I cast downstream at a forty-five-degree angle, let the leech swing toward shore with the current, and prayed for a strike. Walking downstream, I repeated the motion a second time, a third, and a fourth. Then, on the fifth try, I felt that splendid yank that signifies the deceit has worked.

My host, Yuri, had requested fresh fish, so I decided against releasing the *lenok*. It was a fine, eighteen-inch specimen, with subtle hues of copper and rose on its flanks, and I dragged it up on the pebbly bank and bonked it on the head with a rock. For the next hour, I lost myself in pursuit of *lenok*. The bunny leech proved irresistible, and as I moved downstream, a fish would strike my fly every few minutes. On several occasions, I could feel the *lenok* grab the long tail of the leech and miss the hook. I would cast over the fish again—sometimes as many as a half dozen times—until it either was hooked or had fled. In all, I landed three *lenok*, hooked and lost at least that many, and pulled in a pike, as well.

Vitaly lit a fire on the bank, spread out his greatcoat, and produced two cans of canned Russian beef. When opened, these victuals resembled a solid lump of cholesterol, all congealed white fat and gristle. In America, I would rather have dined on Dumpster scraps than dig into this canned beef. But when you've scarcely eaten breakfast and have been on a cold river for four hours, tastes change. Vitaly stuck the tins straight in the coals, and soon the white fat melted into a rich, brown gravy. My nostrils began to pick up the aroma of simmering beef. Vitaly extracted the cans from the fire, cut slices of bread, poured tin cups of vodka, and announced, "Good appetite!" I inhaled the beef and bread; few things have ever tasted better. We chased these comestibles with three fingers of vodka, and the world looked like a finer place. Dessert was black tea sweetened with thick condensed milk.

Leaning back on the greatcoat, I asked Vitaly how his life today compared with the Communist years. To my surprise, he didn't lament the passing of the Soviet Union. What did gall him were the changes he'd seen in the land and on the river. He and other villagers still took their drinking water straight from the Amga, since there were few settlements and no industry upstream. But geologists had been exploring the upper reaches of the river, he said, and one day soon gold mining might come to the Amga.

As we prepared to return home, I asked him what it was like living as a bachelor in a hamlet such as Upper Amga. He smiled and said, "You get used to it."

Trouble was brewing in the village. The previous night, while I slept, a group of drunken Yakuts had joined the party next door. The hulking, belligerent trucker had insulted members of the local Yakut gentry, and in the middle of the night, as the Russian driver slept in his truck, the Yakuts returned, dragged him out of his cab, and beat him to a pulp. Now, as Yuri, Alek, and I prepared to fry the fish I had caught that day, Alek looked out the window of Yuri's shack and said, "Looks like problems."

One of the young Yakuts was walking across the Amga bridge holding a double-barreled shotgun. He intended to kill the Russian driver.

Alek, who had been drinking for three straight days, walked quickly out of the shack and headed for the bridge embankment, which loomed over the meteorological station. Yuri suggested we stay inside, which seemed like sound advice. I watched through the window as Alek scrambled up the hill and confronted the armed, inebriated Yakut. They talked for a minute, after which Alek took the gun from the young man, fired both barrels into the air, and sent the Yakut home across the river. Walking back into the hut, Alek disassembled the gun and hid it. He was laughing. "Those fucking Yakuts, all they want to do is get drunk and fight."

Joined by my fishing partner, Vitaly, and Zoya, we ate fried *lenok* and pike as Brasilian and French soap operas played on Yuri's small TV. After consuming a few pieces of fish, with much bone sucking and chunks of white flesh falling to the floor, Alek downed another tumbler of vodka and resumed his groping of Zoya.

"The drunks weren't humane enough last night to leave us alone and give me a chance to fuck her," said Alek.

"Shut up, Alek!" said Zoya, slapping down his probing hands.

As darkness fell, Alek leapt up and announced he and Zoya were driving to her home in Ulu, sixty miles north. Vitaly left, Yuri went to work, and not long before midnight the village's generator sputtered to a halt, causing the lights to flicker and die.

It was time to move on.

The next morning I stood at the end of the Amga bridge, listening for the rumble of a northbound truck. Several rigs passed in the first hour, but none stopped. Below me, the beaten trucker hobbled around his cab, suffering torments that no doubt far eclipsed the burst of pleasure he had experienced when he lifted off on his vodka high two days earlier.

Around 10 A.M., a mud-splattered truck pulling a brown railway container rolled across the bridge. I flagged down the driver, trying to look every inch the marooned foreigner, and his truck ground to a stop. A thin, unshaven blond rolled down his window and invited me to join him. His name was Gennady, and he and two fellow truckers were returning from a four-day, round-trip run from Yakutsk to Berkakit, near Tynda. They were carrying tens of thousands of Choco Pies, a large, chocolate-covered cookie—imported from South Korea—that was the cheapie dessert of choice throughout the Russian Far East that summer. For his ninety-six-hour effort, Gennady would earn $1,000, which helped explain why he was a staunch supporter of market economics.

He was a talkative, easygoing man of thirty, dressed in soiled brown pants and a dark sweater, and smoking cigarettes named for the old workhorse Soviet civilian airliner, TU-134. As we struggled up steep inclines, Gennady said he was driving almost round the clock these days because the Yakutsk-Tynda road would soon be cut for nearly two months. No bridge crossed the broad Lena River at Yakutsk, and every fall the ferries stopped running as ice floes formed. By early December, the Lena's ice would be thick enough to support a winter road.

Gennady shook his head at the appalling condition of the highway, which was the lifeline for a large portion of northeastern Siberia. To reach Yakutsk, we would have to travel nearly two hundred miles, only about fifteen miles of which were paved. Our average speed would slow to twenty miles an hour. But in a perverse way, the dreadful road was a blessing for Gennady and his fellow truckers. If it were as smooth as an American interstate, he said, then the companies that hired him wouldn't pay nearly as handsomely for the runs.

The two other drivers in the caravan caught up with us in Ulu, where a toothless hunter tried to interest the men in swapping some of their gasoline and potatoes for a jar of bear fat. "This works wonders on coughs," said the hunter. The truckers took a pass on the fat, but gave the man a sack of potatoes anyway.

At midafternoon, the three trucks pulled into a dirt lot in the middle of the taiga, where a vagrant poet was living in hobo splendor. His name was Sergei Kudiyarov, and he had been encamped there for six weeks. Home was a lean-to supported by stacks of old tires and covered with a thin sheet of plastic. His dining room table was a wood plank resting on birch poles. Sergei was a malodorous and moth-eaten man, wearing a filthy, loose-fitting brown sweater and a pair of frayed blue-jean shorts. His dirt-smeared legs were covered in scabs and scales. Gardens of soil had lodged under his fingernails. He had blue eyes, thick glasses, and it appeared as if he had donned a blindfold and taken a pair of dull shears to his light brown hair.

As we chatted, he smoked Marlboros and took swigs of vodka from a grimy, plastic soda bottle.

He lived on the kindness of truck drivers, who traded food, vodka, and cigarettes for the berries and mushrooms he gathered in the taiga. With winter on its way, however, it would soon be time to move.

"Looks like a pretty difficult life," I said.

"What difficult life? Here I have a lot fewer cares than people in the city. A lot fewer. I didn't decide to live here. I just stopped and stayed. It's all the same to me. . . . I don't ever think about food. I have enough food to last two months."

What interested me was not so much his tramp code of conduct, but that he had lived here a month and a half without getting the bum's rush from the cops. In the old days, he would have lasted about two hours before being institutionalized. This fact was not lost on Gennady Zalesny, the trucker who had picked me up. Gennady was generally happy with the changes that had come to Russia, but he lamented the appearance of more homeless people and bums.

"He's not normal," said Gennady as we sat in his friend's cab drinking black tea. "He's a parasite. In Soviet times they would have thrown him in jail for five years."

The morning's overcast cleared, exposing a turquoise sky. We continued north through a hilly terrain, passing trucks kicking up white walls of dust. As Gennady promised, the last thirty-five kilometers—twenty miles—were the worst, the highway a pocked, rutted, washed-out obstacle course. Stopping to drink from an underground spring, the second driver, Volodya Panov, said, "Can you believe that thirty kilometers could be like this? The last ten are hell. After a trip you get home and you're still bouncing in your bed."

Shortly before 8 P.M., the third driver's truck sputtered and died. With Volodya—known as Vova—in charge, the three men pushed up the mud-caked cab, exposing the engine. Vova Panov was a skilled mechanic, brimming with energy and enthusiasm. About five feet eight inches tall, he had a broad, flat face, a pug nose, and blue eyes. Though the temperature was falling through the forties, he wore only a light shirt as he fiddled with the engine. The middle finger of his left hand was bandaged, the result of an accident in which he had chopped off the tip. He worked with a cigarette clamped between his gold teeth, his words punching through the smoke in staccato bursts.

Vova, who was about thirty, was in love with the life of a long-haul Siberian trucker.

"If you're not a good mechanic here, forget it," said Vova, extracting the fuel pump. "You won't last. Imagine it's January and fifty below zero, and you're alone on this highway and have a serious problem. You've got to solve it while the engine is still warm. Otherwise you have to start building fires under and around the truck, burning spare tires so you don't freeze.

"Oh, you should be here in winter! You walk into the taiga when it's fifty below and the branches of the pine and fir trees are crackling from the cold. You stand in the middle of the taiga and there's this amazing hum from the cold. But Russian drivers are tough. If I break down and it's minus fifty, I can go into the taiga and survive the night."

Spoken like a true Siberian. This was a place that had never known the serfdom of European Russia, which helped explain why Siberians possessed a streak of hard-bitten independence often lacking in their compatriots west of the Urals.

The fuel pump was fine. Vova put it back in place and began examining the fuel line.

While he worked, he told the story of how he had gotten into the trucking business. After serving with the Soviet army in Mongolia, he attended mechanic's school, where he assembled two trucks from scrap metal and junkyard detritus. Selling these and drawing on small savings, he had recently purchased a Super Maz truck for 190 million rubles, about $35,000. In a good month, he could earn 25 million, or $5,000.

"I can't even imagine living in western Russia now. My life is here in Yakutia."

As he spoke, a pink sunset shone through the pine forest. After an hour's tinkering, Vova found the source of the problem—a broken line between the gas tank and the engine. He sucked on a rubber pipe to get the gas flowing and wound up with a mouthful.

"Oh, shit!" he exclaimed, spitting out half a cup of gas. "Is that awful!"

At 10:15 P.M., twelve hours and two hundred miles after we had left the Amga, we arrived at the banks of the Lena River. In a large, dirt lot, a half dozen trucks and a dozen cars waited for the ferry. Five miles away, across the Lena, the lights of Yakutsk twinkled. Above the city, where the sun had set, the horizon was a deep blue, giving way to a pitch-black Siberian sky filled with stars.

We had just missed the last ferry and would have to spend the night in the parking area. Vova invited me into his cab, where I slept surprisingly well stretched out on the front seat, with Vova tucked under a comforter in the berth to my back. Trucks rumbled into the lot all night, fouling the cold air with diesel exhaust.

A sharp rap on the door roused us at 6 A.M. The sky was overcast again, and a dirty yellow sunrise smudged the eastern horizon. "I told you that you'd sleep well in the cabin," said Vova, wiggling into his pants. "I always sleep well in the cabin. I love it."

Scrambling into the front seat, he rubbed his face and lit up a cigarette.

"Better to have a hundred friends than a hundred rubles." So goes a Russian saying, the truth of which was brought home to me as the truckers drove onto the Lena River ferry. Gennady, with whom I had traveled the day before, had a friend who worked on the boat. Rather than buy a ticket and pay the full, $200 fare for tractor-trailers, Gennady directly paid his friend $100. The truckers rode the ferry half-price, while the friend and the captain made a fine profit. The only loser was the state-run ferry system, but since the government hadn't paid anyone's salary in months, what choice did workers have but to steal? There was method in Russia's madness.

The ferry wound through a series of islands, which concealed a panoramic view of the Lena. At 2,680 miles, the Lena was Russia's third-longest river, and its width, coupled with the power of the ice floes that tumbled down the waterway every spring, made it virtually impossible to span with a bridge.

Vova invited me home, and we drove through a bleak industrial section of idled concrete factories. He and Gennady lived with their parents on the same street, a narrow thoroughfare with wooden cottages set behind five-foot plank fences. Vova's parents had a neat, spacious home with wooden floors and muted, flowered wallpaper. Galina and Pyotr Panov were about sixty years old and looked classically Russian—short, stout, snub-nosed, blue-eyed, and ruddy-cheeked.

Yakutsk, founded in 1632 by one of the great Russian explorers, Semyon Dezhnev, was—for the most part—standard-issue, Soviet-era, concrete-box dreariness. But there was a difference. In several parts of town, attractive buildings of glass, steel, and concrete were either under construction or had just been completed. There were new banks, hospitals, children's health clinics, a stadium, and a modern university—all being built by legions of Russians and foreign workers from Macedonia, Poland, Turkey, Slovenia, Serbia, Armenia, Tajikistan, and Azerbaijan. This construction boom was easily explained: Yakutsk was the capital of a republic, Sakha-Yakutia, that was one-third the size of the United States and brimming with mineral wealth, including diamonds, gold, and silver. If this much money was trickling down to the masses in the form of new buildings, I couldn't imagine how much was winding up in the pockets of the republic's leaders.

That night at Vova's it was bath time, and several friends dropped by to eat, drink vodka, guzzle high-octane Danish beer, then sweat it all out in the inferno. We took turns lying on a wooden plank in the fiery bath, where we mercilessly swatted one another—front and back—with bouquets of birch branches. Afterward, with towels around our waists, we cooled off in the forty-degree night air, steam rising from our bodies, then returned for more heat and birch-twig torment, a hose-down with icy water, cooling down outside, more heat, a cold-water dousing, heat and beating, night air, another chilly hose-down, then a final stand-to in the courtyard, where everyone sang the praises of the Russian bath.

"It's a necessity of life," said Vova. "I couldn't live without a bath twice a week."

"The key to good health," said Gennady's father. "It opens up the arteries."

"The doctors told me to be careful because it wasn't good for my blood pressure," said Vova's dad, who'd had a heart attack or two. "But I took a bath and I could feel my heart valve open right up. It felt wonderful."

"The leaves pull all the impurities out of your body," opined Gennady.

I doubted none of this. We all felt superb, purified, the rivers of vodka and beer purged from our bodies and washed down the little drain in Vova's bath. What didn't make sense was what came next. After banishing the evil humors that had accumulated in our organisms, we marched into Vova's kitchen and proceeded to poison our-

selves once again, throwing down more vodka toasts and imbibing beer so strong that two bottles left you light-headed and tongue-tied. We drank to everything, including Tank Driver's Day, a holiday that could only have been invented in the Soviet Union. Vova promised to visit me in America, in part to see the wonders of this fabled land, but also to get a first-class set of false teeth to replace his, most of which had rotted.

Inevitably, the conversation turned to trucks, the men trading tales of woe on the road and praising their machines. Shortly before midnight, Vova took center stage and declared, "An engine is like a symphony. I can tell what's wrong just by listening to it."

As it turned out, getting from Tynda to Yakutsk was the easy part. Pushing east from Yakutsk to Magadan required more ingenuity. High water had flooded sections of the Yakutsk-Khandyga road, the first leg of the trip. Even truckers weren't venturing onto the route. So I took to the Lena River, setting out at 4 A.M.—after a bleary good-bye to Vova and his family—for the Yakutsk port, where I boarded a hydrofoil to Khandyga. We jetted 150 miles to the north— downstream—then turned east onto the Aldan River and cruised 250 miles farther to Khandyga. The trip aboard the white-and-blue hydrofoil took twelve hours, the two dozen passengers dozing much of the way. The sky and the river were a uniform shade of gray, the landscape an endless line of fall foliage. Midway through the voyage, I had tea with the captain, a brawny, taciturn Yakut who said, "People have been stealing in Russia for one thousand years and will steal for one thousand more. With the riches we have in Yakutia, if we did things right, we could be a second Kuwait. But all we have now is a fucking whorehouse."

Khandyga was a small town of unrelenting grimness. Its chief characteristic was the hideous coal dust that covered everything, particularly the roads, which were a midnight-black mire. For decades, trucks had brought coal to the port from regional mines, and a good portion of the dust seemed to have settled on the town. Khandyga was a mélange of ramshackle two-story, wooden barracks, low-slung concrete apartment blocks, and dismal wooden shacks slumping into the permafrost. Much of the town seemed to be built on swamps, and a network of decaying, narrow wooden walkways spanned mosquito-infested puddles. Like most larger Russian towns and cities, Khandyga had a centralized heating system, with steam from a coal-fired generator traveling through yard-wide, aboveground pipes to buildings. Khandyga's pipes, covered in asbestos, were falling apart, with shreds of deadly looking insulation dangling from the tubes. Walking around the town on a cool, drizzly evening, I was overcome with melancholy. It was, quite possibly, the most hideous place I'd seen in all of Russia.

My lodgings only added to the sense of gloom. I wound up in a barge that served as a hotel, a place with long, dark corridors and a central bathroom with an appalling stench. My room was about eight feet square, with a bare lightbulb, two metal cots, filthy mattresses, and pillows stained with blood and other unidentified fluids. Barricading the door with my knapsack, I crawled into my sleeping bag and tried to doze, an activity inhibited by the booming shouts that reverberated down the wooden corridor all night. Rain drummed on the roof until dawn. Waking at 8 A.M., I had only one desire: to put as much distance as possible between myself and Khandyga.

I did not go about this wisely. By chance, the night before I had met the deputy head of the regional government, and he promised to help me find an eastbound truck. He was a former Communist Party official, which should have sounded an alarm. When I arrived at his office, he told me that the road to Magadan was temporarily cut by a surging river, and that I'd better think about returning to Yakutsk and flying. I told him that backtracking was out of the question. His chauffeur drove us to the local state-run truck park, where the director curtly told me that the road was cut. Mainly out of hospitality, but partly out of the lingering apparatchik's impulse to control completely a guest's itinerary, the deputy regional director drove me to a friend's business, where we learned that a convoy might depart for Magadan in a few days.

Accustomed to freedom of movement, I felt stifled by the hand of this well-meaning man and told him politely—but bluntly—to drop me off on the eastern edge of town.

"It's impossible to go by road to Kolyma or Magadan now," he told me.

"In Russia," I said, "anything is possible."

We drove down the soot-covered road and stopped where the last apartment building gave way to the taiga. As I retrieved my bags from the back of the jeep, the apparatchik's young chauffeur looked at me as if I had lost my mind. Out of his pocket he extracted a talisman—a little purple troll. "This might help," he said.

The road was quiet. Occasionally, a jeep or car sped by, but none stopped. After forty minutes, an olive green Zil truck came to a halt, and I threw my gear in the back and hopped in the cab. The men were traveling north to work on an electrical generator and could take me as far as Tyoply Klyuch—"Warm Spring"—forty miles east. The man sitting next to me in the cab asked me about America, and my answers about middle-class life—the homes, cars, and jobs—left him speechless.

"Here," he said, "people now basically consider that they don't have a government, at least one that will help them, and so we don't do anything to help the government."

We drove through thick, golden forest. Soon, snow-covered peaks appeared on the eastern horizon. Tyoply Klyuch was a drowsy, muddy hamlet of small wooden houses and apartment buildings. And though it was no more than a speck on the map, it was home to a man whom a friend in America had said I should contact. The Russian's name was Aleksei Chernitsyn, and he was a dispatcher at the local airport. To my astonishment, Chernitsyn was there, a short, slender, brown-haired fellow with a ready smile. He invited me into his home, and after lunch we set out to find an eastbound truck. Soon, local truckers and the man who oversaw the region's road system delivered the bad news: the road to Kolyma was washed out about 150 miles ahead. Three Ural trucks had just returned after being unable to ford a flooded river. The only way to Kolyma was to hop a small AN-24, leaving the next day from Tyoply Klyuch, and fly to Ust Nera, a mining town in the mountains. Ust Nera was at the northwestern extremity of Kolyma, and from there I could hitchhike to Magadan, traveling through the heart of the abandoned Stalinist camps. Ust Nera also had another appeal—it was not far from the "pole of cold," Oimyakon, a town that had once recorded the most frigid temperature in Russia, ninety-six degrees Fahrenheit below zero.

That evening, an unemployed helicopter pilot, Volodya Stetsuk, took me and his family fishing on the nearby Khandyga River. He was a striking man of about thirty, tall, with dirty-blond hair swept straight back, blue eyes, and prominent cheekbones. The skies were clear and the temperature forty-five degrees as we walked the half mile from the town to the river. The Khandyga was a shallow, fast-moving stream, set dramatically against a mountain range in the middle distance, its seven-thousand-foot peaks blanketed with snow. Wading out to a pebble bar at the confluence of the Khandyga and a small tributary, I saw grayling darting to the surface to pluck off unidentified entomological life. I tied on a white mayfly imitation and caught several grayling, two of which—each about nine inches long—I kept for Stetsuk. The grayling were the color of steel with small, dark spots, and after I extracted the hook, I walked with them to the dry, upper end of the bar. Struggling fiercely as I squeezed them and prepared to knock their heads on a rock, these fish were the essence of wildness. The power in their small bodies went through me like an electrical charge. After I stunned them, they twitched a few times on the brown and gray stones, then stopped moving. Two was all I had the stomach to kill.

After the squalor of the town of Khandyga, it was a pleasure to stand knee-deep in the river of the same name, my senses focused on the swift current and the grayling that occasionally rose to my fly. I lost track of time. Soon it was nearly eight, and the sun was down, its last rays illuminating high, scattered clouds with a mellow, lavender hue. Stetsuk, his wife, and their seven-year-old son had lit a fire on the rocky shore, and I joined them. Breaking out a bottle of homemade berry wine, we drank the sweet, tasty concoction from plastic cups as the sky turned a deep blue and the air took on a noticeable chill. Since losing his job as a pilot more than a year ago, Volodya had done a little "trading" in food and other items and soon expected to be rehired at the local airport. He and his wife, Natasha—also about thirty—preferred life in the new Russia, despite its uncertainty.

"Look, we can travel and buy what we want," said Stetsuk as sparks from the fire drifted into the darkening sky. "If you have a head and hands, you can make a living. Last year, we took all our savings and went to London for a week. We loved it. We want to do some more traveling."

As their son stoked the fire, the first star appeared in the cobalt blue sky.

7.

Kolyma

The AN-24 was five miles out, the exhaust from its twin engines tracing a black line across the blue sky. Walking onto the second-floor balcony of the Tyoply Klyuch airport, the controller checked the runway for grazing cattle, which yesterday had interfered with two landings. The cows were gone. The red-and-white propeller plane was cleared to land.

We took off around 10 A.M., heading 225 miles to Ust Nera. Because the road was washed out, it was the only leg of my trans-Russia trip that I would not complete overland, and I was disappointed. But ten weeks of travel in rural Russia, exposed to the likes of Yuri Brodsky and the army colonel in Gorno-Altaisk, had made me something of a fatalist. Whereas once I might have struggled against the inevitable, I now surrendered to it.

The AN-24 flew over jagged, snow-covered mountains that rose to nine thousand feet, range after range unrolling to the north and east. I had read about the severely beautiful landscape of Kolyma, but only now, as I approached it from the air, did I get a sense of the striking natural backdrop against which the mines and labor camps were set. The Khandyga and other rivers coursed through the terrain, their banks lined with brilliant yellow trees. On the lower slopes, the mountainsides were thick with golden larches. For fifteen minutes, we followed the Magadan road, a dirt track paralleling a river. Not a car or a truck was in sight.

As we approached Ust Nera, the copilot—a stocky, young blond— invited me into the cockpit. The plane followed a wide valley, and looking down, I saw a cloudy green river devastated by gold mining. Mile after mile of the stream had been excavated, its course altered, its banks littered with mountains of waste rock and sand. To the north, I spied another river, similarly denuded. Both flowed into the Indigirka, whose waters—fouled by tons of mining sediment— wound several hundred miles north to the East Siberian Sea.

Ust Nera, a town of about ten thousand, lay straight ahead, situated in a bowl surrounded on three sides by jagged mountains. The winds were high, and the plane was pitching as we descended and touched down on a gravel runway. I was the last passenger off. Tossing my black knapsack on the ground, I descended the metal ladder. No sooner did my feet touch the runway than a plainclothes policeman approached and said, "Where are you from?"

"America."

"You have entered a closed Yakutian border zone. Follow me."

Border zone? We were five hundred miles from the nearest border. I knew the Sakha-Yakutia Republic was trying to exercise its autonomy, but this was absurd, as if a Russian had flown into a small Texas town, only to be told he had entered a restricted Longhorn border zone. Several scenarios ran through my mind, including the distinct possibility I might be placed on the AN-24 and sent back to Yakutsk.

The affable copilot accompanied me, explaining that Ust Nera was in the heart of a vast gold-mining area and was therefore a closed city. Walking into the airport building, we strolled down a dark corridor and into a tiny office. There, the policeman showed me a resolution of the government of Sakha-Yakutia, listing Ust Nera and other towns as closed. He took my passport, visa, and accreditation card.

Now he had my attention. Contrition, I concluded, was the only way out of this predicament.

The man returned, and I apologized and announced my intention to get out of Ust Nera as quickly as possible. His look softened. "I think things might work out all right," he told the copilot, "but he'll have to go with the head of criminal investigations and register at the police station."

Gleb Kharkov, the chief of criminal investigations, walked into the cubbyhole. He was a slender, dark-haired man of about thirty-five. Sizing me up, he asked me to follow him to his car and grabbed my gear bag.

"It's heavy," he said. "What's in here?"

"Fishing tackle and waders. I'm a fisherman."

"So am I."

The threat of deportation was receding.

Riding in his Volga sedan across the Indigirka River, Kharkov said, "The gold mining has ruined so many rivers. They're totally polluted. You have to go far away from towns and mines to catch fish now. When I was a boy, you could go right to the river here and catch loads of fish."

Ust Nera was a nasty little town in a sublime setting. Hovering above the burg was a six-thousand-foot peak, atop of which was a small meteorological station plunked down in the snow. In the distance, white mountains stretched to the horizon. The town was all dusty streets, run-down wooden barracks, and gray concrete buildings in various stages of decay.

Kharkov was a busy man, investigating his third suicide in a month, a distraught nurse. Suicides were running twice as high as the previous year, which he attributed to hard economic times. He drove me around for fifteen minutes, trying unsuccessfully to help me find a southbound truck to the heart of Kolyma. Then he dropped me off at the edge of town, promising to swing by in a few hours to see if I was still around.

For four hours, I sat on the side of the road near a shabby filling station, waiting for a truck heading to Artyk or Susuman. Normally, coal trucks moved up and down the highway in September, delivering the winter's supply of fuel to Ust Nera. But the local government didn't yet have the money to pay for coal—temperatures were already in the twenties at night—and the trucks weren't running. The day was mercifully warm, near sixty degrees, and I rested in the sun on my knapsack, gazing at the mountains.

At five-thirty, Kharkov returned. With him was another policeman, who told me that a rarely visited Stalinist labor camp was located about one hundred miles north of Ust Nera in a high valley. Known as Alyaskitovy, the camp was hard to reach and well preserved. He knew a friend with a truck sturdy enough to make the rugged trip. I met the friend, we agreed on a price, and arranged to meet the following morning at seven-thirty.

I spent the night in the Hotel Sunny, a concrete structure on the main street. In need of a bath, I asked the middle-aged receptionist if there was any hope of hot water. None, she replied. No coal.

"The hotel belongs to the regional government, and we haven't been paid since February," she said. "Sometimes they give us some food."

"What do you live on?" I asked.

"Enthusiasm," she replied with a weary smile.

Anatoly Sadykov had the face of an ex-con: a thin Fu Manchu mustache, a broken nose, greasy brown hair flopping over his forehead, green eyes, and an expression—revealed from time to time—that told you this was not a man to cross. I liked him from the start.

His green Zil flatbed truck was parked in front of the Hotel Sunny at the appointed hour. Dressed in a brown leather jacket and blue jeans, Anatoly was smoking as he waited for me with his eighteen-year-old son, a friendly, blond kid named Aleksei. The elder Sadykov's mood was upbeat, which could be explained in part by the $250 he was about to earn driving me to the gulag camp.

We were scarcely out of Ust Nera when we came to a swollen creek whose bridge had been swept away not long ago. In the middle of the creek was an old, white Moskvich car, water up to its doors. A man and a woman were inside, waiting—however long it took—for the help they knew would eventually come. No one said a word; it was understood in this part of the world that if your car was swamped in a flooded creek, whoever happened along would help. Hooking a metal cable from his Zil to the Moskvich's bumper, Anatoly extracted the car. The man thanked him, then waited along the cool, sunny bank for his engine to dry.

We traveled north along one of the defiled river valleys I had seen from the air. It was an awesome and depressing sight—huge pyramids of sand and rock lined the riverbank, the leftovers from the vacuuming and sifting process used to separate gold from the riverbed. The stream and its spawning grounds were dead.

Leaning forward as we bounced along, Anatoly, who was thirty-six, looked my way and said, "We literally walk on gold here, and yet we're poor. Can you imagine that? We mine tons of gold, and what do we have to show for it?"

The Zil wound its way up a mountainside to five-thousand-foot Olchasky Pass, from the top of which we had a stunning view north—mile after mile of mountains and valleys. Here, in one of the coldest spots in Russia, the peak of fall was past, and the radiant gold of the larches—the dominant tree—had faded to a rusty brown. From the top of the pass you felt as if you could almost see to the Arctic Circle, one hundred miles to the north. Magadan, the port city that served as the gateway to the Kolyma gulag, was nearly seven hundred miles to the southeast, and from where we sat, all the way to the Pacific, mines and labor camps were strewn along the Kolyma highway. The road was originally built by prisoners. "We're riding on bones," said Anatoly.

Hurtling down the other side of the pass, we rocketed around hairpin turns with sheer, five-hundred-foot drops and no guardrails. At the bottom, in the shade of a mountain, we got out of the truck and drank coffee from a thermos. I asked Anatoly whom he had voted for in July.

"Gorbachev," he replied, a surprising answer, since only about 1 percent of the voters had supported the former Soviet president, a pariah in the land he helped liberate.

"He turned us around. Now people are saying he's to blame for everything falling apart. But he opened our eyes to the rest of the world. Now we have freedom for the first time. We can buy anything we want. My wife can travel overseas and do business. We can dress well; we used to be clothed in such shit. Before it was a nightmare. We had nothing. We couldn't open our mouths. People who say Gorbachev tore everything apart are idiots who can't see far into the future."

Climbing higher, we followed a narrow river valley with scree slopes rising steeply up the mountainsides. On the dirt road, we came upon a stalled truck. Two men, dressed in soiled, green coats, stumbled up the road, one carrying a bucket of water. Two other men were passed out in the back of the truck amid a heap of clothes, tents, fishing gear, and food. A fifth man sat dumbly behind the wheel. All were in various stages of inebriation, which amused Anatoly, since he hadn't taken a drink in four years. After helping jump-start the engine, Anatoly clambered into his Zil and drove away.

"They left Ust Nera on a fishing trip last night, and this is as far as they've gotten. They'll get to their fishing camp later today and won't even start fishing for a couple of days until they drink all their vodka. They brought two cases of vodka—that's twenty-four bottles for five guys, about five bottles apiece. That's a two-day supply. When the vodka's gone, they'll drink some strong tea, do a little fishing, and go home. That's fishing, Russian style."

At 10:30 A.M., Anatoly turned off the main road onto a track strewn with boulders and downed trees. To our left, down an embankment, was the Arangas River. One bend in the stream, perpetually shaded by the mountain, was still clogged with a thirty-yard shelf of ice from the previous winter. Anatoly related how he had killed a bear along the Arangas recently.

"Didn't you shoot him out of season?" I asked.

"For us, it's much easier to do things outside the law," he replied. "In America, you have reliable laws that work for the people. Our laws are just the opposite. It's easier for us not to pay attention to laws."

Soon, we came to a rock slide blocking the road. Anatoly gingerly maneuvered the Zil over the pile, scaling three-foot boulders. The track veered away from the river and into the woods. Now, beneath a yellow carpet of larch needles, I could see that the road was built on thousands of timbers laid across the permafrost. "*Zeks* did this," said Anatoly, using the slang for gulag laborers.

Enveloped by trees, the road ran through bogs and streams. Soon we came to an open stretch, and before us was a bridge, about ten feet long. A sizable section of the span—about three feet—had rotted away. Anatoly jumped out of the cab and inspected the bridge, which spanned a ravine eight feet deep. He climbed back into the cab, flashed me a smile, and—without a word—backed up about forty yards. He was not retreating. Suddenly it dawned on me that he planned to get up a sufficient head of steam to carry the Zil over the hole in the bridge. I considered asking permission to hop out and walk across the span, but held my tongue.

Jamming the Zil into gear, Anatoly floored it, and we charged ahead. The truck lurched over the road, my head slamming into the roof of the cab as we prepared for liftoff. Before I knew it we were at the bridge. As we hit the near side, I glanced into the ravine and held my breath. With one last stomp on the accelerator, Anatoly willed his huge machine over the rickety bridge and the gaping hole. He had pulled it off, and grunting with relief, he lit up a cigarette. Alyaskitovy was just around the corner.

The first thing I saw were the remnants of the fifteen-foot wooden gate at the entrance to the forced-labor camp. The vertical posts were upright but listing. In most Kolyma camps, a sign hung above the entrance and probably did here, too: "Labor is a matter of honor, courage, and heroism."

To the left, I caught sight of a beige mountain of slag that rose forty yards in the air, was at least as wide, and stretched all the way to the Arangas River a quarter mile below. These were the leavings of the tungsten mined at Alyaskitovy. The mineral was used in making high-quality steel and lightbulb filaments.

We drove father into the camp, and halfway up a hill were the rusty remains of the plant's iron superstructure. Strewn along the slope were several burned-out buildings of stucco and stone. Tilting electrical poles and the remnants of a barbed-wire fence climbed up the mountain.

Anatoly parked, and we jumped out of the truck. Though the camp had been closed since 1957, and though hunters and souvenir-seeking locals had been coming to Alyaskitovy over the decades, the ground was still littered with debris from the gulag. Spread out at our feet were old wheelbarrows, buckets, black boots, shovels, respirators, tin cups, machinery parts, stoves, sieves, and carts filled with rock corings from exploratory drilling.

Alyaskitovy, which once held fifteen hundred prisoners, possessed an end-of-the-world beauty. On the opposite side of the Arangas valley, perhaps a mile away, was a rocky gray wall, its surface broken by streams and coulees thick with aspen and birch. The clear, green waters of the Arangas lay below us, sheltered by a band of trees. The river flowed northward through a scenic valley, heading toward a snowy range about ten miles in the distance.

White clouds rode high in the turquoise sky. It was *babye leto*, "woman's summer"—*Indian summer* in English—and the temperature was near sixty degrees. The only sound was that of the Arangas murmuring in the distance.

For many Soviets, the word *Kolyma* was synonymous with Stalin's terror. As Robert Conquest, the renowned scholar of the terror, has noted, the gulag took root among the monasteries of the Solovetsky Islands and reached its zenith in the mines of Kolyma.

Kolyma ingested its first gulag prisoners in 1932, when the regional network of mines and labor camps gained a foothold in Magadan, the port city on the Sea of Okhotsk. From then until 1957—four years after Stalin's death—the Kolyma system metastasized throughout northeastern Siberia, eventually occupying an area nearly as large as Western Europe. Hundreds of thousands of innocent political prisoners made a long and terrifying journey to Kolyma, crammed in boxcars on the Trans-Siberian Railway, held in railway cars and transit camps in Pacific Ocean ports such as Vladivostok, and finally stuffed—sometimes three thousand to a ship—into the holds of freighters, which then made the weeks-long voyage to Magadan. On the sea journey, prisoners died by the score of starvation, disease, and exposure. Some were executed. Others were raped by the common criminals, who—with the consent of the secret-police guards— terrorized the political prisoners throughout Kolyma.

Kolyma grew because of the need for slave labor to excavate the thousands of tons of gold that lay just beneath the ground. Eventually, the gulag prisoners would extract not only gold, but also uranium, silver, tin, lead, and tungsten. At the peak of the Kolyma system, in the early 1950s, roughly one hundred mines and labor camps operated in the region. Pinpointing how many prisoners were shipped to Kolyma, and how many died there, is difficult, for the Russians were not as meticulous record keepers as the Nazis. Using shipping records and the testimony of workers and prisoners, Conquest estimated that from 1932 to 1957, as many as 3.5 million prisoners were fed into the Kolyma slave-labor camps. Of those, he said, a minimum of 2 million are believed to have perished from starvation, disease, exposure, and execution. At its peak, Kolyma held 300,000 to 500,000 prisoners, Conquest has written.

Some Russian scholars say that while Conquest's numbers are

high, as many as 2 million prisoners may have been shipped to Kolyma, and hundreds of thousands died. Others contend that figures on the Kolyma gulag are inflated. Alexander Kozlov, an expert on Kolyma at the Magadan Regional Museum, said his analysis of ship and gulag records indicates that roughly 800,000 prisoners came to Kolyma. Of those, he said, approximately 150,000 perished.

On one issue—the cruelty of the Kolyma system—there is absolute accord. Until 1937, when Stalin ratcheted up his terror and ordered that gulag prisoners stop being "coddled," the main purpose of Kolyma was to dig gold. After 1937, said Conquest, the NKVD secret-police overseers at Kolyma had two aims—to dig gold, and to kill off political prisoners. They died in myriad circumstances, some building the hundreds of miles of roads that would spread through Kolyma, some making the five-hundred-mile forced marches to the far gold mines, some in summary executions, and many in the mines and camps.

Why they died is no mystery. After 1937, the Far Northern Construction Trust—the NKVD organization that ran Kolyma—starved and worked them to death. The overseers replaced felt boots with cloth, and fur coats with cotton, quilted ones. They increased the workday to twelve or sixteen hours, while often cutting food rations to a bowl or two of hot broth a day, a salted herring, and less than a pound of bread. They made men work in temperatures of up to sixty below zero Celsius, increased the daily production quotas, and summarily executed those who became too weak to carry on. They scarcely heated the drafty wooden barracks and often refused sick prisoners admission to camp infirmaries. Every year, at least one-quarter of the prisoners perished, according to Conquest. For the inmates, life became a daily struggle to stay one step ahead of starvation, disease, and enervation.

Varlam Shalamov, who spent seventeen years in Kolyma and became its most vivid chronicler, wrote in *Kolyma Takes:*

> *Potashnikov felt his strength leaving him every day. A thirty-year-old man, he had difficulty in climbing onto an upper berth and even in getting down from it. His neighbor had died yesterday. The man simply didn't wake up, and no one asked for the cause of death, as if there were only one cause that everyone knew.*

He didn't want to die here in the frost under the boots of the guards, in the barracks with its swearing, dirt, and total indifference written on every face. He bore no grudge for people's indifference, for he had long since compre-hended the source of that spiritual dullness. The same frost that transformed a man's spit into ice in midair also penetrated the soul. If bones could freeze, then the brain could also be dulled and the soul could freeze over. And the soul shuddered and froze—perhaps to remain frozen forever. Potashnikov had lost everything except the desire to survive, to endure the cold and remain alive.

Toting a shotgun in case we crossed paths with a brown bear, Anatoly led the way up the narrow, wooded valley to the main camp. Midway up the rocky mountainside was the entrance to an old tungsten mine. On our left, in a broad, sunlit meadow, was the village where several hundred camp officials, engineers, and other civilians who worked at the gulag once lived. Scattered about the dun-colored grass were the rusting carcasses of a half dozen Soviet trucks from the late 1940s and early 1950s. On one of the green hoods was a steel tag that read "ZIS," the Russian initials for the Factory in the Name of Stalin. Several buildings made of stucco and wood had collapsed in a gray heap.

We proceeded up the valley, shedding our coats in the warm, afternoon air and passing fresh bear tracks. The valley floor was covered with honey-colored larches, and patches of the trees crawled up the lead-gray slopes. Wandering through the ruins of a kindergarten for the children of the mine's civilian employees, we found in the long grass a wooden wagon, a wooden doll sled, a plastic truck, and a swing in the shape of a boat.

At last we came to the main camp, a barbed-wire enclosure—perhaps two hundred yards by one hundred yards—bounded on both sides by precipitous slopes that blocked out the sun much of the year. The arched entrance gate, about twenty-five feet high, was well preserved. A twenty-foot guard tower was in excellent condition, but two other towers were listing sharply. Parallel, fifteen-foot barbed-wire fences still ringed the camp, with rusty tin cans—placed there to alert the guards—dangling from the wire. The barracks and other buildings inside the compound had long ago been razed.

"This was the zone," said Anatoly. "Imagine how many lives were ruined here, so many good minds destroyed. People lived here. They dreamed of a good life, they made plans, all the while knowing their fate was in the hands of the NKVD. They understood their fate, but still dreamed of home, their families."

I climbed the watchtower and could discern—in the yard-high grass—the outlines of about a dozen barracks, aligned in two rows. Inside several of the foundations were lone, rusted, iron stoves. Years later, a survivor of Alyaskitovy wrote the local museum recounting an incident that took place in one of the barracks. In 1951, several young women graduates of a mining institute came to work as civilians at the camp. The women took pity on the famished prisoners and surreptitiously gave them food. The survivor recounted how he and one of the women, a pretty girl he identified only as "N," took a liking to each other. One day, after bringing him some food, the girl and the prisoner lay on opposite bunks, gazing at one another for several minutes. Then the woman left. Someone informed on her, and several days later a group of guards and criminals, who worked as trustees, took the girl into the taiga and gang-raped her on the snow. The common criminals frequently gang-raped women prisoners; the practice was so widespread the criminals even had a slang expression for it: "She fell under the trolley."

At the upper end of the valley, not far above the barracks, was the main tungsten mine—a forbidding zone flanked by two stony mountains whose surfaces had been stripped of trees. Tons of rusting mining equipment lay in heaps between the two slopes. Some of it was American, including a large, boxlike piece of machinery stamped, "Gardner-Denver. Quincy-Denver. Made in USA." On one slope was the main mine, with a shaft leading into the mountain. An intact set of rails ran a short distance out of the shaft. Nearby, on its side, lay a large steel cart once used to carry ore.

In the narrow ravine between the mountains, we came upon dozens of wooden lockers, many with doors, where the prisoners had changed before heading into the mountain. Nearby was another ruined building with a sign that read, "Window for Lamp Distribution." Hundreds of old headlamps and batteries lay scattered on the ground, some marked with a date, 1948. Metal tags for the lamps still hung neatly on hooks; the numbers went as high as 980.

Decaying wooden steps wound more than two hundred yards up a barren scree slope. Once, a guard post stood at the end of the steps.

Looking at the desolate mountains, it was not hard to picture the scene a half century before, with winter winds whipping down the canyon and, as one ex-Kolyma prisoner described, "human ants carrying their heavy load up the rugged mountain." Even on an Indian-summer day it was a forlorn place that still imparted, to some small degree, the sense of abandonment that Kolyma's prisoners must have felt.

"Nothing remained for them but to die and they died without thinking of escaping," wrote Shalamov. "They died, showing once again this national quality . . . which all politicians have abused—patience."

The following evening, back in Ust Nera, I met Svetlana Petrovskaya, who spent several years in Alyaskitovy—not as a prisoner, but as the daughter of the mine's chief engineer.

"I was five or six at the time, and I remember prisoners calling me to the barbed-wire fence and giving me flowers and little hand-made toys. I think they just craved human contact. The guards didn't interfere. Even they didn't begrudge the prisoners this little bit of human contact."

Svetlana, a stout, lively woman with bleached-blond hair, said that supervising the work in the mines took a heavy toll on her father.

"He never spoke with me about it. It was a closed subject. My mother said he used to come home from work, put his head in his hands, and say, 'Olga, what wretched people are working in the mines. What wretched people.' He would just sit there, staring. He drank some when we lived there. But when he left the camp, he started drinking terribly.

"He was a cultured, intelligent man. He read a lot. I think he was having a big argument within himself. To have spoken out against what he saw would have meant death. He would have ended up a prisoner, working in the mines himself."

In Ust Nera, Svetlana was vice chairwoman of the tiny chapter of Memorial, a nationwide organization founded during perestroika and dedicated to exposing the horrors of the Stalin era and rehabilitating its victims. Shortly before sunset, she took me to a hillside near town where hundreds—perhaps thousands—of gulag victims were buried in unmarked graves.

Turning off the main road, we bounced down a short dirt track to a site covered in larches and scrub pine. In front of us, a panoramic vista opened up—the expansive, yellow valley of the Nera River, and behind it a line of white-topped mountains. Bounding out of the car, Svetlana explained that in 1991 she brought a group of eleventh graders to the gravesite, and they helped her rebury the scores of bones that had surfaced over the years.

Hurrying along the road, she stopped. A human femur bone was at her feet. Casting her gaze into the nearby scrub, she spotted an open, shallow grave containing arm, leg, and rib bones.

"We covered this grave up, and we came back a month ago and it was fine," she said, throwing handfuls of stones and dirt over the bones. "What barbarism! Who would do such a thing?"

She led the way into a tangle of shrubs. Slowly, I began to make out dozens of mounds. Some of the rises, no more than five feet square, were marked by a half dozen sticks, indicating that five or six people had been buried in one small plot.

"No one's interested in this history anymore," said Svetlana. "They have far more pressing problems to worry about these days, like when they will receive their salary, and how they will feed their family."

That night, after dinner, Svetlana and I negotiated the muddy streets on the way to the hotel. The air was filled with wood smoke, emanating from stoves in greenhouses, where townspeople were rushing to squeeze the last bit of ripeness out of their tomatoes. Svetlana had raised one hundred plants in her greenhouse, harvesting a thousand pounds of tomatoes. Pickled and eaten fresh, they would be her family's staple vegetable in the winter.

"The government puts no goals or ideals in front of us now," she said as we felt our way down pitch-dark streets. "Our kids are in confusion. You should never kill all traditions as we have, kill all that came before, completely wipe out groups like the Young Pioneers, and leave our children with nothing, no moral support, no spiritual ideas.

"Like the Communists, we're now trying to do away with everything that came before. We want to destroy not only all that was bad in the Communist era, but all that was good. It's such a Russian trait—just rip the shirt right off your back and start over with nothing."

On Saturday morning, I was back where I started three days before, waiting for a ride south to Susuman. Fishing near Ust Nera was scarcely worth the effort. I had caught one grayling in the Arangas River on the way back from Alyaskitovy. But for the most part, gold mining had rendered the region's rivers unfishable.

For hours, no trucks appeared, and I sat and watched families fanning into the taiga to pick mountain cranberries. From time to time, trucks from the local collective farm lumbered past, workers sitting on piles of cabbage and potatoes in the flatbeds.

Finally, at midafternoon, a trucker from Magadan stopped and gave me a ride. He was only going as far as Artyk, three hours to the southeast, but even that short hop seemed an improvement over another night in the Hotel Sunny. We followed the Nera River through a mountainous landscape, passing miles of riverbed ravaged in the search for gold.

Artyk convinced me that I had indeed entered some northern, post-Communist twilight zone of unrelenting grimness. A neglected backwater plunked down under a vast Siberian sky, Artyk was a mining town that had steadily lost population in recent years as the gold enterprises plundered the area's rivers and moved on. Its dirt streets were potholed and black with coal. Half the town seemed to be dilapidated wooden homes, the other half Stalin-era, two-story barracks with peeling stucco facades.

The driver dropped me off at a Sakha-Yakutia "border check-point," an odd little outpost that highlighted the autonomy mania sweeping Russia. The Magadan region was fifty miles to the south-east. Since there was nothing between Artyk and the regional bound-ary, Sakha-Yakutia had established a police and customs checkpoint at Artyk. The post was nothing more than a box atop a pile of coal, dirt, and trash. Ill-tempered stray dogs—two of them missing a leg—wandered through this moonscape. Looking south at sunset, I saw a road winding through a wide valley to infinity. Nothing stirred.

Introducing myself to the two border guards—young men dressed in camouflage fatigues and carrying AK-47s—I entered their post and stowed my bags in a corner. The station was small and stuffy, with an iron stove in the center of the floor and some pinups on the walls. Settling in behind a table, the guards resumed playing cards.

Outside, perched on a pile of wood, smoking as he took in the sunset, was a young, blond man dressed in blue track pants and a black leather jacket. I asked how long he'd been waiting for a south-bound truck. Five hours, he replied, noting it was unlikely there'd be another truck that night. But all was not hopeless. The weekly bus from Ust Nera to Susuman would arrive at 3 A.M.

His name was Sasha Kutyeminsky, and he was a twenty-eight-year-old former miner with an intelligent, if slightly weary, expression. Now he was a "trader," importing fresh foods and vegetables into Kolyma. He said he didn't much enjoy the business of buying and selling, but that the money was decent, and it was the only way he'd found to support his wife and two children.

After waiting an hour for a truck, Sasha and I strolled to the town center, which was dominated by two Stalin-era, columned structures, a Palace of Culture and a school. In the twilight, I could make out a mural painted on a tile wall. It showed a miner, hard hat on head, hand pointing toward the shining future. "To You, Motherland, We Give Our Inspired Work."

Clouds had moved in, and as we walked, a light rain began to fall. The rot of the old system was palpable, and Sasha was moved to pronounce two words, which translated literally as "green melancholy." What he meant was, "Depressing beyond belief."

"And so everyone drinks," he went on, "because then it seems for a while that they're not surrounded by all this, and that they have no problems. It's all falling apart. For ten years now no one has been looking after any of this."

Growing chilled, we headed back to the border post. The air was filled with the smell of coal fires, and a ghostly layer of smoke hung in the air.

"Honestly, though, it's so much more interesting to be living now than it was before," he continued. "It's so much freer, there's nothing holding us back. I remember the grayness of the way it used to be, the uniformity—kindergarten, school, army, work. It was all the same."

We entered the post, and the guards offered us some fried potatoes. I heated a can of meat on the stove, and Sasha and I shared a few bites. After napping briefly on a grimy sofa, I joined Sasha outside and waited for the bus. He was from the town of Kadykchan, about four hours south. In recent years, as mines closed, the population had fallen from seven thousand to thirty-five hundred, many families fleeing the brutal Kolyma winters and heading for the relatively mild climate of European Russia in search of opportunity.

"What kind of life is there here? My grandparents have been bouncing around Kolyma their whole lives, going from village to village. I certainly don't want to do that. I want to get out of here, too, but the question is to where, and how."

He said that many of the mines were so poorly run, the technology so backward, that companies were actually losing money digging gold.

The bus arrived at 3:30 A.M., and I slept fitfully until eight, when we pulled into Kadykchan. We rode past razed wooden homes, gutted and vandalized stucco apartments, rusting trucks and tractors. Trash and old tires were scattered along the road. On a hill overlooking the town was a Communist-era billboard. "Glory to Miners," it proclaimed.

Susuman, a dingy town near the heart of the Kolyma gulag, struck me chiefly as a place that still displayed an unusual number of coma-inducing Soviet-era slogans on buildings and billboards. I spent my first afternoon there perusing the fare.

"Northern Citizens—the Strengthening of Socialist Labor Discipline Is the Duty of Each of Us."

"To Susuman—Our Urgent Labor!"

"In Each Workplace—a High Level of Organization, the Ability to Work With Full Efficiency."

The next day, an out-of-work engineer turned taxi driver drove me to the nearby town of Maldyak, where thousands of prisoners once labored in gold mines. I hadn't planned to visit Maldyak, until I found out that one of the Soviet Union's most illustrious citizens, Sergei Pavlovich Korolev, had been imprisoned there. Little known in the West, Korolev was the father of the Soviet space program, the chief designer of the first ICBM and other rockets whose launchings shook the United States. Korolev was the moving force behind not only the 1957 launch of the satellite *Sputnik*, but also the April 12, 1961, flight that made Yury Gagarin the first man in space. Those two achievements were the high-water mark of Communism, a heady epoch when the entire Soviet Union seemed to believe Khrushchev's mantra: "We will catch and overtake America!" But this great figure in postwar Soviet life was not exempt from Stalin's terror. Like nearly everyone else of intelligence and achievement, he, too, was persecuted.

Korolev's turn came on June 27, 1938. He had been working with a talented group of aviation engineers in Moscow, men who were designing the Soviet Union's military aircraft. Fueled by paranoia, Stalin carried out a series of purges in the engineers' ranks, not unlike the arrests and executions that devastated the Soviet general staff.

Interrogated at various Moscow prisons, Korolev was told by the NKVD that "our country doesn't need your fireworks. Or maybe you're making rockets for an attempt on the life of our leader." He expected to be shot. Instead, he was given a ten-year sentence and shipped to Kolyma in the summer of 1939. He traveled about three hundred miles from Magadan to Susuman and was put to work digging gold in an aboveground mine. The prisoners lived in tents and suffered high death rates. Soon, Korolev grew weak and ill. Later, he said he would almost certainly have perished were it not for the kindness of a woman doctor at Maldyak, who saved him from the mines, placed him in the infirmary, and nursed him back to health. The woman doctor said that at the peak of the terror about three thousand prisoners died a year in Maldyak—roughly a third of the camp's population.

As the threat of war with Germany grew, top engineers in Moscow—including aviation designer Andrei Tupolev—persuaded the secret police to recall the brilliant Korolev from Kolyma. On December 23, 1939, after less than six months in Maldyak, he was sent back to European Russia, where he worked—still as a prisoner—in a bureau designing warplanes. To the end of his life, he kept the battered aluminum cup he had used in the Kolyma gulag.

The road from Susuman to Maldyak meandered through a wasted landscape of open-pit gold and coal mines. Maldyak was a collection of two-story, white stucco buildings strung out on a hillside above the river of the same name. None of the gulag barracks remained; they had long ago been razed to get at more gold.

Pyotr Makarov, a mine executive who had studied Korolev's brief stay at Maldyak, pointed to the opposite hill, where the aviation designer had scrabbled the earth for gold. These days, miners were reprocessing the old slag, extracting gold that the rudimentary equipment used by Korolev and his fellow prisoners failed to wring from the rocky ground.

Two Kamaz dump trucks, filled with coal, sat on the side of the Tinkinskoye Highway, the main route south to Magadan. I was heading to Ust Omchug, where I hoped to find a fish-filled stream unmolested by mining, and to visit one of Kolyma's most infamous labor camps, Butugychag. The trucks were parked in a turnaround black with coal dust, and they seemed to be heading my way. I approached one of the drivers, a slender man of about thirty with curly, black hair, a black mustache, a week's growth of beard, elliptical sunglasses, dark trousers, and a pair of fingerless Michael Jackson gloves. He offered me a ride.

The Tinkinskoye road was one of the most rugged in Kolyma, with numerous high passes that frequently were unnavigable in winter. Within a few minutes we were creeping at ten miles an hour up a mountain covered in scree, lichen, and scattered larch. At the top, a dramatic view opened up, with a wooded valley directly below us and a range of rugged, snowy mountains stretching to the north.

After an hour, we came to the Aryan River, where a dozen Russian workers had temporarily closed the bridge to dribble asphalt into the myriad cracks and holes in its surface. After we had sat for half an hour, the second driver wandered onto the bridge to ask the workmen when the span would reopen. A few minutes later, he reported, "They said, 'It all depends. If our throats are parched, it could be at least an hour. If we get something to drink, it will be a lot quicker.' "

The two drivers were out of vodka, so we had to wait. On the other side of the bridge, a pair of drivers had less patience. Deciding to bypass the bridge, they ventured instead over an adjacent span, a rickety wooden structure with holes in its planked surface. My driver, Volodya, and his companion watched in amazement as the trucks bumped over the old bridge. "Shit!" said Volodya. "They're out of their minds."

Within an hour, we were on the other side, where Volodya and the second driver, Yuri, pulled over for lunch. It was three-thirty; we had traveled thirteen miles in three hours.

We crawled over two more passes, gently negotiating vertigo-inducing curves with sheer, fifteen-hundred-foot drops. Rounding one bend, we spotted, far below, a red truck that had slipped off the road and rolled to a stop about a thousand feet down a ravine.

In the evening, with a cold rain falling, we rolled into Omchak, a down-on-its-luck mining town that was squalor personified. I had contemplated spending a day or two there, but the truckers said the local streams were befouled. Surveying the drab, stucco barracks, the dirt roads pocked with puddles, and the abandoned, tar-paper shantytowns, I told Volodya I wanted to keep moving. He replied that if I didn't mind a tight fit, I could spend the night in his cab.

After buying German beer and Dutch vodka in a small store, we drove south of Omchak, pulled off the road, and parked next to a small river. It was dusk, but light enough to see that the stream was loaded with mining sediment. We peeled potatoes in the headlights, then dumped them into a pot with canned Russian beef. Accompanied by cucumbers, two tins of sardines, and onions—which the locals jokingly referred to as "Kolyma apples"—it was a fine meal, chased with ample quantities of vodka.

As Sade played on Volodya's grainy boom box, he and Yuri explained that they were not in the same league as the trucking tycoons I'd met in Yakutsk. They were employed by a company in Magadan, and work was not abundant. Still, their lives were better than before.

"Every day you have to think, 'How am I going to feed my family tomorrow?' " said Volodya, who was twenty-seven and had two children. "But at least now, if you have the money, you can get whatever you want—a two-story dacha, a jeep, travel abroad. All that was closed to us before. At least now it's possible."

He and I spent the night in his cab in an intertwined, vodka-plagued state of semi-slumber. I awoke parched and dazed to a gray dawn and was revived only by a sponge bath in the river and a cup of strong tea. At midmorning, heading for Ust Omchug, Yuri picked up a pair of hitchhikers—a criminal investigator from the prosecutor's office, and his prisoner, a man accused of stealing 650 pounds of meat and attempting to sell it for about $1,000. When we stopped at a small store, the investigator—a short, well-built man of about forty-five with doleful blue eyes—wandered up to me. I asked him about the fate of his prisoner, who stood nearby with a passive expression on his mustachioed face. "He has a prior conviction," said the investigator. "He'll probably get three to four years."

Looking at me with a mixture of exhaustion, anger, and despair, the investigator said, "What a nightmare. Everyone is stealing. I have been a criminal investigator for twenty-two years, and I'm sick of this place. I've got to get to the mainland, where there is a little civilization." (In Kolyma, a place so out-of-the-way it might as well be an island, locals refer to the rest of Russia as the mainland.)

"The whole system is rotten. The police are ignorant, have no education. They're totally corrupt. The Mafia is running the country. Everyone is drinking himself to death. No one is paying salaries. At least under the old system there was some stability. People knew what tomorrow would bring. They received their pay regularly. Now people work and have no idea what will be. There is utter uncertainty and chaos. I'm sick of it all. Kolyma is falling apart before our very eyes."

He sighed, shook his head, and turned away.

For nearly three months, I had avoided falling into the hospitable clutches of the former Communist Party big shots who still ran things in much of rural Russia. In Ust Omchug, my luck ran out.

My plunge to the depths of the apparatchik world—a purgatory of endless merrymaking, autocratic hosts, and grating inefficiency—was occasioned by my acquaintance with a plump, officious, blacktressed boss by the name of Svetlana Kovalenko. A friend of a friend in Magadan had given me Kovalenko's name, and when I arrived in Ust Omchug, she became my dominatrix.

Kovalenko held a position of utmost importance in the region— she ran the company that trucked in the food and booze from Magadan. In Soviet times, such a person attracted Communist bosses like flies to honey, for as much as the old Party hacks liked their power, they cherished even more their God-given right to enjoy the very best in victuals and vodka. Though the market economy had arrived, the fact remained that Ust Omchug was still run by a small, cozy group of big shots. Svetlana, as the chief procurer of life's bounties, was at the center of this cabal.

All I wanted, I told her, was to visit Butugychag, the labor camp, and to go fishing on a far-off river or lake. She smiled and nodded, but she wasn't listening. I was a novelty item, and for the next thirty-six hours I would be at the center of a storm of flat-out revelry.

Ground zero for the fun-making was Svetlana's café and store, incongruously located on the first floor of the regional police building. There, stout women in white coats and caps served up goulash, fried fish, and pickled cabbage. They also sold vodka, champagne, chocolates, and other delicacies from the restaurant's amply-stocked shelves. That first evening, after settling into an unoccupied apartment owned by one of Svetlana's friends, I joined a group of Ust Omchug's power brokers at Chez Svetlana. In attendance were the deputy head of police, the chief of the highway patrol, the head and deputy head of the local administration, and the deputy chair of the Magadan regional legislature. Many of them had been Party officials in Soviet times.

The café, otherwise deserted, was our private dining room. The night began with Svetlana and the two police chiefs carrying fistfuls of vodka and champagne to the tables. My fellow revelers were a decent bunch, but the two law-enforcement bigwigs—burly, block-headed, overfed men in their thirties—had unfortunately not shed some old apparatchik habits. Perhaps the most annoying was their tendency to watch, hawklike, what I drank, and to immediately call to the group's attention my failure to drain the three-ounce shots of vodka.

"Oh, Mr. Fan, what's that?" the deputy police chief would say, wagging his head in grave disappointment. "You didn't drink it all up. You offend Olga by not downing your glass to her toast."

At first, I politely told the big police boys that I was doing the best I could and was sorry if I offended them by not ingesting every drop of vodka. But they were not to be deterred, and the drunker these men got, the more persistent they became.

"Mr. Fan, in our country, people consider it very rude if you don't empty your glass after someone makes a toast. Why aren't you drinking?"

"In my country," I replied, "it's considered very rude to force a guest to drink when he doesn't want to."

"Ah, but you're in Russia now."

Svetlana, who had long black hair, a busty figure, and a stern visage that could give a recalcitrant husband nightmares, was becoming inebriated and overbearing.

"You don't go anywhere with anyone else while you're in Ust Omchug," she said to me at one point. "You don't do anything without my permission. We'll take care of everything."

Around 11 P.M., I noticed that people were loading vodka, champagne, and food into cardboard boxes.

"So you want to fish, eh?" asked the deputy police chief, who had a porky face and a little blond mustache. "Well, we're going fishing—Russian style."

We piled into a few police jeeps, picking up my fly rod along the way. Driving through town to the Detrin River, I began to experience a heady sensation of omnipotence. Hah! I thought. No one can arrest us. We *are* the authorities!

The caravan of jeeps drove to the rocky shore of the Detrin. In the headlights, I could make out a narrow river, and behind it a steep hillside. We were in pursuit of a creature known as a *sig*, a type of whitefish the deputy chief said was officially listed as a threatened species in the region. Stringing up my fly rod and tying on a baitfish imitation, I tried casting into the river. But it was shallow and slow moving, and I fished with little confidence of catching anything.

"You're not going to get a fish with that thing," said the deputy chief. "You've got to fish Russian style, with a net."

Two men dragged the river, pulling in a dozen fish. The *sig* were sleek, up to sixteen inches long, and had puckered mouths. Soon, a bonfire was roaring on the beach, and the men were preparing a big pot of *ukha*, fish soup, which was superb. People milled about, singing, sloshing vodka, slurping soup. Then the deputy chief brought out his AK-47. "Anybody want to take a shot?"

There were a half dozen volunteers, and under the deputy chief's tutelage they fired off rounds into the river, the red tracers pinging off the stones and streaking with awesome beauty up the opposite hillside. The deputy chair of the regional legislature, so drunk she could scarcely stand, grabbed the AK-47 and began waving the barrel. Instinctively I ducked. Steadying her arm, the deputy chief helped her unload a few rounds in the direction of the Detrin. I, too, fired into the hills, the gun jerking upward with every "Pop! Pop! Pop!" I was beginning to see the allure of being a boss in a place like Ust Omchug. You could party endlessly, drive drunk, and shoot up the joint, and nobody was going to get in your way.

Svetlana, barely ambulatory, insisted on walking me up to my fourth-floor apartment. Sitting down on the couch next to me, she looked my way and said, "Is everything okay? You don't need anything? You must be tired."

She declined my offer to escort her home. I heard her crashing down four flights of concrete steps.

I felt as if I had been taken hostage and wondered whether I should set out tomorrow on my own. But there was reason for hope. Earlier, at a more sober hour, Svetlana had mentioned that a truck driver would be carrying supplies to an elderly hunter and trapper who had lived alone for decades in the taiga. He was a survivor of the gulag and resided on a splendid lake. She promised to see if I could tag along.

Russians are relentless. At noon the next day, Svetlana and the two police bosses showed up at my apartment and unloaded bread, cheese, butter, and three bottles of champagne. "We've brought you breakfast," said Svetlana, who looked wobbly from her hangover. Standing in the tiny kitchen, which had a view of concrete apartment buildings and a playground, they popped the champagne, filled glasses to overflowing, and chugged it down.

We returned to the café, where the usual suspects pushed tables together and dove into goulash, meat dumplings, salad, and more vodka and champagne. It was 2 P.M., we were supposed to visit the former labor camp, and I was mired with this group of big shots. In the old days, the apparatchiks in the countryside drowned visitors in alcohol to avoid showing them Soviet reality. This group had no such agenda; they just liked to get drunk. Refusing to throw back a tumbler of vodka at midday, I angered a low-ranking policeman. "People who don't drink are sick," he said.

This movable feast took flight around three-thirty, giving me hope that at last we were going to Butugychag. But they were not finished yet. We repaired to the office of the deputy chief, who ordered a secretary to walk downstairs to Svetlana's for champagne and chocolates. We drank some more, which was unfortunate, for the added champagne pushed Svetlana's blood alcohol level past the point of obnoxiousness. After berating a policeman who was moving to western Russia, she turned to me and said, "There are bad people here, but they get selected out. All those who remain here are good. . . . We are more proud of our nation than you are of yours. . . . There was a lot of good in Communism."

I scowled at her.

"You're sick of us, aren't you? Tired of us already."

Finally, as evening approached, we set off for Butugychag. The crew was going to make a party of that, as well, loading boxes of food and booze into jeeps that would take us to one of the deadliest gulag mines in all of Kolyma.

Twenty miles out of Ust Omchug, we turned off the main road onto a rutted dirt track. Climbing higher, the two jeeps splashed through creeks and rattled over shaky log bridges that dated to Stalin's days. As the jeeps headed up a narrow valley, the route hemmed in by scrubby birches, I caught my first glimpse of Butugychag—a mountain of gray scree, stripped of vegetation. Here, prisoners mined tin and uranium.

A mile ahead, our driver came to a halt near a swift stream. Peering through the underbrush, I could see on the opposite bank the shell of a long, low building made of stucco and stone. "That's the uranium processing plant," someone said.

Thousands of laborers excavated uranium from the surrounding mountains, then carted it to this building to be refined. Some journalists have written that Butugychag's uranium was used in the manufacture of the first Soviet atomic bomb, but experts in Magadan disputed that. There was no disputing, however, that thousands of prisoners died of radiation sickness, many within months of arriving at the mine.

With typical Russian fatalism, my hosts announced that there was still a robust level of radiation all over Butugychag, particularly inside the processing plant. I could see a pile of beige sand, the size of a football field, next to the plant. "The tailings from the processed uranium," said Svetlana.

"Don't worry, it's safe to be here awhile, especially when the sun's not shining," said one of the police chiefs.

"Just the opposite," someone opined. "Radiation is higher when it's cloudy."

"A Japanese delegation came here once," said a third of our group's rocket scientists. "They were all wearing radiation detection badges. As soon as they set foot in Butugychag, their badges started showing high levels of radiation. They ran to their helicopter and took off."

I figured a quick run through the plant couldn't do too much harm. Svetlana led the way, falling knee-deep into the creek, then scrambling over a concrete wall and into the factory. It was a dank, decaying concrete hulk, and moving briskly through it, I felt as if I had stumbled into the sarcophagus at Chernobyl. One room held enormous concrete tubs where, according to Svetlana, the uranium was stored before processing. Chunks of debris littered the interior. I hustled up concrete steps to the third floor, where there was a row of eight-foot metal gates and more evil-looking concrete tubs. This, said Svetlana, was the final uranium-processing hall. From the third-floor windows, I looked out on the vast mound of tailings, piled up around a row of wooden vats. It was one of the eeriest places I'd ever been, and after five minutes I told Svetlana I'd had enough.

The jeeps headed farther up the valley, surrounded on all sides by rocky, charcoal-gray mountains. Butugychag was made up of several mines and camps, and high to our right, on a ridge partially covered in snow, I could see the most infamous, known as Black Rock. We passed clusters of ruined stone buildings—surrounded by collapsing barbed-wire fences—that once made up the heart of the camp. One of them, still largely intact, housed the punishment cells, about a dozen, ten-by-five-foot cubicles arrayed off a central corridor. Bars still remained on the windows and many of the doors. The only heat came from a stove at the end of the hall. In winter, the death rate was astronomical.

The group scrambled up a slope covered in pine bush. On a low ridge, stretching for a hundred yards, was one of the camp cemeteries, a collection of individual and mass graves dug into the rocky soil. The graves were marked by short sticks, attached to which were tin-can tops stamped with identification numbers. One shallow grave was open, and bones were scattered nearby. The graveyard commanded a lovely, bleak view of miles of craggy mountains, some shrouded in clouds. A steady wind rattled the rusted can tops.

At dusk, on the way back to Ust Omchug, we stopped near a river, and the chiefs hauled out the food and vodka. After Butugy-chag, I wanted a drink. The deputy police chief said I'd be foolish not to have one. "It takes away the radiation," he said, only half-joking.

He was known by his patronymic, Fyodorovich. For years, he had been on his own in the taiga, surviving by hunting and trapping. Living in a cabin that was hours from the nearest road, he was virtually cut off for months once the heavy snowfalls began in November. Every fall, the local government sent him a load of staples—tea, cigarettes, flour, sugar, canned fish and meat—to tide him over until spring.

Sergei Kaftan, a local trucker, was driving the supplies to Fyodorovich's and had agreed to take me along. The fishing there, on Sunny Lake, was supposed to be superb. Kaftan had hoped to leave around 6 P.M., but the endless dillydallying of the local lords had made me hopelessly late. When we finally climbed into his green Ural truck at ten-thirty at night, he was furious at the debauched potentates. "Everything with them is always me, me, me," he said.

After forty minutes on the main road, we turned onto a dirt road that grew progressively worse, finally degenerating into a barely discernible track through the forest. The truck bounced in and out of craters, lurched over downed trees, and plunged through streams. We rumbled up and down hills, and once a ptarmigan—already costumed in its white winter plumage—flew spectrally across the road in our headlights.

Kaftan was about forty and married to the nicest of the government officials I'd met, an attractive, middle-aged woman named Valentina. A quiet, likable man, he hadn't had a drink in three years. I asked why he'd sworn off alcohol.

"Family problems," he replied, his cigarette glowing in the darkened cab. "I had the same problem as your president, Clinton. Other women. I'd drink and get around them and couldn't resist. It was like hypnosis."

Around 3 A.M., the track to Fyodorovich's seemed to disappear altogether, and the Ural struggled through bogs and dense forests of larch, birch, and pine. Bracing myself on the dashboard as we lurched forward, I caught sight of a log hut, its roof covered in tar paper. This was Fyodorovich's guest cabin, Kaftan explained. The old trapper himself lived deep in the sheltering forest.

Kaftan leaned long and hard on the horn, a jarring note in the middle of nowhere, and one that set the ducks on Sunny Lake squawking. We sat and waited. For five minutes, we saw nothing. He honked the horn again. Several more minutes passed. Then, to my right, I saw a lantern bobbing slowly through the forest. The light glided toward us, and soon a ghostly figure emerged from the darkness and into our headlights. Sergei and I hopped out of the cab and walked to meet Fyodorovich.

In the lamplight, his face was a revelation: craggy, toothless, the cheeks hollow and leathery, the nose raptorlike, the chin covered in snowy whiskers stained with tobacco, it was the countenance of a man who had drifted far from the amenities of civilization.

His body was swaddled in layers of wool and canvas, his head wrapped in a brown, turbanlike cloth. I went to shake his hand, and Kaftan said, "Fyodorovich, I've brought you a guest from America."

He held the lantern up and looked me over. "America!" He laughed, exposing his bare gums. "You're joking. All the way from America? Come in. Come in."

Removing the padlock on the door, he ushered us into a tidy, low-ceilinged, one-room cabin. It was furnished with an iron stove, a small desk, and two beds, both of which were covered with cotton bedspreads. He lit a kerosene lamp and threw kindling and wood into the stove. Soon the fire was blazing, taking the chill off the room.

Crouching next to the stove, Fyodorovich began relaying the news from Sunny Lake, where he was the only human inhabitant. Just yesterday, he had seen deer tracks in the mud, followed by the paw prints of a large wolf. A brown bear had been prowling around the guest cabin lately, "a big, beautiful fellow with shades of silver in his fur." In the spring, a young bear pounced on a guest-cabin window to get at some food inside. He retreated, his injured paw leaving blood in the snow. Last winter had been a mild one, part of a warming trend that Fyodorovich had noticed in his corner of Siberia.

"The climate is changing for the worse," said Fyodorovich, offering up his interpretation of the greenhouse effect. "It has to do with a film over the earth. It's all those gasses in the air."

I had feared he might not want to discuss his years in the gulag, but talk of the climate reminded him of the hard frosts in the labor camps. "We worked outside, summer and winter, blasting the earth and sifting it for gold. Those were real frosts then, fifty-five or sixty degrees below zero. Now there are a few days of real cold like that, and then it warms up to forty below."

Sensing the conversation might last awhile, Kaftan walked out to the truck and returned with a plastic bag filled with red packages of Prima cigarettes. Fyodorovich—whose full name was Vladimir Fyodorovich Afanasiev—opened up a pack, sniffed one of the nonfilter cigarettes, lit up, and took a deep pull.

"It looks like good tobacco . . . smells okay," he said, rolling the cigarette between his fingers. I had the sense he had run out of smokes.

"There's a lot of bad tobacco and vodka now. Before the war— well, that was good tobacco. Oh, it was aromatic! I've smoked since the war and now I couldn't live without it. I could live without vodka, but never without cigarettes. Since I was a boy, I have loved the aroma of tobacco. Before the war, they made these long cigarettes, and they were so aromatic. My father smoked *mahorka* [a homemade tobacco].

"Before the war, all the products tasted better. They were real. How I remember the bread! That was real bread! You'd be walking toward a village and someone would be baking bread at home and you could smell that bread from several kilometers away. Now you put bread right up to your nose and it hardly smells like anything."

He had been resting on his haunches for twenty-five minutes, lighting up several cigarettes in that time. His weather-beaten face was softened by his big, toothless laughs and twinkling blue eyes. They gleamed when he spoke about a childhood—lived at the peak of Stalin's terror—that he nonetheless remembered with fondness.

There was silence in the cabin, save for the crackling of the fire.

"I've gotten used to the quiet here, the honking of the geese and the swans, the sound of a bear when it growls. . . . But there's more poaching around here now, and the poachers are mainly the big bosses. They come here, shoot up everything, take what they want. Hell, they've stolen everything—there isn't anything left to steal."

"How long have you been living here?" I asked.

"I was released from the [labor] camp in 1949. I had no clothes, no transportation, no money, nowhere to go. So I stayed. I'm an aborigine now!"

He laughed hard at his own joke. It was 4 A.M. Sergei Kaftan walked to the truck and retrieved some bread and a package of hot dogs. The old man—he was seventy—gummed them, and he and I had a shot of vodka. Fyodorovich would have talked until dawn, but Sergei and I were tired.

"Well, Fyodorovich, it's late," said Sergei. "We ought to try and get some sleep."

"Of course, of course," said the old man. "Please, please, sleep all you want. Is it warm enough in here for you?"

I walked out with him. The temperature was just above freezing, the sky overcast, the night black as pitch. Sunny Lake was a few feet from our cabin, and the ducks in the middle of it were jabbering away, disturbed by our presence. I thanked Fyodorovich for his warm welcome, said good-night, and watched as he returned to his cabin in the woods, his lantern swaying in the forest.

Sergei was already asleep, and I crawled into my bag, extinguished the guttering lamp, and listened to the silence outside. A swan trumpeted on the lake. Drifting off, I felt at home for the first time in months.

. . .

Fyodorovich crept in at eight-thirty. The fire had gone out, and the cabin was freezing. As Sergei slept, I shimmied into my clothes and walked outside. In front of me was Sunny Lake, its waters still and black. The sky was overcast, and as I surveyed it, Fyodorovich said, "Before, in September, the air had a beautiful clarity about it. Now it seems to rain a lot."

I looked over Fyodorovich's realm in the daylight. The guest cabin, set in a clearing, was a log hut, painted green, with a peeling, tar-paper roof. It had two small windows, one on each side, and a front porch. Nearby, a few feet from the lake, were a table and benches made of wooden planks. Next to them was an outdoor stove, coated in white stucco. Behind the cabin, blending into the forest, were an outhouse and sheds where Fyodorovich stored firewood and supplies.

Sunny Lake was a tranquil, picturesque body of water about two miles long and a mile and a half wide, surrounded by slate-colored hills that rose to perhaps two thousand feet. Many of the slopes were barren scree, others were clothed in larches whose needles had turned brown and were spilling on the ground. Flocks of ducks rafted on the water and flew, with rapid wing-beats, around the lake. A small group of whooper swans—enormous white birds—could be seen on the far side of the lake. From time to time, small squadrons of the swans trumpeted mournfully overhead, bound for southern China.

In the pebbly shallows, two small, metal boats were tethered to the shore.

Forty yards from the guest cabin, Fyodorovich had built a log bathhouse, and next to it was a spring. It bubbled out of the permafrost and meandered, gin-clear, in front of the bath. There, Fyodorovich had built a wooden dam. Above the dam was an inviting pool about three feet deep and six feet across. Below it was an even deeper pool, and just beyond that, the stream emptied into the lake. Kneeling next to the dam, I splashed water on my face, cupped my hands, and drank several mouthfuls. It was uncommonly sweet and cold, and drinking it brought on a momentary, stabbing pain above my eyes. Beyond the bath was the forest, and the path to Fyodorovich's cabin.

Returning to the table by the lake, Fyodorovich stoked a fire and prepared tea. He had strung out his nets early that morning and promised that after breakfast we would check them and fish for arctic char.

Kaftan emerged, and we breakfasted in the chilly morning air on canned beef, hot dogs, bread, and tea. Fyodorovich drank his tea black, a brew so strong it would have sent my heart into fibrillation. "We have a saying," he said. "Before you drink tea, you feel weak. After you drink tea, you are completely without strength."

He laughed again. In the light of day, I studied him more closely. He was about five feet nine, wiry, and wore a soiled green coat, a tattered brown sweater, gray pants, and rubber boots. His brown, turbanlike cap was of a type worn by Russian construction workers, and underneath it was a full head of gray hair. His beard was white and wavy, his cheeks sunken and etched with lines. Fyodorovich's hands belonged to a man who had spent a life outdoors—gnarly, calloused, and scarred. The digits of his right hand were stained orange from a half century of tobacco.

After breakfast, we unloaded Fyodorovich's supplies, storing them in the guest cabin. The old man grabbed a 120-pound sack of sugar, tossed it over his shoulder, and carried it twenty yards into the cabin.

Before setting out for Fyodorovich's, I had worried about encountering an eccentric, taciturn recluse. Instead, sitting in front of me was a quintessential Siberian *muzhik*, or peasant, a gregarious figure who—in his striking, bearded appearance and unsullied way of life—seemed like a character from the pages of Tolstoy. Even more, he struck me as a Russian version of Dersu, the aboriginal hunter in the classic work *Dersu the Trapper* by turn-of-the-century Russian explorer V. K. Arseniev. Both Fyodorovich and Dersu lived alone in the wilds of the Russian Far East, both were on intimate terms with the natural world, and both were dismayed by the incursion of modern life into their domains.

As Sergei went to work on his truck, Fyodorovich settled in next to the stove, leaned back on his haunches, lit his pungent Primas, and told me about his life.

He was born in 1926 in the Lipetsk region, about three hundred miles south of Moscow. His father, who fought in World War I, was a factory worker and musician. His mother worked on a chicken farm. In 1933, the family lived through a famine, and six years later Fyodorovich's mother became ill, forcing him to drop out of school in the sixth grade to work at an electric power plant.

The German army invaded Russia on June 22, 1941, and by late summer the Nazis were rolling over Fyodorovich's village of Livny. Only fifteen, he joined a Russian sapper unit, helping build trenches and fortifications. He last saw his family in September 1941. The following month, as he sat atop an army truck spotting Nazi planes, his convoy was attacked from the air. Wounded in the legs and buttocks, Fyodorovich was thrown from the truck and buried under a pile of dirt and debris. A soldier rescued him when he saw the boy's hand protruding from the earth, its fingers wiggling.

Burned and badly wounded, he spent eight months in the hospital, then was transferred to Sverdlovsk in the Urals, where he sorted metal at a steel plant. Later, he was sent to work at a munitions factory, where he spent the duration of the war. There, he learned that his father, brother, and sister had been killed by the Germans. His mother was still alive.

"There were a lot of families like that in the war," he said.

In 1946, with the war over, he met a young woman and married her. They were together for about a month when he sought permission to visit his mother and was turned down. Deciding to go anyway, he hopped a westbound train with some friends, and was arrested at the second stop. Thus began his trip into the gulag.

Sentenced to eight years for deserting his job at a military factory, he was held two months at an ancient prison in Sverdlovsk. Next came a grueling, two-month train ride in the fall of 1946 to the Pacific Ocean port of Nakhodka. Packed like livestock into the cars, shitting in buckets, their food often commandeered by hungry soldiers, the prisoners became emaciated and ill. Some died.

In the early spring of 1947, Fyodorovich was crammed into a ship with several thousand other prisoners and sent to Magadan. During the journey, which took more than two weeks, the prisoners had little food, even less water, and were vomiting and defecating everywhere. They sat for a long time in Magadan harbor, waiting for the ice to clear.

"Many, many died along the way," said Fyodorovich. "The sailors

the hills silent. Several times, flights of swans crossed high overhead. Once, a pair glided to a landing about three hundred yards away. I had little desire to row to shore. If I had been catching fish, I would probably have stayed on the water until evening.

Fyodorovich and Kaftan were frying the pink-fleshed char on the outdoor stove. They had laid out bread, butter, and vodka on the scarred wooden table. When the fish were done, Kaftan placed them on newspaper and we broke off chunks of the steaming flesh. Just an hour out of the lake, it was succulent, ambrosial.

"I like these fish in tomato sauce," said Fyodorovich. "What's that new tomato sauce from America? Kapsup?"

"Ketchup," I replied.

"That's it. Kapsup. Yes, that's very tasty."

I poured glasses of pepper vodka for Fyodorovich and myself, and we toasted everyone's health. In the winter, he would sometimes go weeks or months without a drink—last winter he even ran out of sugar—and he luxuriated in the company of guests.

It was time for a bath. Kaftan and I wandered over to the small, log bathhouse, a two-room structure with an inner sanctum for steaming, and an outer room for drinking, smoking, and drying. Fyodorovich had been stoking the fire since morning, and even the outer room was hot. As Kaftan and I stripped down, I noticed Fyodorovich placing several green champagne bottles in the spring-fed stream outside the bathhouse door.

Kaftan was first into the bath, emerging lobster red five minutes later, trails of steam rising from his glistening, muscular body. Fyodorovich ducked out of the bathhouse and returned with one of the champagne bottles. There was no label on the old bottle, and its mouth was sealed with a plastic cap, held in place by a piece of cloth.

"Kvass!" announced Fyodorovich, sliding a few chipped teacups across a wooden table.

Kvass is a traditional Russian drink made from fermented bread or rye flour, and is sometimes mildly alcoholic. I had tried some commercially produced kvass in Russia and found it sour and repugnant.

"Fyodorovich's kvass is the best," said Kaftan. "The rest doesn't compare."

The old man popped the top and a gusher of brown foam shot

two feet into the air and splatted on the floor. Half the bottle was lost in the opening burst, and Kaftan rushed to get the cups under the lip. We each wound up with a few ounces. I took a sip. The taste was pungent and magnificent, a little like cider, a little like dark beer, but mainly unlike anything I had ever had before. It was tangy, sweet, rich, yeasty, and earthy. It tasted like Russia.

Fyodorovich described how kvass should be made—dark bread, boiling water, sugar, yeast, raisins, honey, mint, and the essence of apples and pears. He made do with what he had at Sunny Lake.

"Yes, that's real kvass!" he said. "We call that Petrovsky kvass, from the time they made kvass under Peter the Great. For real Petrovsky kvass, you need to use beet sugar. Earlier, nearly all Russians drank kvass. Now they drink your Coca-Cola."

I ducked into the steam room and sat down on the upper wooden shelf. Within minutes, sweat began dripping from my pores. I stood it as long as I could, then flayed myself with birch leaves. As I emerged from the steam room, Fyodorovich urged me to take the full cure, which included a plunge in the stream. I walked into the ice-cold pool above the dam, squatted down, and poured water over my crimson, steaming body. As an experience, it was somewhere between invigorating and life-threatening.

Hustling back into the bath, I returned to the steam room. Fyodorovich followed me in and hollered, *"Na polok! Na polok!"*—"On the shelf! On the shelf!"—which meant it was time to clamber onto the top deck and flagellate myself again with birch leaves. He tossed several more ladles of water on the red-hot stones, filling the chamber with scalding clouds of steam, what the Marquis de Custine called "boiling fog." My hide seared, barely able to breathe, I lashed myself with the birch leaves. Fyodorovich tossed another ladle of water onto the stones. His eyes burned with joy.

"Davai! Davai!"—"Let's go! Let's go!" he shouted. He shook his fist and laughed as I peeled off skin with the birch twigs.

"That's it! That's it! Keep it up! You got it! . . . Sergei, look, he's just like a Russian."

I bolted from the steam chamber into the forty-five-degree air. Standing there, the steam billowing like smoke from my flesh, I braced myself for the stream. I jumped in, rolled around, threw water over my face, head, and back. It was bracing beyond words.

The three of us sat in the dimly lit drying room, filled with the odors of tobacco smoke, sweat, and kvass. Fyodorovich opened another bottle, and I drank several cups and listened to the rambling, free-associating monologue pour out of the contented, mildly inebriated old man.

It was midafternoon, and Kaftan had to drive back that evening to Ust Omchug. I wanted to stay longer at Fyodorovich's, so we worked out a plan. Kaftan would return and send another truck driver, whom I would pay to fetch me in a day or two.

Fyodorovich nodded off in the bathhouse, and Kaftan drove off in his truck. The bath, the vodka, and the kvass had drained me, and at 5 P.M. I lay down in the guest cabin for a nap. I awoke three hours later when Fyodorovich stepped into the hut. Outside, night was falling.

We walked in the twilight to Fyodorovich's cabin. Along the way, we heard swans squawking and trumpeting on the lake.

"That's the young ones raising a fuss," said Fyodorovich, holding a lantern in his right hand. "They want to stay here. They like the motherland. They don't want to migrate. They don't understand it's time to go because soon there won't be any water here. It will all be ice. . . . Even if I was hungry, I wouldn't shoot a swan. They're very trusting. They'll take a piece of bread right out of your hand.

"In the last twenty years, people have killed nature around here. They don't understand you have to respect and preserve it, not kill it. All our local game warden understands is how to kill. Even the lake has become poor."

His cabin, located about three hundred yards from the lake, was a one-room log structure with a front porch supported on one side by a massive larch tree. A table, covered in oilcloth, and a wooden bench sat on the porch. Jackets and pots and pans hung under the eaves of the cabin. A raised garden plot sat in front of the house. In the dusky light, I could make out traps, sleds, and other doodads hanging from the porch, cabin, and trees.

Producing an old shovel that he had taken with him when he left the gulag, he said, "This is a real American shovel from Roosevelt's time. It's built to last. It dug blasting holes at the mines beautifully."

Inside, the cabin—which Fyodorovich had built in 1965—was neat and cozy. The ceiling was about five feet high, the room about eight feet by ten feet, the logs ten inches in diameter, with moss chinking in between. There were two single beds, a desk, a chair, a small bookshelf, and a framed drawing of a fairy-tale Russian witch, Baba Yaga. He showed me several old black-and-white photographs of him and his friends hunting and fishing. In one, he was pictured with a brown bear cub, Masha, whose mother was killed. He then raised the cub for several months.

I asked if he had any pictures of his family. "They didn't last," he said. "They took them away at the camp."

We walked back to the lake in the dark, Fyodorovich carrying a bucket of mountain cranberries, which I had told him I fancied. He lit a fire in the stove, and we ate leftover char and drank a few shots of vodka.

"People have become synthetic, and what is synthetic is destroying man. I live in nature, but everywhere people are moving away from nature. People are destroying themselves. They have become extremely educated and invented computers. But nature gave birth to man, and man has forgotten that. Man is the highest reflection of nature, but he is destroying himself.

"Nature teaches me and tells me what is real and what isn't. I can read nature, but now it's becoming more difficult to read. . . . I don't need television. That's not real. I need a squirrel jumping on the table and eating out of my hand. That is truth."

Fyodorovich said he was suffering from hernias, ulcers, and other ailments. "I don't see much more time in front of me," he said.

He was nodding off, and I proposed that we go to bed. He rose, a little wobbly, and I held his elbow as we walked out of the cabin. I suggested he stay with me and avoid the long walk back to his cabin in the dark, but he declined. The lantern disappeared into the taiga.

The wind had risen, and between swiftly moving clouds I caught a glimpse of the Big Dipper. Lulled by the sound of the breeze in the pines and the waves lapping against the metal hulls of Fyodorovich's boats, I went to sleep. At 4 A.M., I walked out in bare feet to relieve myself. The night was still. Thinking of the "big, beautiful" bear that was fond of wandering around the guest cabin, I hustled inside and slipped into bed.

. . .

We went fishing the next morning. Fyodorovich rowed me across the lake to one of his favorite spots for netting char, his powerful strokes propelling the boat swiftly across the calm surface of the water. Once again the weather was overcast and cool, and swans were on the move.

As he rowed, Fyodorovich pointed out his trapping route in the surrounding hills. Nearly every day in winter, he strapped on skis and completed a twelve-mile circuit, checking his one hundred sable traps. Occasionally he trapped ermine or squirrel, but the previous year he'd only snared thirty-three squirrels, far from his peak of thirty-five hundred in the 1950s. Increased hunting pressure and poaching were reducing the numbers of fur-bearing animals, as well as moose and bear. Still, the area around Sunny Lake provided a subsistence living for Fyodorovich: ample fish in spring and summer, some occasional game, and enough sable—which he sold for about $80 apiece—to supply him with cigarettes and staples.

We drifted along a rocky shore, casting into the clear, green-gray water. Fyodorovich used a primitive spinning rod. We caught nothing and after two hours decided to quit. Fyodorovich said the fish did not take the hook well this late in the year. The time for angling on Sunny Lake, he said, was in late spring, when the ice had melted and the char gulped insects off the surface.

Checking his nets, we discovered they held two dozen char.

Fyodorovich prepared fish soup, tossing in the char, potatoes, onions, and greens he had grown in his garden. It was delicious, and sitting by the lakeshore I ate three bowls and joined him in a few toasts. He told a story—confirmed later by Sergei Kaftan—of adopting an orphaned moose. The moose stayed with him for a year, finally dying when it choked on a plastic bag it found in the taiga.

Two shotgun blasts sounded from the far end of the lake, and Fyodorovich wheeled around, fretting that the men were illegally bagging whooper swans.

That evening, at 6 P.M., my ride arrived. The driver's name was Gleb, a bearded, bucktoothed outdoorsman who knew Fyodorovich well. With him were his brother and thirteen-year-old nephew. I had enjoyed having Fyodorovich and the lake to myself, and their presence was unsettling. At one point, the boy turned on the radio in his uncle's jeep, disturbing the peace. I asked him to turn it off. Later, I took the boy fishing. He wore a Walkman. We caught nothing.

The heavens cleared that night, and the lake reflected the light of a sky full of stars.

The next morning, we breakfasted outside under gray skies, eating berries, fish soup, bread, and sausage. The men asked Fyodorovich about his trapping.

"With furs today, everyone is putting money in their pockets from my work. All that's left for me is cigarette money. I could sell fish. But that's not right. The lake doesn't belong to me."

Gleb and his brother rowed several hundred yards into Sunny Lake, checking the nets they had set the night before. They returned with about fifty char, which, at Fyodorovich's urging, they threw into a burlap sack and loaded into their jeep. A nonstop breakfast, complete with vodka, continued. Fyodorovich plainly did not want us to leave, proposing one toast after another. He wished me success in my career, and I wished him health and a long life. I told him I'd be back, with a bottle of ketchup for his fried fish.

The time came for the last toast, and he grabbed my arm and linked it with his. I had barely been sipping the vodka all morning, but this glass I drank to the bottom. As we said good-bye, Fyodorovich and I enveloped each other in a bear hug.

The jeep bounced down the rutted trail, and I turned around in my seat, hoping for one last glimpse of the old man. Framed by the lake and the gray hills beyond, he was on his haunches, next to the stove, smoking a Prima.

8.

KAMCHATKA

The Utkholok River was far from civilization, but not so far that the brown bears
didn't recognize the sound of an outboard
motor. They knew its whine meant trouble,
usually in the form of hunters. So it was not surprising that soon
after our expedition arrived on this tundra river in western Kamchatka, the bears ceased gorging on the last of the coho salmon run
and cleared out. What remained were scattered, rotting fish carcasses,
and enormous bear tracks. Stamped deep into the muddy bank, these
paw prints were the size of a man's head. They were everywhere,
stretching for miles up and down the Utkholok, so thick in places
that the shore had the churned-up look of a horse paddock. The high
mud walls that flanked the river bore signs of bear, as well—deep
notches scratched into the earth, marking the spots where the animals clawed their way to the khaki-colored tundra above.

The awesome size and implied power of these bear tracks left me
with conflicting desires; I wanted to see one of these beasts, but from
a respectable distance.

Alone on the upper reaches of the river, Misha Skopets and I
passed scores of fresh tracks and whiffed the rotting coho. From time
to time, in the clear, tea-colored waters of the Utkholok, we would
catch sight of a red-tinted, spawned-out, dying salmon drifting downstream.

Misha Skopets was one of the more original and likable characters
I had met on my trip. He possessed a droll detachment that came
partly, I suspected, from his being a Jew in Russia, accustomed to

the role of outsider. He was from a family of intellectuals—his father was a film director, his mother a musician—but Misha himself was difficult to categorize. He was a respected fish biologist who had discovered a new genus of char in the Russian Arctic. He was, perhaps, the best fly fisherman in all Russia. And he ran a small eco-tourism company, based in Magadan, that catered to foreign naturalists and fly fishermen visiting the Russian Far East. Inevitably, as I prepared for my journey across Russia, I began to hear about Misha and telephoned him. His advice turned out to be excellent.

After a dozen conversations, via phone and E-mail, we met at last in Petropavlovsk-Kamchatski, the capital city of the Kamchatka Peninsula. It was late September, my trip was nearly over, and as I prepared to meet Misha and join a Russian-American expedition, I felt conflicting emotions. I was happy to have emerged unscathed from the overland journey and delighted not to be troubled with the daily concerns—where I would sleep, eat, and go to the bathroom—that had nagged me for three months. Still, I was wary of joining a formal expedition, and uncomfortable, after living for so long among the Russians, with the prospect of being thrown together with Americans.

Landing in Petropavlovsk-Kamchatski, I took a taxi to an apartment where Misha was staying. I trudged up several flights of steps, rang a buzzer, and waited. Soon, the door swung open, and there stood Misha, a short, well-built man of forty-two with cool, green eyes, a closely trimmed beard, and a rapidly thinning head of brown hair. His voice was slightly nasal, his manner gentle, his gaze steady. Around Misha, I often felt I was talking too much.

As we waited for word of where we would meet our fellow expedition members, Misha and I talked about his life in Russia. His father, mother, and sister had emigrated to America and were flourishing. Misha could have joined his family at any time, but he declined. Given the number of Russians—and Russian Jews—eager to flee the uncertainty of their homeland for stable, more prosperous shores, I asked Misha why he remained in Magadan.

"The simple reason is that I don't like to live in a country where there are too many people and not enough nature," said Misha, who spoke excellent English. "I ask my American friends, 'How many days did you spend fly-fishing last year?' and they might reply, 'Fifteen.' Well, I spent ninety days fly-fishing last year, not to mention the time ice-fishing and hunting.

"I am used to the kind of forests we have in Siberia—forests that don't end. If there is a highway at the other end of a forest, there is a different feeling. You know that when you walk into our Siberian forests, you can just keep going and going, and you'll never meet anyone coming into the woods from the other side."

Misha and I weren't sure where we were heading, but we knew what we were after: steelhead trout. After being ferried upstream in a Mercury jet boat, we left Misha's rubber raft on a pebble bar and walked farther upriver, aiming for a high, rocky cliff, the presence of which usually meant a steelhead pool in the river below. The pool looked more promising than expected: about one hundred yards long and fifty yards wide, it was dark and deep and flowed gently beneath the rock ledge. The weather was cool, the skies gray.

Steelhead are like Atlantic salmon—anadromous fish that are hatched in freshwater, migrate to the open ocean, and return to their native streams to spawn. Unlike Pacific salmon, all of which die after spawning, Atlantic salmon and steelhead often survive spawning and can return many times to their native rivers. You fish for steelhead the same way you do for Atlantic salmon—wading into a pool where they may be resting on their upstream migration, casting your fly downstream at a forty-five-degree angle, letting it swing toward shore, stripping in your line, taking a step downstream, and casting again. Like salmon, steelhead don't actively feed on their spawning run, so catching one of these fish is a matter of mystical serendipity. A steelhead a day is a heroic angling achievement.

Fisherman's intuition is an unreliable thing. Often, I approach a stretch of river with a strong sense that it holds fish, and that I'm going to catch one. Just as frequently I come away empty-handed. But as I waded into this pool on the Utkholok, I did so with the absolute certainty that it was home to steelhead. As far as Misha and I knew, no one had ever fly-fished this section of the river. Given my general ineptitude, I cast surprisingly well, and my fly swung through the pool in a crisp, straight line, with none of the bows that can make a fly look unnatural.

The steelhead took my artificial on the fifth or sixth cast, in the middle of the swing. It did not smack the fly in one stunning blow. Rather, in the blink of an eye, I felt the fly stop, my line tighten, and the rod bend. Instinctively, I lifted the rod, setting the hook, and the fish took off. It ran downstream, peeling line off my reel, and I could tell from the bow in my rod and the resistance of the fish that it was sizable, perhaps fifteen pounds. It stopped near the bottom of the pool. The line thrummed. Misha walked up and told me to begin slowly forcing the steelhead upstream, warning that it was still "green" and not to apply too much pressure. I reeled, and the fish gradually followed. Then the line went slack. The steelhead was gone.

"Reel in, let me see your fly," instructed Misha.

I complied.

"Your hook's dull—that's why it came off. It was never really hooked properly."

This was the fourth steelhead I had hooked and lost in three days. The reasons were myriad—dull hooks, failure to give the fish slack when it jumped, acts of God. Once there was the inexcusable sin: the fly slipping off because of a poor knot. I got back a piece of leader, on the end of which was a curlicue that looked like a pig's tail. Steelhead are powerful and unforgiving, and when you fish for them, you'd better do everything right.

"It happens," said Misha. "Go through the pool again. There are steelhead in here."

On my second pass through the pool, I was nearing the end of the run when a steelhead grabbed my fly. It ran across the pool and downstream, and for more than five minutes I fought the fish, which felt larger than the previous one. My hook was sharp, and the knot—tied by Misha—infallible. Gradually, I muscled the fish over to the pebbly shore. Then I caught sight of it in the shallows, a striking silver creature, about a yard long, with tinges of green and a faint, rose-colored stripe on its flank. The fish—less than ten feet away—was tiring, and I backed up on the bank, pulling it steadily toward shore. Then, in about a foot of water, its flank scraped the rocky bottom, and it bolted. Streaking toward deep water, the steelhead shook its head angrily and spit out my fly. Number five was gone.

If the Kola Peninsula was the great redoubt of Atlantic salmon, then Kamchatka—four thousand miles to the east—was the stronghold of the salmon's Pacific Ocean cousin, the steelhead trout. From the moment I hatched the plan for my trip, I knew I wanted to fish for steelhead in Kamchatka. There was only one way to legally do that— to participate in a joint Russian-American scientific expedition studying these fish. Though still numbering in the tens of thousands, Kamchatka steelhead had been heavily poached for several decades, spurring the Soviet government to declare the fish threatened in 1983. Catching them was illegal; in all of Russia, only the Russian-American scientific team had authority to do so.

The expedition was the brainchild of two strong-willed characters, a Russian scientist and an American conservationist. The Russian was Dr. Ksenia A. Savvaitova, a Moscow State University fish biologist who had first come to Kamchatka thirty years ago to study steelhead. The American was Pete Soverel, president of the nonprofit Wild Salmon Center. An angler and naturalist, he had arrived in Kamchatka with the ardor of a man who had seen steelhead trout populations decimated in America's Pacific Northwest and was determined not to let the same thing happen in the Russian Far East.

Together, they cooked up an unconventional but effective funding scheme. Like nearly everyone else in the Russian scientific establishment, Savvaitova had seen her research budget wither away in the post-Soviet era. So they hatched a simple plan: American anglers would pay $5,500 apiece to fly-fish for the steelhead used in the study. That money would underwrite Dr. Savvaitova's work, while also allowing the American fishermen to be the lead specimen gatherers for the Kamchatka Steelhead Project—catching the fish, taking scale and fin samples, measuring them, and tagging them before release.

For me, the appeal of traveling to unspoiled tundra rivers, filled with steelhead, was immense. For three months, I had fished with Russians in inhabited areas and had witnessed unchecked poaching across the country. Poachers had hounded salmon on Kola's accessible rivers, had nearly wiped out taimen in many parts of Siberia, had hauled out grayling by the bucketful from countless streams. After pursuing salmon, grayling, and char across Russia with decidedly mixed results, I was beginning to think that to fish this country properly you needed three things: a rod, a reel, and a helicopter.

Steelhead also had a special appeal. These wild fish—closely related to the rainbow trout of inland waters—carried out epic migrations, inhabited lovely rivers, and often were huge. Unfortunately, a host of heedless actions—the unrestrained damming of rivers, pollution, logging, overfishing, and misguided hatchery programs that had genetically contaminated wild stocks—had devastated steelhead populations in California, Oregon, Idaho, and Washington. Once, millions of wild steelhead had migrated up rivers such as the Columbia, Deschutes, and Umpqua. By the mid-1990s, wild steelhead populations had fallen in the Pacific Northwest to the point where most populations were listed as extinct, endangered, or threatened. Alaska and British Columbia had more steelhead, but even there overfishing—largely as a by-catch of Pacific salmon—had taken a heavy toll.

Kamchatka was a different story. Every fall, steelhead still migrated from the Sea of Okhotsk into at least a dozen pristine rivers on the western coast. The peninsula's steelhead run was still relatively healthy for two main reasons: Kamchatka was remote and, in Soviet times, had been closed to most foreigners and many Russians because of a plethora of military installations. But everything had loosened up in Russia, including access to Kamchatka and control over poachers. Bands of fish pirates strung nets across the mouths of the Utkholok and other rivers during the peak of the fall migration, hauling out steelhead by the ton. Savvaitova and Soverel were hoping to put a stop to this. I wanted to see this steelhead paradise, and to gauge whether Russia—where conservation was still a dim concept—might be able to do more for the fish than we had.

Failing to hook another steelhead in the first hole, Misha and I returned to his raft and began floating down the Utkholok. Dr. Savvaitova and her colleagues had asked the anglers to catch and kill a few dozen rainbow trout, for they were intent on studying the relationship between the so-called resident rainbows—which stayed in the river year-round—and their cousins that had taken to the ocean. Farther down, near the Sea of Okhotsk, the Utkholok was a slower-moving, whiskey-colored stream, surrounded by flat tundra that stretched to the coast. But where Misha and I were, a dozen miles from the sea, the Utkholok was narrower, swifter, and prettier. The upper river ran through a hilly landscape with stunted birches and pine bush covering the slopes. It looped back around on itself and had numerous long, shallow riffles with gouged-out banks. The water possessed a slight greenish cast. It was a superb spot for rainbow trout.

Fishing from gravel bars, Misha began catching the biggest rainbow trout I'd seen in my life. Some were nearly two feet long, and all had prodigious girth. (That evening, when the scientists began studying our trout, they discovered that two of them weighed five pounds.) They were a chrome color with hues of copper and green and had vivid pink bands running down their sides. I caught several myself, and they fought with stirring wildness, often dancing on their tails as they tried to throw the hook.

In addition to the rainbow trout, we caught a couple of coho salmon, a mess of white-spotted char, and numerous Dolly Varden char, two of which we grilled over a campfire for lunch. As we ate, Misha continued the story—begun days earlier—of how he'd wound up in Magadan.

He was raised in Sverdlovsk, where he avidly read Jack London and resolved to live a life that would take him into the wilderness. "Jack London was like mother's milk," said Misha. "In the Communist period, the only way we had to find freedom was to go into the toilet, lock the door, and read."

After graduating from Ural State University in Sverdlovsk, he wrote biological institutes across Siberia, hoping to work in a remote region. He was accepted at an institute in Magadan, where he remained, eventually marrying and fathering a son. Misha had spent months in the wilds of the Russian Far East, traveling along hundreds of miles of rivers. On four occasions he had visited the far-flung lake Elgygytkyn, above the Arctic Circle, where he discovered a new type of char.

"I can say that in my family I am something of a black sheep. Everyone is a musician or a doctor. But my great-grandfather was the chief forester in Simbirsk in the czarist era. Maybe it's genetic in that sense, I don't know."

For me, Misha was a window on Russia, and something of an oracle. For three months, I had been assaulted with impressions of the country and was struggling to make sense of it all. Misha—who once said, "I don't feel comfortable with most Russians"—intuitively understood his native land, yet remained at a distance from it.

Discussing the widespread inability of the government and factories to pay salaries, Misha said, "There is the story of the gypsy who was teaching his horse not to eat because it would be cheaper that way. And it almost worked, if the horse hadn't died."

Referring to Russia's Byzantine laws and punitive tax codes, Misha quoted from a nineteenth-century traveler: "Russian laws are harsh, and the only thing that softens their impact is that no one enforces them."

When the conversation turned to the Russian character, Misha said, "The main thing that separates Russia from the West today, and perhaps always will, is the absolute lack of respect for laws among Russians, the belief that laws have no relevance to their lives and are not to be followed."

Later, an American fisherman asked Misha if Russia would ever set its house in order. "No," he replied. "For the last thousand years Russia has been an example to the Western world of how not to do things. So that to believe that now, all of a sudden, Russia is going to go straight, well, I don't think so.

"It's like having an animal in the zoo that is fed every day in a cage. Now the cage is open. For me, the important thing is the freedom. Some people got freedom, but just asked, 'What can I do with this freedom?' and stayed in their cages. It has never been a problem for me. I know what to do with it.

"I'm not optimistic. I'm pretty optimistic about myself. But I don't think Russia will ever be a happy, wealthy culture."

Misha seemed to place his faith in only a few things, including the restorative power of Siberia's wilderness. He was fond of quoting a line from Pushkin:

"There is no happiness, but there is peace, and freedom."

. . .

In late afternoon, Misha and I floated down a narrow branch of the Utkholok, shooting past high peat banks. Blasting out of a swift-moving chute of water, we found ourselves in a lovely pool, about forty yards wide and more than one hundred yards long. An island and gravel bar stood at the head of the pool, and looming over the hole was a high bluff. A steelhead porpoised on the river, near the far side. I couldn't reach him, but Misha could, making a dozen casts to the fish with his two-handed Spey rod. Once, the steelhead toyed with his fly, but nothing came of it.

Jumping in the raft, I paddled ten yards to the gravel bar, where I could cast into the pool from another angle. Standing on the pebbly spit of land, I heard a splash to my left and saw a disturbance in the boiling, emerald green water. A fish of sizable girth had roiled the waters just fifteen feet to my left. I stood motionless, hoping it would reappear. As I stared at the water, I noticed an odd thing. From the opposite bank, perhaps thirty feet away, a little animal was paddling furiously across the pool toward me. The creature—a mouse or a lemming—made it to the middle of the pool, swimming frantically across the strong current. Then, just as it dog-paddled over the spot of the earlier disturbance, a chunky rainbow trout rose and, with a tidy splash, devoured the frantic mouse. Now I understood what the earlier fuss was about. I had heard that Kamchatka's gargantuan rainbow trout had a fondness for mice. I had just witnessed their gluttony.

It is difficult to describe the effect of such a scene on a fly fisherman. I was standing on the shores of a wilderness stream, and just a few feet from me a greedy horde of rainbow trout—huge beyond imagining—were popping disoriented mice into their mouths like so much tundra junk food. Backing up stealthily, tittering to myself and muttering, "Match the hatch! Match the hatch!"—the fly fisherman's credo to cast a fly that closely resembles what the trout are actually eating—I retreated toward the island, knelt on one knee, and pulled out Big Bertha from my fly-box. It was a brown, two-inch mouse imitation made of deer hair, and it looked remarkably like the real thing.

Crouching down, I walked a few yards onto the gravel bar, cast the mouse to the top of the pool, and let it drift like a six-course banquet over the heads of the voracious trout.

Nothing.

I tried again, the mouse floating irresistibly on the current.

Still nothing! Were they sated? Napping? Had they moved?

I tried a third time. And on this go, as the mouse bobbed like a cork on the Utkholok, the rainbow trout struck. It happened so fast I scarcely recall the attack: a barely discernible silver flash, no splash, just the hairy mouse being sucked down a mysterious trout vortex. Then my line went tight, the rod doubled over, and in a minute a fat rainbow trout, perhaps twenty inches long and weighing three pounds, was lying on the gravel bar. Later, an autopsy confirmed that he and his friends were dining on mice.

Shortly before 7 P.M., Misha and I floated the rest of the way to the camp in his raft. Drifting silently through a landscape of hillocks and muted tundra, we heard the trumpeting of swans. The sky was overcast, with a faint yellow streak on the western horizon. Listening to the gurgling waters of the Utkholok, I told Misha, "This is paradise."

"It is," he replied. "In part because any definition of paradise starts with the fact that there aren't a lot of people."

Ksenia Savvaitova did not fish, although she had a passion for steelhead that surpassed that of the American anglers in the Utkholok camp. She spent many of her days in a white tent just a few feet from the Utkholok, dead steelhead and rainbow trout laid out on a specimen table in front of her. Savvaitova was an elfin woman of about sixty with dark hair cut in a pixie style, large glasses, and an earnest gaze that often seemed just one step from a look of concern. She was energetic, quick-witted, and a good listener.

A member of the biology faculty at Moscow State University, Dr. Savvaitova was one of the most respected ichthyologists in Russia and had traveled extensively in Siberia and the Arctic studying char and other salmonid fish. She was in Kamchatka to solve the riddle of what had happened to this wild population of steelhead in recent decades, and what its fate might be in the future.

"The most important thing is that here there are fish still preserved as they were in the wild, without the effects of the hand of man," said Savvaitova. "There have been no hatcheries, no people living along many of the rivers. Here we can study this fish in its wild state."

Wild, perhaps, but not unmolested. In 1965, Dr. Savvaitova had been part of a small expedition that came to the Utkholok to study steelhead. They found an abundance of fish.

"The most striking thing is that there are a lot less steelhead in the river now," said Dr. Savvaitova as she and a colleague dissected a fish, placing samples of fins, scales, tissues, and sex organs in test tubes. "There has been a sharp fall. The main reason, we believe, is poaching. It has always gone on, but before it was more difficult to get here, and that had saved the fish. But now people can drive to the mouth of the Utkholok from [the town of] Ust-Khairyuzovo. They drive along the shore and stay for several days, even pitching tents. At the peak of the fall migration they string nets across the mouth of the river. We saw the nets last year."

Some of the worst poachers, she said, were the local fish inspectors and political bosses, who either consumed the steelhead themselves or sold them. Dr. Savvaitova was worried that if poaching intensified on rivers like the Utkholok, Kamchatka steelhead could go the way of America's. Her problem was a lack of information. After her 1965 expedition, she never received additional funding to come back to Kamchatka, returning only when she teamed up with Soverel and the Wild Salmon Center. Kamchatka's steelhead had been so little studied that she and her colleagues didn't even know all the rivers they inhabited, or in what numbers. They had only begun to work in four rivers, all of them about halfway up the western coast of Kamchatka—the Utkholok, the Tigil, the Kvachina, and the Snatol-veyem.

What they found was fascinating. Kamchatka steelhead were huge, an average of fifteen pounds, about twice the size of a typical wild steelhead of the Pacific Northwest. The Kamchatka steelhead caught by the American fly fishermen represented nineteen different age groups; in North American rivers, only three or four age groups are customarily found. And about 75 percent of the Kamchatka steelhead were repeat spawners—fish that had migrated from the ocean to their natal rivers more than once. In North America, the repeat spawning rate was usually less than 5 percent.

All this meant that Kamchatka's steelhead, though under threat, were still relatively robust, certainly in comparison with steelhead populations in the Pacific Northwest. Kamchatka's steelhead appeared to be the last large, healthy population of such fish in the world, a finding that not only spurred Dr. Savvaitova and Soverel to broaden their research to other rivers, but also to intensify conservation efforts. They had to convince the locals—hoi polloi and bosses alike—to reduce poaching. In particular, they had to win over Ivan Myknov, whose firm, Wise Raven, owned one of the largest fishing fleets in the Sea of Okhotsk, catching vast quantities of salmon and crab. Myknov was the most powerful man in western Kamchatka, the "czar and father" of the region. Much of the steelhead poaching was occurring at the mouths of rivers where his firm had fish-processing plants. Without Myknov's help, the poaching would never end.

"If we start a frontal attack, they'll just kick us out of here," said Dr. Savvaitova, author of *The Noble Trouts of Kamchatka*. "We have to work the other way, to try to enlighten them, to try to explain the ecology. . . . For a long time Russians thought that their resources were inexhaustible. But recently people have realized that our natural resources are finite. Still, we are living in a different world. Your people can feed themselves. We are on an absolutely different level, the way your people were in the last century."

The call came over the radio telephone at nine-thirty in the morning: the Wise Raven company was sending a helicopter to take Soverel and a small group to the Sopochnaya River, about seventy-five miles to the south. Myknov, perhaps hearing of the small fortunes being made from the salmon camps of the Kola Peninsula, had decided to get into the recreational-fishing business in Kamchatka. Although without Savvaitova and Soverel he couldn't legally catch steelhead, Myknov could bring in anglers to catch rainbow trout, salmon, and char. He had chosen the Sopochnaya as the site of his first venture and, after losing a newly built camp to a flood, was scouting a second location. Myknov wanted to bring Soverel and his expedition to the river the following year, and Soverel was interested: the Sopochnaya was a steelhead river, and no one had fly-fished it before. Soverel also wanted to meet Myknov.

The gray MI-8, its sides smeared black with engine exhaust, touched down behind the Utkholok camp at 11 A.M. On board was Zhenya Poloskov, Myknov's representative and the man building the camp on the Sopochnaya. Several people from our camp, including Soverel and Dr. Savvaitova, boarded the helicopter, and we flew south, skimming the bluffs along the Sea of Okhotsk. Shallow, muddy flats lay near the shoreline, and beyond, in the gray water, I saw a white beluga whale rise to the surface. The temperature was in the forties, the sky covered with a high, silvery overcast. The MI-8 flew over Ust-Khairyuzovo, a ragtag harbor that sheltered part of Myknov's fishing fleet, then continued south for ten more minutes. To the east, as far as the eye could see, the tundra was a maze of rivers and streams, stretching to a line of mountains on the horizon. There was no sign of civilization.

Soon we were over Ust Sopochnoye, where a ramshackle fish-processing plant and an abandoned border guard post were plopped down on a sandy spit of land. The site was a jumble of wrecked wooden buildings and dozens of rusted fifty-gallon drums. Turning inland, we flew low over a landscape that was only beginning to show its fall colors—chartreuse birch and aspen, and tundra grasses going from green to gold. Soon we were over the Sopochnaya, a dark stream that followed a wildly meandering course through a flat landscape, broken occasionally by low hills. The noise of the helicopter drove flocks of ducks off the river, which was about fifty yards wide.

The makeshift camp was at a bend in the river that had been swamped by a freak September flood. What once had been a grassy riverbank was now a field of foot-deep, shark-gray sand. Set in the middle of this loam were several tents and a wooden bathhouse. Touching down in the sand, we quickly unloaded our jet boat and stowed our gear in a yellow tent. The helicopter took off, shooting sand in all directions, and soon there was no sound but the whisper of the Sopochnaya flowing past the camp.

The camp staff included a bearded Crimean Tatar cook named Anatoly and a Koryak native named Andrei. He was a haunted-looking figure—skinny, largely toothless, with matted, collar-length hair and a scraggly mustache and beard. Poloskov wasted no time informing us that it was a bad year for bears—the mushroom, pine nut, and berry crops had been poor, and the salmon run was over.

The brown bears in the area were hungry. A week before, as the Koryak was setting up tents, a female bear and her cub had wandered into the camp. She charged Andrei and was about to pounce on him when Poloskov's dog, a fearless laika, went after the cub. Just a few yards from the Koryak when she saw her cub being pursued, the bear broke off her attack to shoo away the dog. Andrei was unharmed.

The Sopochnaya was a pretty river, located in hillier, more forested terrain than the Utkholok. That first afternoon Soverel and I fished some promising-looking steelhead water—long pools that lay below undercut peat banks—but caught nothing. Heading back to camp at dusk, we saw a Steller's sea eagle, a relatively rare bird found on Kamchatka and in the Russian Far East. Perched on a dead tree, the enormous creature had a brilliant yellow beak, a dark body, and white patches on its shoulders. Soverel cut the engine and we drifted toward the eagle. Eyeing us as we approached, the bird showed no alarm. Finally, when we closed to about forty feet, the Steller's hopped off its perch, unfurled its enormous wings—their span was easily six feet—and with a slow, majestic whoosh, whoosh, whoosh flew to the opposite bank and circled us, its white tail and distinctive white shoulder markings plainly visible. The Steller's wing-beats were so powerful we could feel their concussive flaps as the bird flew overhead.

In the evening, Zhenya Poloskov—an affable, slender, dark-haired man of about fifty—rose to deliver a toast in the long, blue mess tent.

"We have waited a long time to cooperate with you," he said, raising his glass in Soverel and Savvaitova's direction. "We are businessmen. I say that openly. But I can tell you that if businessmen like us, with an interest in preserving steelhead, don't work together with people like you, then the steelhead will be wiped out. They will be poached out of existence."

Later, Poloskov informed Soverel and the Russian scientists that workers at the fish-processing plant at the mouth of the Sopochnaya were poaching liberally. After the Pacific salmon run had ended in September, they stayed on, netting steelhead entering the river to spawn. At times, their nets contained forty or fifty of the fish. Poloskov estimated they killed at least two tons of steelhead every fall.

That night, as rain pattered on our tent, the laika patrolled the perimeter of the camp, barking wildly on several occasions. I had no idea if the dog was repelling bear or figments of its imagination, but the laika's presence was comforting.

Under cloudy skies, we searched the river for steelhead. Mergansers scrambled across the river's surface and took flight as we approached. Peregrine falcons glided out of birch groves. One morning, in a half-mile stretch of river, five Steller's sea eagles lifted off their perches and circled overhead. As we rounded a bend, a brown bear clambered up the bank and disappeared into the tundra grass.

For two days we caught nothing. Finally, on the third, in a wide, dark pool flanked on the far side by a fifteen-foot earthen bank, Soverel caught the first steelhead on a fly in the Sopochnaya. It was a large female, weighing close to twenty pounds. Dragging it toward the pebbly shore, he dug a small pool with his boot and maneuvered the steelhead into the hole. It was a gleaming silver color, indicating it had recently entered the river from the Sea of Okhotsk. The fish lay there quietly, half-submerged, its gills opening and closing, its wild eye looking at the human shapes hovering overhead. Soverel—a tall man of fifty-five with strawberry blond hair and a closely cropped beard going gray at the chin—took samples of the steelhead's scales and fins, from which the scientists could determine its age and how many times it had entered freshwater to spawn. He measured its length and girth. Then he inserted a yellow "Floy tag" below its dorsal fin, held it upright in the stream for a minute, and let it go. The steelhead waved its tail, then lazily disappeared into the copper-colored pool.

A half hour later, Soverel—a Vietnam veteran, retired navy captain, and professor at the University of Washington—landed a second steelhead and tagged it.

That night, the vodka and the toasts flowed liberally as the group celebrated Soverel's angling success. The cook, Anatoly, was at the table, too. At dusk, as the clouds had broken up and blue skies appeared, he had watched us fly-fish in the pool by the camp. After dinner, Anatoly raised his vodka glass to make a toast.

"I'm not a fisherman," said Anatoly, a swarthy man with curly, brown hair and beard. "I don't own a fishing rod. But just seeing you fish tonight, seeing the joy I saw in your eyes when you fished, was a real pleasure."

Soverel was in fine mettle, talking expansively about the Kamchatka Steelhead Project, which he hoped would continue for twenty years. I translated his words, and as I did, Anatoly's visage turned cool. After a few minutes, Anatoly—a friendly man with a proud bearing—wandered out of the mess tent into the black night and lit up a cigarette. I joined him. Standing in the chilly air, we talked, and he scorned Soverel's crusade. He worked on commercial fishing boats as a cook and said that steelhead were plentiful in the waters around Kamchatka.

"So maybe you have lost all your steelhead in America, but don't come here telling us how to save ours," he said. "I sit here and listen to all this talk about steelhead and saving these fish, and I can't take it seriously. Is this really a problem, given all the truly serious problems in our country today? We have all these problems, and you're worried about the fish?

"What is poaching, after all? I live on the river and you're trying to tell me I can't fish here? All those toasts you make about the fish you are protecting! It seems to me that a bunch of rich people are sitting around in America and they don't have enough to do, so they're inventing all these problems."

Soverel appeared outside the tent, trying to explain his position to Anatoly. But the Russian just shook his head. The pair stood awkwardly for a moment and smiled wanly at one another, two men from two worlds, speaking entirely different languages.

The helicopter arrived the next afternoon and flew us to Ust-Khairyuzovo for a meeting with Ivan Myknov. Approaching the airport, we skimmed low over the seedy town and its crumbling docks. No one had much time, and Soverel decided to speak with the fishing magnate at the airport.

Wandering away from the helicopter, I saw a delegation approaching from a low-slung wooden building. In the center of the group, trailing a half dozen assistants, was Myknov. He was a short, dapper man, dressed in a dark suit, a blue-striped shirt, a blue-and-gold print tie, and sparkling black shoes. He appeared to be about forty, with a full head of dark brown hair, a pleasant-looking, slightly pudgy face, and a couple of gold teeth. His expression was relaxed and intelligent, his presence charismatic.

Myknov, Soverel, and Savvaitova stood in a circle. This was Soverel's initial opportunity to impress Myknov with the goals of the Kamchatka Steelhead Project, and to convince him that the region would be better off if the steelhead were unmolested and a series of tightly controlled angling camps established. Soverel gave his abbreviated spiel, and Myknov listened attentively. When the team finished, Myknov said he supported their scientific efforts and would do whatever he could to help. He said he was all for preserving steelhead populations. And he noted that although the potential income from angling camps was minuscule compared with his high-seas crab operations, he intended to establish several "first-class" camps on the Sopochnaya and other rivers. Local officials had given him the exclusive rights to develop camps along a handful of streams.

Soverel and the Russian scientists heard what they wanted to hear during the fifteen-minute meeting, and after warm farewells Soverel's group boarded the helicopter and returned to the Utkholok camp.

Soon thereafter, Myknov and a small group flew by helicopter to the Sopochnaya camp, where they met an American businessman interested in bringing anglers to western Kamchatka. Later, a man who was present told me that members of Myknov's entourage illegally netted steelhead, hauling them back to Ust-Khairyuzovo in burlap sacks.

"I don't think Myknov has a clue as to what Pete's doing," said the man. "There's no way Pete's going to stop Myknov from doing what he wants on the river."

Steelhead were running in large numbers up the Utkholok, and the seven or eight anglers in camp were sometimes catching and tagging a total of a dozen a day—a high count, given the difficulty of landing steelhead. Of the dozen American anglers in two camps, there was only one who, after eight days, had failed to catch a single steelhead. That was me. The nobler side of my character was delighted that so many fish were being caught for the greater good of science. My baser side was stewing. Group angling can be bad for the psyche, particularly when all around people are catching fish, while you couldn't land one with a stick of dynamite.

The day after returning from the Sopochnaya, I traveled to one of the most productive pools on the river. Given my abominable record, I was allowed to fish first, and about two-thirds of the way down the pool I was treated to a stirring sight. As I stripped in my fly, a massive, unseen steelhead followed it for about five feet, creating a wake. I cast again, and once again this Moby Dick followed my fly, literally making waves. I cast twice more, but the wake did not materialize.

Deciding to change flies, I reeled in my orange-and-red General Practitioner, only to discover the terrible truth. Due to poor casting, my fly had become tangled with my leader, and the end of my line was a hopeless mess. No wonder the steelhead never took the fly; I might as well have been tossing out a Tootsie Roll Pop.

The following angler through the pool caught a steelhead in the exact spot where I had seen the wakes, no doubt the very fish I had spooked. It weighed twenty pounds.

My despair knew no bounds.

The following day, I floated down the Utkholok with fellow American angler Michael Blakely. For seven hours I tried, and failed, to hook a fish, contenting myself with the grassy vistas of the lower Utkholok and sightings of geese and swans. At 5 P.M., in the last hole, I stood on a gravel bar and cast across a deep, narrow pool, watching as my line swung crisply through the water. Suddenly, I felt a slow, steady tug, followed by a hard yank. In a daze, I watched as line unspooled wildly from my reel. The fish stopped, then ran again. After losing a half dozen steelhead, I was giving no quarter in this fight and was not about to wait for a hook to come out or a knot to slip or a head-shake to send my fly into orbit. I reeled and walked backward on the bar, and within a minute the steelhead—a lovely, silver female weighing about twelve pounds—was on dry land. I let out a series of war whoops that carried for more than a mile over the tundra. At last, I had my steelhead.

As I muttered incoherently and steadied the fish in a shallow indentation in the gravel, Blakely took the fin and scale samples and tagged the steelhead. I suggested we collect some sea lice, ocean parasites that latch on to the fish's gills, and that were also a subject of study by the Russian team. Then Blakely and I made an unpardonable error. Forgetting Soverel's admonishment to extract sea lice only from the outside of the gills, I held the steelhead as Blakely lifted open the gill flap with his forceps. Just as he was about to pluck a lice from the crimson, cartilaginous mass, the steelhead jumped. The hemostats punctured the gills, and the fish began to bleed uncontrollably.

"Fuck!" shouted Blakely, flinging the hemostats. "We're going to have to bop her with a rock."

"Hold on," I said. "Let's see if she stops bleeding."

"No way she's going to stop, not with a wound to the gills."

I held the fish in the pool we'd scooped out for her. Every time her gills opened, blood pumped into the water. Soon the pool was red, and Michael kicked open a channel to the river. Every few seconds her gills would open, and I would hold my breath thinking that, at last, the bleeding had stopped. But the blood would inevitably come, pulsing into the Utkholok. I made Blakely wait another minute or two, until it was clear he was right. Grabbing a rock, he knocked her twice above the eyes. She twitched, then lay still. Blood trickled onto the gray stones.

Dr. Savvaitova's team, which had government permission to kill twenty-five steelhead, still needed to dissect a few fish, and my catch would not go to waste. But this was one of the few times an angler had killed a steelhead on the expedition. I was disgusted with myself and regretted my silly celebrating, which had led to the death of the fish.

The following morning I caught, tagged, and released three steelhead, banishing the curse that had dogged me for ten days.

Dr. Savvaitova, a half dozen American anglers, and I flew out under overcast skies, the gray helicopter circling once as we waved goodbye to those remaining in the Utkholok camp. The pilot headed southeast for the eighty-minute flight to Esso, where we would take a bus to the capital, Petropavlovsk-Kamchatski. Our flight took us over miles of rust-colored tundra, where dozens of rivers and streams snaked toward the Sea of Okhotsk. The foothills of the Middle Range were covered with pine bush and scrubby birch, most of which had lost their leaves in the twelve days we had been at camp. The MI8 glided low over stony plateaus, their surfaces covered with pale green moss and lichens.

As we neared the mountains, the wind rose and the helicopter began to sway. Below was a green river, wider than the Utkholok and churned by long riffles. In the pools I could see dark shadows. Most likely they were grass. I imagined they were steelhead, running upstream.

When we hit the Middle Range, the weather worsened. The lead-gray clouds just above us were spitting ice and rain, and the ground was covered in a fresh layer of snow. Visibility dropped to about five hundred feet, and the pilot was forced to follow a river and thread his way through the mountains. We flew down a steep valley, the helicopter one hundred and fifty feet from the ground, the rocky, sparsely forested hillsides rising sharply above us on both sides. The sky darkened, and everyone grew silent, staring at the pine trees and boulders that whizzed past our windows.

In a remote valley, a Koryak hunter stood by a wooden shack and waved.

Civilization announced itself in the form of tracks from dozens of all-terrain vehicles, fanning out from a valley into the tundra. Farther on, we passed a power line and a gravel road. Shortly after noon, we landed in Esso.

Epilogue

I left Russia the following evening, walking up the steps of an Alaska Airlines jet as great, fleecy clouds sailed across a cool, blue sky. The flight, bound for Anchorage, was full of Americans staking their claim in the new Russia—businessmen, mining engineers, commercial fishermen, evangelical preachers. A Mormon missionary—blond, crewcutted, wearing a white shirt and dark tie—sat across from me, showing someone photos of the brick church he had helped build in the Siberian countryside. Later, he opened a tome called *Practical Christian Theology*, reading with care the section entitled "The Post-Tribulational Rapture View."

Sipping a bourbon, picking at the bland beef served by a cheery stewardess, I felt relief and exhilaration at having finished the trip. I had wanted to lose myself in the Russian countryside, and as I sat in the cabin of the MD-80, I began to realize how thoroughly I had done so. For three months, I had lived in another world, a place of log cabins, of outhouses, of sprawling gardens, of forests that seemed to go on forever, of wild, northern rivers. But these were merely the physical outlines of the land through which I had traveled. The people made more of an impression. If we in America had become utterly dependent on a complex network of governments, corporations, institutions, and stores, then the denizens of the Russian countryside depended upon—and counted on—almost no one but themselves. This was not necessarily a good thing—the lives of the people I had met were far too arduous to romanticize—but it was a fact that struck me with great force nearly everywhere I went.

What struck me, as well, was the brazen poaching I had witnessed from one end of the country to the other. Time and again, I had traveled to remote rivers, only to find that local inhabitants or gangs of poachers had decimated fish populations for miles around. As I watched people netting Atlantic salmon on the Kola Peninsula or hauling grayling after grayling out of Siberian streams, I wanted to tell them there was an end to the game. But with what moral authority could I speak, coming from a country that had driven the passenger pigeon to extinction, nearly wiped out the buffalo and the pronghorn, and all but extirpated grayling in the Lower 48? Still, it was painful to witness Russians repeating our mistakes, and depressing to travel through a country where conservation was an alien concept. I knew that some Russians indiscriminately bagged game and fish because they needed the food. But there were other reasons for the unfettered poaching. Many Russians were skeptical that a land so vast could be despoiled. Others were not convinced that an individual could make a difference. And seven decades of Communist rules, regulations, and slogans had left a sizable portion of the masses believing that only fools obeyed laws.

After such a voyage, reentering America was at once pleasant and unsettling. How smoothly everything appeared to work, and how spoiled we all seemed. I returned to American reality in stages. The first was the Kamchatka camp, where, for the first time in months, I was in the company of my compatriots. My fellow anglers were a decent, intelligent, and enjoyable bunch. But after a summer of journeying on my own among Russians, I felt uncomfortable once again being a gringo, lumped together with the other Americans, viewed by the camp staff as a well-to-do tourist in the "country of wonders." I had come to Kamchatka seeking unspoiled wilderness and unsurpassed fishing. I got that. In the bargain, I began to lose Russia. Sitting in the camp, I remembered the advice of a former teacher, a delightful eccentric and world rambler who insisted that real travel must be undertaken alone.

"Two people talk to each other," said the teacher. "One person talks to the world."

The second stage of reentry was the Alaska Airlines flight, a hurtling chunk of America. The cabin struck me as a sane, clean, friendly, and alien place. Already, rural Russia seemed like another planet, another century.

I had hoped that a trip across Russia would offer profound insight into a country that had long fascinated me, but, truth be told, there were no blinding revelations. Flying home, grappling with a swirl of impressions and memories, I began to realize that understanding a place like Russia doesn't come in epiphanic bursts. It comes with a steady accretion of experiences and relationships, so that gradually a stranger can set aside a lifetime of looking at the world through his own prism and begin to see it through another. This process has its limits, however, for ultimately the traveler is a voyeur, able to fly home when the whim strikes.

One thing I learned was to quit looking at Russia with optimism or pessimism, but rather to see her as she was. As a correspondent during perestroika, I found myself viewing the titanic struggle in the Soviet Union as a kind of spectator sport. I cheered on Gorbachev and Yeltsin as they battled the Neanderthals who wanted to preserve the Communist past. Standing just fifteen feet from Yeltsin when he climbed atop a tank to face down the Communist coup leaders of August 1991, how could I *not* root for him? When he and his economic wunderkinds freed prices, busted up the Soviet economy, and began willy-nilly to privatize Russian industry, of course I cheered them on. Wasn't it great that, from the ruins of the Evil Empire, these bright young men were building a Slavic version of America?

I know now that I was a fool. My first mistake was thinking the Russians were just like us. The second was believing that charging ahead with reforms was the right thing for Russia. As a naive American of limited vision, I failed to see that corruption, inefficiency, and bureaucracy would make a mockery of many of the reforms. Yeltsin's brand of economic "shock therapy" seemed like a grand idea: get the pain over quickly, then move on to the shining capitalist future. But three months of traveling through rural Russia had stripped me of my certainty; I had seen too much upheaval, too much poverty.

· · ·

In the end, I came back to the words of nineteenth-century writer Fydor Tyutchev:

> *Russia can't be fathomed with the mind,*
> *She can't be measured with your common yardstick.*
> *She has a special status,*
> *You can only believe in her.*

The place was too big, too unruly, too contradictory for neat summations. What could you say with certainty? That this was the richest country in the world, yet one whose people often lived in squalor. That this was a nation trying to cover in two decades as much ground as America had covered in two centuries, yet lacking any semblance of democratic traditions. That this was a great civilization with brilliant achievements in the arts and sciences, yet one that found itself, at the end of the twentieth century, humiliated and impoverished. And that the Russian people were among the most stoic and long-suffering in the world—I often found myself grateful we had never gone to war with them—yet somehow seemed unable to live in a civilized manner during peaceful times.

I knew another thing, as well. In the eight years since I had first set foot in Russia, the country had made remarkable progress. Only a fool would predict the future of such a place, but I finished my journey with the same conviction I had when I started: there was no way back for Russia, and slowly, over the coming decades, it would continue to lurch forward.

For the most part, that notion comforted me. But as I saw American and Western culture flooding into Russia, I was glad I had made my trip when I did. In many ways, the country was changing rapidly; the backwaters through which I had traveled were bound to change, too.

As I flew home, such lofty thoughts of Russia were muddled, half-formed. What really stuck with me from my journey was the succession of characters I had met along the way. I thought of Yuri Brodsky and pictured him in the bow of a pitching skiff, smiling at the storm that had terrified me. I thought of Viktor Chumak and saw him cursing and smoking in his stalled truck, the boundless Russian steppe unrolling behind him. I thought of Lev Bobolev,

hunched over a broken outboard motor on the Volga, and pictured the Russian army colonel in a dingy hotel room in Gorno-Altaisk, going dreamy as he talked about his trek into the mountains. I thought of Vova Panov, the long-haul truck driver in Yakutsk, spitting out a mouthful of gasoline and laughing as he took apart an engine. And I remembered Misha Skopets, standing waist-deep in the Utkholok, his fifteen-foot Spey rod bent in half as he fought a huge steelhead trout.

The four-hour flight took us along the coast of northern Kamchatka and the Koryak Autonomous Region, a wild expanse of snow-covered mountains stretching for hundreds of miles. Countless rivers ran to the Bering Sea, their dark channels—not yet frozen—tracing dark, meandering lines in the white landscape.

Not long after midnight, I arrived in Anchorage, setting foot on American soil for the first time in one hundred days. There was no hope of sleep in the antiseptic quiet of the Lakeshore Motel, so I wandered over to a 7-Eleven store for a soda and a bag of chips. Sickly-looking desperadoes with long hair and cowboy hats—men for whom Alaska was no doubt the end of the line—wandered aimlessly up and down the aisles, either stoned out of their minds or casing the joint.

The selection on cable at 2 A.M. was not heartening. There seemed to be an unusual preoccupation with building good abs. Tony Robbins and other TV hucksters wearied me with their energy. I flipped through cooking shows, fire-and-brimstone preachers, yoga demonstrations, Jean-Claude Van Damme. Then I turned off the TV.

In the darkness I thought of Fyodorovich, deep in the Kolyma taiga. It was the eleventh of October, and already, I imagined, the first light snows had dusted the area around Sunny Lake. I pictured the old man sitting alone in the sun by the lakeshore, smoking a Prima and gazing skyward as the last of the whooper swans flew south, squawking and trumpeting as they went.

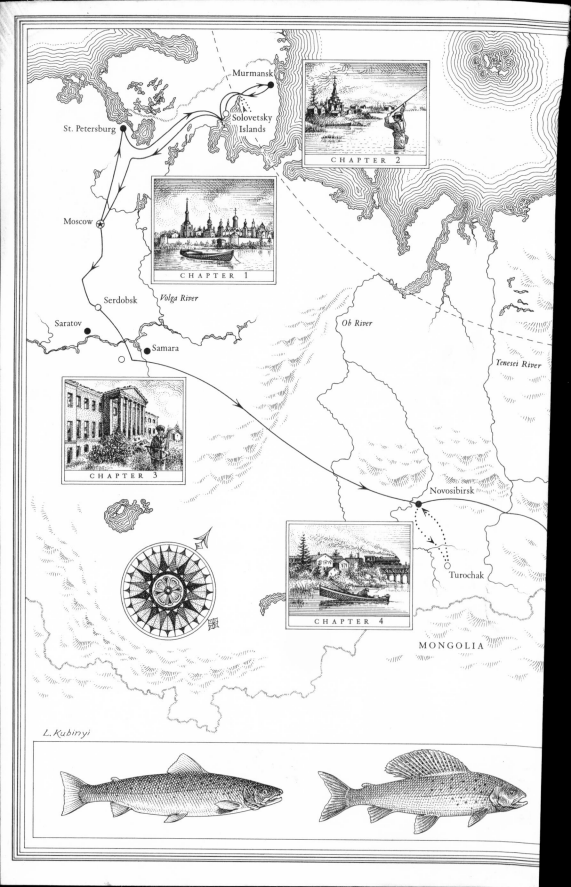

Murmansk

Solovetsky
Islands

CHAPTER 2

St. Petersburg

Moscow

CHAPTER 1

Serdobsk

Volga River

Ob River

Saratov

Samara

Tenesei River

CHAPTER 3

Novosibirsk

CHAPTER 4

Turochak

MONGOLIA

L. Kubinyi